Modelling in Behavioural Ecology

Studies in Behavioural Adaptation

Series Editor: John Lazarus, Department of Psychology,
   The University of Newcastle upon Tyne

*Gulls and Plovers: The Ecology and Behaviour of Mixed Species
Feeding Groups*
C.J. Barnard and D.B.A. Thompson
(Croom Helm, London & Sydney/Columbia University Press, New York)

Modelling in Behavioural Ecology:

An Introductory Text

DENNIS LENDREM, Department of Psychology,
University of Newcastle upon Tyne

CROOM HELM
London & Sydney

TIMBER PRESS
Portland, Oregon

© 1986 Dennis Lendrem
Croom Helm Ltd, Provident House, Burrell Row,
Beckenham, Kent BR3 1AT
Croom Helm, Australia Pty Ltd, Suite 4, 6th Floor,
64–76 Kippax Street, Surry Hills, NSW 2010, Australia

British Library Cataloguing in Publication Data

Lendrem, Dennis
    Modelling in behavioural ecology: an
    introductory text.—(Studies in
    behavioural adaptation)
    1. Ecology—Mathematical models
    I. Title   II. Series
    574.5′0724   QH541.15.M3

    ISBN 0-7099-1691-4
    ISBN 0-7099-4119-6 Pbk

First published in the USA 1986 by
Timber Press,
9999 S.W. Wilshire,
Portland, OR 97225,
USA

ISBN 0-88192-031-2
ISBN 0-88192-032-0 Pbk

Typeset in Plantin by Leaper & Gard Ltd, Bristol, England
Printed and bound in Great Britain

Contents

Series Editor's Foreword

In the early years of this century a Scottish doctor speculated on the evolutionary origin of human tears. It seemed to him that with the increase in brain size and cognitive powers of our early ancestors many events in the struggle for existence would be just too distressing to observe. How comforting then, for the mother, distraught by the sight of her child being devoured by a lion, to cloud her vision with a flood of tears!

Just so, though if the good doctor had pondered further, the following picture might have occurred to him, comfortable in his speculative armchair, and given him some pause for thought.

These stories do not, of course, get us very far in explaining the evolution of tears or anything else, but they do remind us how far the study of behavioural adaptation has come this century. This is, in fact, an exciting time for students of behaviour. The last twenty years have seen a great advance in the theoretical armoury for tackling problems of behavioural evolution and adaptation, and a parallel expansion in empirical studies, particularly in the field. The concepts of inclusive fitness and evolutionary stability, for example, have helped to explain major features of social behaviour and have generated entirely new questions and predictions for the field worker to examine. Cost-benefit analysis and optimisation theory have done the same for behaviour in general, and links with population biology and population genetics are becoming stronger.

The heady days which saw the birth of behavioural ecology and sociobiology are now over, the new concepts have been refined and consolidated, and field data and comparative studies have accumulated at an impressive rate. Now seems a good time to take stock, to review the state of the art and to point some directions for future work. These are the aims of the present series, which will examine questions of behavioural adaptation and evolution in depth. As for our intended readership, we hope that all those interested in such problems, from advanced undergraduate to research worker and lecturer, will find these books of value. Some contributions to the series will encompass particular areas of study, reviewing theory and data and presenting fresh ideas. Others will report the findings of new empirical studies of an extensive nature, which make a significant contribution by examining a range of interrelated questions. The richness, but also the difficulty, of functional enquiry results from the multiple effects of selection pressures and the complex causal relationships between the behavioural responses to evolutionary forces. Studies which measure a comprehensive set of behavioural attributes, and their ecological correlates, are therefore particularly valuable.

The present book holds a special place in the series since it deals with the methods of modelling in behavioural ecology, methods that are common to all areas of the subject. For any behavioural problem it is possible to develop a model that predicts the strategy that maximises the individual's fitness, or some more immediate consequence of its actions. Since natural selection favours behaviour that increases fitness, such models allow us to see how far evolutionary forces have gone towards optimising the individual's answer to a particular behavioural problem, be it feeding, mating, territory size or whatever. In addition, when the success of a behavioural strategy is frequency-dependent, evolutionarily stable strategy theory can be employed to predict the outcome.

These methods now play a central part in the development of all branches of behavioural ecology and research workers are consequently finding it increasingly important to learn these methods in order to develop their own models and to understand those of their colleagues. Students, too, can benefit greatly from a working knowledge of these techniques, both for their intrinsic importance to the subject and as a creative aid to understanding the essentials of a problem, and the inevitable assumptions and simplifications required if a solution is to be formulated.

In the pages that follow, Dennis Lendrem sets out the general techniques of behavioural modelling, taking great pains to explain the mathematical principles fully so that even the novice can use this book as a primer in the subject. His method is to use published models to illustrate more general behavioural problems. Drawing on discussions with many of the modellers concerned he is also able to illuminate the process by which a model is developed, as well as explaining the nature of the finished product. By working with both examples and general principles it is hoped that intending modellers will be able to use this book to transform their ideas into quantitative and testable models.

John Lazarus
Newcastle upon Tyne

Acknowledgements

This book began as a series of lectures delivered to final year zoologists at the University of Nottingham and the University of Newcastle upon Tyne. I am indebted to Chris Barnard, and Pete Garson for letting me try out chunks of the book on their final year behavioural ecologists; my thanks to those students who helped make the book better than the lectures.

In order to gain insight into the development of mathematical models and counter the feeling that they are plucked from thin air I have been careful to augment the published models with much unpublished (and some unpublishable!) material. I am especially grateful to John Krebs, Alex Kacelnik, Tom Caraco, Richard Sibly, David McFarland, Ron Ydenberg, Alasdair Houston, and Professor John Maynard Smith for free and frank discussion of their models ('warts and all' as one of them put it).

A great number of people helped get this book off the ground. I would especially like to thank Alex Kacelnik, Tom Caraco, Chris Barnard, Des Thompson, Andy Hart, Richard Sibly, Robin McCleery, David McFarland, Ron Ydenberg, Alasdair Houston, Professor William Hamilton and John Lazarus for reading various chunks of the manuscript. I am especially grateful to John Lazarus for working his way through the entire book, discussing modelling in general and games theory in particular. David Stretch fed me with ideas, and Philip Jones gave me a crash revision course on solving differential equations. My thanks also to Rebecca Torrance for preparing the chapter vignettes. My greatest debt is to my wife Wendy and son Tom without whom I would probably have completed this book long before the contract deadline.

Chapter 1
Introduction

1.1 Introduction

There is a story that during his stay at the court of Catherine II of Russia, the great Swiss mathematician Euler got into an argument about the existence of God. To defeat the Voltairians in the battle of wits, the great mathematician called for a blackboard, on which he wrote:

$$(x + y)^2 = x^2 + 2xy + y^2$$
Therefore God exists.

Unable to dispute the relevance of the equation (which they did not understand), and unwilling to confess their ignorance, the literati were forced to accept his argument!

Much of the vigour of behavioural ecology stems from the use of mathematical models. But, as this little story illustrates, there is a certain mystique surrounding mathematics and mathematical modelling. The aim of this book is to take some of the mystique out of modelling in behavioural ecology.

There are two major problems when teaching modelling. The first is that the models themselves often appear to have been plucked from thin air. The highly sanitised accounts which eventually make publication give little feel for the background work, or the development of the model. In order to get around this problem each chapter opens with a brief resumé of modelling in that area. I then look at one or two models in great detail. To give a feel for model development these accounts are augmented by unpublished material.

The second major problem is that it is difficult to grasp mathematical modelling unless you sit down and do some yourself. Modelling is a dirty business! Only hands-on experience can give you a feel for what is going on. There are several excellent textbooks presenting brief descriptions of the important models. These books serve a very useful function. However, they are very skilfully edited; the tricky (and even the not so tricky) algebra is frequently glossed over. The result is a heavily bowdlerised account of those models. In contrast, this book attempts to spell out how the various equations are derived. By specifying the nuts and bolts, it is very easy to substitute for various parameters and actually try out the models. I include several worked examples which give a feel for how the models behave.

In the next few pages I shall introduce some general ideas about the evolution of behaviour and about mathematical modelling of that behaviour.

1.2 The Economic Animal

The field of behavioural ecology owes a great deal to the application of economic thinking to animal behaviour (McFarland, 1985). Krebs (1978) traces the development of the economic or 'cost-benefit' approach to the pioneering work of Niko Tinbergen. Tinbergen and his colleagues attempted to measure the survival *value* of behaviours with simple, ingenious field and laboratory experiments.

This early work revolutionised the way that scientists tackled behaviour. It meant that one could attempt to measure the costs and benefits of behaviours, and put the two together to predict how animals *should* behave. And we expect that animals should behave in such a way as to maximise their benefits, or minimise costs; we expect to see *economic animals*. Why? Because evolution is directed by natural selection, and natural selection favours efficient, economic animals. Efficient, economic individuals are more likely to survive and reproduce than their companions. And in the tooth and claw atmosphere of natural selection, inefficient uneconomic individuals fall by the evolutionary wayside.

Most of the models in this book are optimality models. Optimisation is the process of minimising costs, maximising benefits, or obtaining the best compromise between the two (that is, maximising (benefits − costs)). Optimality models make assumptions about the costs and benefits of various behaviours and seek to predict which particular combination of costs and benefits will give the maximum *net* benefit. It is important to remember that optimality models do *not* test the optimality assumption. Optimisation models *assume* that an animal's behaviour is adaptive; that it contributes to the survival of the individual or its offspring. They assume that individuals are designed in such a way as to maximise their net benefits. We are *not* testing the hypothesis that great tits or shrews are optimal animals. We assume that they are. We shall return to this point in the final chapter.

1.3 Modelling Behaviour

The basic defining characteristic of all models is that they represent some aspect of the real world by a more abstract system. Logically enough this process is called *abstraction*. And the abstract system adopted by the models in this book is mathematics. In the rest of this book I hope to flesh out this rather bland definition. However, in this section I want to raise one or two general points about modelling behaviour. In particular I want to ask the question 'Why model behaviour?'

Mathematics provides a broad framework for modelling events in the real world. The reason we use mathematics is because it is a well-worked system with known properties. And once we have identified events in the real world with a branch of mathematics we can exploit the mathematical legwork performed by previous generations. We can take advantage of these known properties to *derive* predictions (the process of *derivation*). We then compare these predictions with data. If the data do not conform to the predictions then we can reject the model and start again. From a logical viewpoint it is worth noting that a model can only be *rejected* on the basis of data, *not* proved. It is quite possible for two models to make the same predictions and so prove to be indistinguishable.

So what are the advantages of mathematical modelling in behavioural ecology?

Krebs and Davies (1981) identify three advantages to modelling behaviour. They suggest that one advantage is that it forces us to make explicit our assumptions. To a certain extent this is true; there is little room for woolly-minded thinking in a mathematical model. However, as we shall see, many models make implicit assumptions which are difficult to identify. And these assumptions can lead to misunderstandings. Mathematical modelling may be more rigorous than other disciplines, but there is still considerable latitude for wrong-thinking!

The second advantage is that modelling emphasises the generality of simple decision rules. The Marginal Value Theorem in Chapter Three for instance has been applied to foraging in great tits, copulation in dungflies and courtship feeding in red-backed shrike. However, I would be wary of making too much of this kind of generality. *We* impose this mathematical homology — not the animals (McFarland and Houston, 1981). It may bear absolutely no relationship to how the animal actually makes decisions; emphasising the generality of these rules may fool us into thinking that it does.

The third and most important advantage of mathematical modelling is its precision. Mathematical models allow us to test our ideas about the costs and benefits of various behaviours. The advantage of modelling behaviour is that it gives us precise predictions. Systematic departures from these predictions usually mean that we have overlooked some rather important feature of the animal's behaviour. It is the precision of mathematics which allows us to test our understanding of a problem.

Do our animals actually carry out the various calculations?

As you make your way through the various models it will soon become apparent that we are asking quite a lot of our animals. It is, for instance, hard to imagine a pied wagtail slowly picking its way through the calculus in Appendix 7.1. Can we really believe that our animals solve the various equations? The answer is no. But then we are *not* asking them to solve the equations. Just because we can describe their behaviour mathematically does not mean that they are capable of performing the mathematics. There is a classic example to illustrate the folly of this kind of thinking. We can describe the trajectory of a ball which is tossed in the air and caught again, using some fairly complex quadratic equations. However, nobody that I know uses those calculations to catch the ball! Another example is that of a beam of light refracted by water. We can describe the path of light using some fairly simple equations, but the beam of light does not make those calculations.

However, in recent years, interest has shifted away from optimality modelling toward the *heuristics* or 'rules of thumb' which animals use in order to solve optimality problems (Krebs and McCleery, 1984; Ydenberg, 1984a; Ydenberg and Krebs, in press); this is a shift in interest which parallels that in psychology from questions about how *well* people perform to *how* they perform (Slovic, Fischoff and Lichtenstein, 1980; Einhorn, 1982; Tversky and Kahneman, 1982).

1.4 Preview

Each chapter takes an area in behavioural ecology and outlines various mathematical models in that area. I then concentrate on one or two models in great detail. In addition I include lots of worked examples. In this way I hope to overcome two of the major obstacles to understanding mathematical modelling; namely, understanding how the models arise, and grasping how the models actually behave once you start substituting for parameters. At the end of each chapter I trace the development of the models and attempt to identify some of the general principles behind modelling in behavioural ecology.

The book assumes very little knowledge of mathematics other than a little elementary algebra. For many biologists their last encounter with mathematics may have been some 4 or 5 years previous to their behavioural ecology. To get over this problem I have gone to great lengths to spell out the algebra. For those readers already adept at algebra, these sections may seem rather long-winded and they may wish to omit them. Some of the trickier algebra is relegated to short appendices at the end of the chapter, not because it is fiendishly difficult, but because it interrupts the flow of the text.

In the next chapter (Chapter 2) I introduce the mathematical methods employed in this book. Chapter 2 not only introduces the mathematics, but also spells out (with the aid of some very simple examples) exactly how we can use that mathematics to model behaviour.

Chapter 3 starts with some very simple optimality models. These look at an animal's behaviour after it has decided to feed, copulate, or whatever and then asks questions about how best to perform that behaviour — questions about what to eat and how much time to spend eating; in short, questions which involve optimising a single behaviour. The chapter opens with what are probably the best known group of models in behavioural ecology, those from optimal foraging theory. These models are all fairly straightforward *deterministic* models; once the model parameters have been measured the animal's behaviour is specified completely by the equations. The models deal with a number of general problems about feeding behaviour. Which prey should an animal prefer? Given a variety of prey types at different densities should an animal take them all? If not, how many types should be eaten? And given that food is patchily distributed how long should a predator stay in a patch? Having answered these general questions we use the theory to solve a problem facing many animals delivering prey to hungry offspring; how many prey should it take back in order to maximise offspring growth?

Chapter 4 stays with optimising a single behaviour and with optimal foraging theory but considers a radical change in the optimisation criterion: risk minimisation as opposed to rate maximisation. In making this switch we are introduced to some *stochastic* (that is, probabilistic, statistical) models of behaviour. In real life, patches of food do not always yield the same amounts of food. On some days food may be abundant in a patch; on other days it may be scarce. This chapter tackles general questions about how such variability affects an animal's chances of starvation? Starting with a very simple model of how animals should behave if they are to minimise the chances of starvation, we then develop a more general model and look at the effects of variability in travel times between patches on the time an animal should spend in a patch.

Chapter 5 considers what happens when we have a conflict between two (or more) behaviours. The foraging models in Chapters 3 and 4 were fairly straightforward. The animals were required to optimise single behaviours. However, if you watch an animal feeding it frequently interrupts feeding to perform other behaviours such as drinking or scanning for predators. This chapter looks at the conflict between feeding and scanning for predators, and traces the development of mathematical models of scanning behaviour and predator detection. The aim of these models is to calculate the probability of an animal detecting a predator given a certain scanning *pattern*.

Trading-off two (or more) behaviours is an important general problem, and Chapter 6 takes up the trade-off between feeding and vigilance where Chapter 5 leaves off. The simple descriptive models of Chapter 5 do not tell us the best way to combine these two behaviours. On the one hand if an animal spends all its time feeding there is a good chance that it will fall victim to a predator. On the other hand if it spends all its time looking for predators it will starve to death. The best solution must be to alternate the two. Can we predict precisely how the animal should alternate between feeding and vigilance? It is a question of balancing two very different behaviours. Chapter 5 describes how the *state–space* approach can be used to tackle this kind of problem. Furthermore, this balance between feeding and vigilance will change with time since the cost of not feeding will fall as an animal approaches satiation. This chapter introduces the reader to *dynamic* models of behaviour — models which describe changes in time.

Chapter 7 describes another method for combining two very different behaviours (feeding and territorial defence). These models simply express defence costs in terms of their effect on feeding rates. These models are then used to predict the time budgets and optimal territory sizes of various species. They tackle questions such as how much time should an animal spend feeding and how much time in territorial defence? What is the optimal territory size? When should a territory owner share its territory, and how much time should it spend on territory?

In Chapter 8, we go on to look at situations where the optimum behaviour depends upon what everyone else is doing. An animal's social behaviour may be largely influenced by its conspecifics. Chapter 8 shows how games theory models have been applied to the analysis of social behaviour. In particular we look at the evolution of aggressive behaviour and at the evolution of co-operation. Why are aggressive contests in the natural world so heavily ritualised? How can cooperation evolve in the tooth-and-claw atmosphere of natural selection? In addition, Chapter 8 describes some very specific models of aggressive contests between spiders. These models attempt to capture something of the complexity of such disputes.

In the final chapter (Chapter 9) we consider some of the problems with modelling and some of the general lessons to be drawn from the previous chapters. In particular we take a look at the modelling process itself and the evaluation of models in behavioural ecology.

Chapter 2
Mathematical Methods

2.1 Introduction

Before moving on to the models I want to introduce some of the mathematics upon which they rest, and the aim of this chapter is to outline some of the more important mathematical ideas used in this book. Much of it may already be familiar to many readers. However, if you have forgotten all about differential calculus, Poisson processes etc. then this chapter should jog your memory!

This chapter serves a double purpose. As well as gently introducing the mathematics, I illustrate (with the aid of some very simple examples) how that mathematics can be used to model behaviour. In the process, some very general points about modelling in behavioural ecology emerge.

2.2 Differential Calculus

In Chapter 1 I said that many of the models used in behavioural ecology are simple optimality models. Optimality models make various assumptions about the costs and benefits of a behaviour, and then predict how an animal should behave if it is to maximise benefits or minimise costs. As soon as we start talking about maximisation and minimisation we start talking about calculus. In this section I want to introduce the mathematical principles, and in the next section show how these principles can be used to construct optimality models.

Figure 2.1 shows a graph of $y = x^2$. Consider two points very close together on this curve. Let us call these points (x, y) and $(x + \delta x,\ y + \delta y)$. The symbols

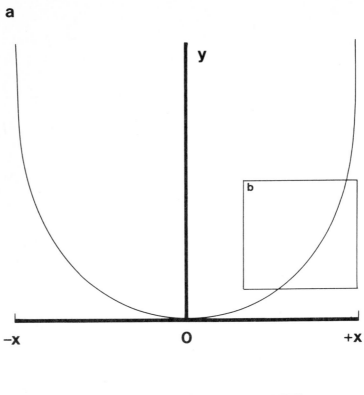

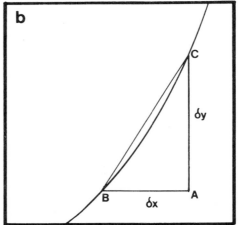

Figure 2.1: (a) Graph of y = x²: y is minimised when x = 0. (b) The slope of the curve BC is almost the same as the slope of the line BC (Δ = δy/δx). In this case, the slope is minimised when x = 0.

δx and δy mean a small increase in both x and y respectively. So these points are very close together indeed. The gradient (Δ) of a straight line joining these two points is simply the distance between y and $(y + \delta y)$ divided by the distance between x and $(x + \delta x)$. That is,

$$\Delta = \frac{(y + \delta y) - y}{(x + \delta x) - x}$$

That is,

$$\Delta = \frac{\delta y}{\delta x}$$

Now, the smaller our value of δx the more nearly Δ approximates the *true* gradient of the curve at the point (x, y). And if δx is infinitesimally small then,

$$\frac{\delta y}{\delta x} = \frac{dy}{dx}$$

and dy/dx is known as the *first derivative*. There are a number of different conventions for representing the first derivative. In this book I alternate between dy/dx and $\dot{y}$ ('y dot') according to which makes the equations look simpler.

Often we want to differentiate the first derivative to find the *second derivative* (in the next section it will become clear why we might want to do this). In this book I write these second derivatives as,

$$\frac{d^2y}{dx^2} \text{ or } \frac{d\dot{y}}{dx}$$

depending upon which is the more convenient. In other books, the latter term is more usually written as $\ddot{y}$ ('y double-dot').

(It may help to think of these derivatives in terms of the classic examples taken from physics. These consider the movement of an object in space and time. The main interest is in linear motion in which y is the distance travelled by an object in time x. The first derivative (dy/dx) gives us the rate of change of y with x; in other words it gives us the object's *velocity*. The second derivative (d^2y/dx^2) gives us the rate of change of velocity; in other words it gives us the *acceleration* of an object.)

Returning to our example, if $y = x^2$ then,

$$y + \delta y = (x + \delta x)^2$$
$$= (x + \delta x)(x + \delta x)$$
$$= x^2 + 2x\delta x + (\delta x)^2$$

This means that,

$$(y + \delta y) - y = (x^2 + 2x\,\delta x + (\delta x)^2) - x^2$$
$$\delta y = 2x\delta x + (\delta x)^2$$

So the gradient of the line between (x,y) and $(x + \delta x, y + \delta y)$ is simply,

$$\frac{\delta y}{\delta x} = \frac{2x\delta x + (\delta x)^2}{\delta x}$$

And δx cancels leaving,

$$\frac{\delta y}{\delta x} = 2x + \delta x$$

Now, if δx is infinitesimally small then the δx on the right-hand side tends to zero and can be neglected, and so

$$\frac{\delta y}{\delta x} = \frac{dy}{dx} = 2x$$

In other words the slope of the curve at point (x,y) is $2x$.
Using this kind of argument it can be shown that if

$$y = kx^n$$

then,

$$\frac{dy}{dx} = nkx^{n-1}$$

So, in our example where $k = 1$ and $n = 2$, then

$$y = x^2$$

$$\frac{dy}{dx} = 2x^{2-1}$$
$$= 2x$$

which is what we calculated earlier from first principles!
Similarly, if

$y = kx$	$dy/dx = k$
$y = kx^3$	$dy/dx = 3kx^2$

And there are one or two particularly useful derivatives which crop up time and again (especially in Chapters 6 and 7). These are,

$y = k/x$
$\quad = kx^{-1}$ $\qquad dy/dx = -1kx^{-2}$
$\qquad\qquad\qquad\qquad = -k/x^2$

$y = e^x$ $\qquad dy/dx = e^x = y$

$y = e^{kx}$ $\qquad dy/dx = k(e^{kx})$
$\qquad\qquad\qquad = ky$

In this last case dy/dx is actually proportional to y (see also sections 2.4 and 2.5).

A particularly useful rule is that for the differentiation of a product. If y and z are functions of x, and

$$u = yz$$

then,

$$du/dx = z.dy/dx + y.dz/dx$$

This little trick comes to our rescue in Chapters 6 and 7.

In the next section I shall outline how differential calculus can be used to model behaviour.

2.3 Maxima and Minima

In building optimality models we are often called on to find the minimum cost or maximum payoff and we can do this using the differential calculus outlined in section 2.2 above. To do this we take advantage of the fact that if a function is at a maximum or a minimum then the first derivative equals zero. That is, $dy/dx = 0$. If we look at our curve of $y = x^2$ (See Figure 2.1) then we can see that when:

$x < 0$ the gradient of the curve will be negative,
x $= 0$ the gradient will be 0, and when
x > 0 the gradient of the curve will be positive.

So, for the function $y = x^2$, y is minimised when the gradient $= 0$. That is, when $x = 0$.

With such a straightforward function it is a fairly simple matter to draw the curve and identify the minimum point. However, with more complex functions, we do not want to draw out the curves every time. Instead we can identify that value of x which minimises y by setting the first derivative $= 0$. We know that if the curve is at a minimum (or maximum) then the derivative $= 0$.

$$dy/dx = 0$$

Now if $y = x^2$ then

$$dy/dx = 2x$$

(see section 2.2).

We want the value of x for which y is minimised. And x is minimised (or maximised) when:

$$dy/dx = 0 = 2x$$

And so y is minimised when $x = 0$, which is what we found by plotting the curve.

The next obvious question is how do we distinguish a maximum point from a minimum point? This is an important distinction — we want to discriminate animals which maximise their payoffs from animals which minimise their pay-offs! To do this we need to look at the second derivative.

At a *minimum* point $dy/dx = 0$ and d^2y/dx^2 is *positive*.
At a *maximum* point $dy/dx = 0$ and d^2y/dx^2 is *negative*.

Returning to our earlier example, if

$$y = x^2$$
$$dy/dx = 2x$$
$$d^2y/dx^2 = 2$$

The second derivative is positive when $x = 0$ (and indeed for all values of x) so we know that y is at a *minimum* when $x = 0$.

We use this approach to solve several problems in Chapters 6 and 7. However, in order to show how the principles outlined above can help us to model behaviour I am going to discuss two very simple models — one of sleeping behaviour and another of flight in birds.

Example 1

An animal spends a certain amount of time, t, sleeping. The benefit (B) of sleeping for t hours is known to be a linear function of time spent sleeping. So,

$$B(t) = 10t \tag{1}$$

However, sleeping also carries a certain cost. An animal cannot for instance sleep and eat at the same time. So time spent sleeping occurs at the expense of time spent eating. The relationship between the cost (C) and time is not known exactly, but it is thought to increase exponentially with time spent sleeping such that sleeping for 10 hours is more than twice as costly as sleeping for 5 hours. So,

$$C(t) = t^k \tag{2}$$

where $k > 0$.

As a first guess, let us assume a *quadratic* cost, $k = 2$. Assuming that the costs and benefits are measured in the same currency (see later) we can combine these two functions to find the net benefit (N). Thus,

$$N = B - C = 10t - t^2 \tag{3}$$

The obvious question is how long should our animal spend sleeping if it is to maximise its net benefits? What is the optimal time spent sleeping $(t^\star)$.

To answer this question we start by differentiating equation (3) with respect to t,

$$dN/dt = 10 - 2t$$

And this is at a maximum (or minimum) when $dN/dt = 0$. That is, when,

$$dN/dt = 0 = 10 - 2t$$

Solving for t,

$$t^\star = 10/2 = 5 \text{ hours}$$

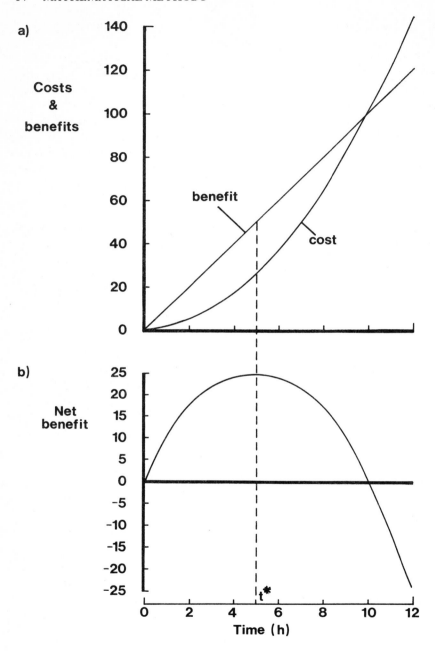

Figure 2.2: Costs and benefits of sleep as a function of time spent sleeping (a). The benefit is a linear and the cost a quadratic function of time spent sleeping. The optimal sleeping time is that maximising the net benefits (b). (In this example t* = 5 hours.)

The next question is 'Is this the time which maximises or minimises the net benefits?' (an important distinction). To find this we must differentiate again,

$$d^2N/dt^2 = -2$$

which is negative, confirming that $t^\star$ *maximises* net benefits.

Figure 2.2 illustrates what is happening diagrammatically. The benefit of sleeping is a linear function of time spent sleeping. The cost is a quadratic function. The optimal sleeping time is that which maximises the net benefits.

Although this is a model of sleeping behaviour, we could have applied the same kind of thinking to other behaviours. We might have been talking about time spent feeding, time spent in amplexus, or time spent grooming. Of course the cost and benefit functions would look rather different for these behaviours, but in principle we can apply the same kind of mathematical methods. The goal is to identify the costs and benefits, fit appropriate functions, and then express them in the same currency so that we can calculate net benefits.

Note also that we have an arbitrary component to this model. We assumed a quadratic cost,

$$C(t) = t^2$$

That is, $k = 2$ in equation (2). But how sensitive is our model to the *parameter* k? We can find out by trying other values of k. If,

$$C(t) = t^3$$

then,

$$N = B - C = 10t - t^3$$

Differentiating,

$$dN/dt = 10 - 3t^2$$

And this is at a maximum or minimum when $dN/dt = 0$. So,

$$0 = 10 - 3t^2$$

Solving for t gives us an optimal sleeping time,

$$t^\star = (10/3)^{1/2}$$
$$= 1.826 \text{ hours.}$$

(see Figure 2.3).

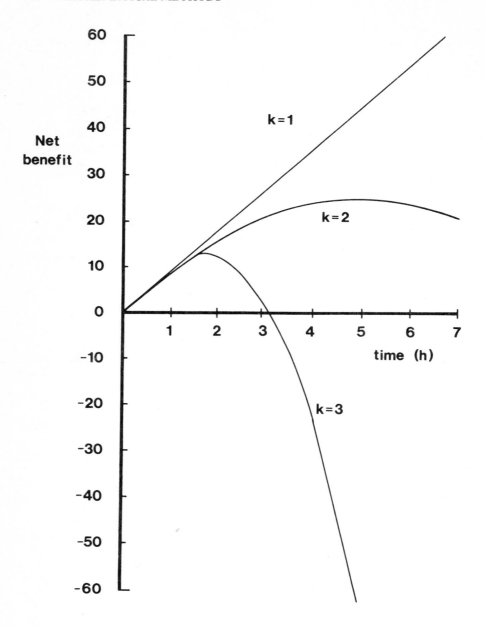

Figure 2.3: Our model of sleeping behaviour is very sensitive to the arbitrary parameter k. When k = 2 the optimal sleeping time is 5 hours. However, when k = 3 the optimal time is 1.83 hours.

And,

$$d^2N/dt^2 = -6t$$

(which is negative for all positive values of t, confirming that this is a maximum point).

So the model is very sensitive to the parameter k. We might like some direct experimental estimate of k before taking the model any further.

In the next sample we look at an optimality model which minimises costs rather than maximises net benefits.

Example 2

By analogy with aeroplane flight (McNeill Alexander, 1982) the power required to propel a bird in level flight at constant velocity v is made of up two components: the *profile* power and the *induced* power. The induced power (P_i) is that needed to keep the bird in the air, and,

$$P_i = BL^2/v$$

where B is a constant and L is the *lift*. The lift is the upward aerodynamic force which supports the weight of the bird. The profile power (P_p) is the power required to move the bird through the air, and,

$$P_p = Av^3$$

where A is a constant.

So the total power required,

$$P_t = P_p + P_i$$
$$= Av^3 + BL^2/v$$

And the *energetic cost* required to travel unit distance at velocity v,

$$E = P_t/v$$
$$= Av^2 + BL^2/v^2 \qquad (4)$$

So, here we have a fairly simple equation relating energetic costs to a behaviour (in this case, the speed at which a bird flies). What, we might ask, is the flying speed (v^*) which minimises the energetic costs? What is the optimal velocity?

The first step is to differentiate equation (4) with respect to v. So,

$$dE/dv = 2Av - 2BL^2/v^3$$

And we know that E is either maximised or minimised when $dE/dv = 0$. So E is maximised or minimised when,

$$2Av - 2BL^2/v^3 = 0$$

Multiplying through by v^3,

$$2Av^4 - 2BL^2 = 0$$

And rearranging,

$$v^4 = BL^2/A$$

So,

$$v^\star = (BL^2)^{1/4} \tag{5}$$

We can confirm that this is the point *minimising* energetic costs by a second differentiation.

$$d^2E/dv^2 = 2A + 6BL^2/v^4$$

which is *positive* for all positive values of v confirming that our bird minimises its energetic costs at a flying speed of $v^\star$.

If we let A, B and L adopt some fairly arbitrary values (let them all equal one) then the optimal flying speed is

$$\begin{aligned} v^\star &= (BL^2/A)^{1/4} \\ &= (1.1^2/1)^{1/4} \\ &= 1 \text{ ms}^{-1} \end{aligned}$$

And we can confirm this visually by inspecting Figure 2.4.

These two models illustrate the role of differential calculus in modelling in behavioural ecology. In the next section I want to move on to some other useful mathematical methods.

2.4 Integration

The integration employed in this book is fairly trivial, but this section should refresh your memory.

Perhaps the easiest way to tackle integration is by working through an example. Figure 2.5 shows the relationship between the velocity of a free-falling object and time. The classic example is of a free-falling stone, but since

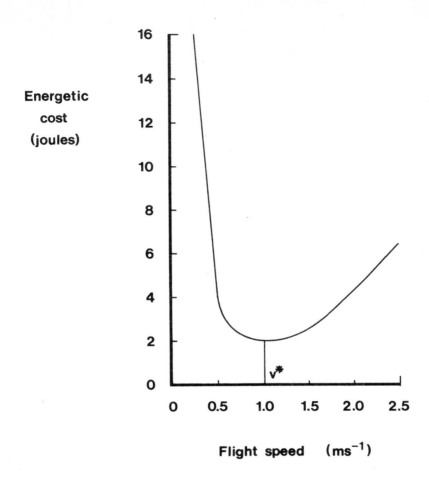

Figure 2.4: Optimal flight speed. The graph shows how the energetic cost (E) depends upon flight speed (v). When A = B = L = 1, the cost is minimised when v = 1 ms^{-1}.

this is a book on behavioural ecology perhaps we should think of a free-falling gannet. (I feel sure that the reader can imagine many reasons why this would be an oversimplified model of gannet diving behaviour!)

The velocity,

$$v = u + at$$

where v is the velocity at time t, u is the initial velocity of the object, and a is the acceleration due to gravity. If the initial velocity of our gannet is $0\,\text{ms}^{-1}$

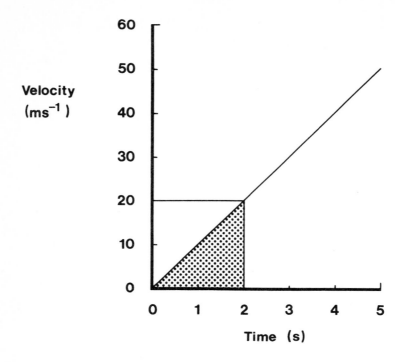

Figure 2.5: Velocity of a free-falling gannet. The distance travelled by the gannet in 2 s is given by the shaded area beneath the curve.

and it drops (like a stone) with an acceleration due to gravity of $10 \, \text{ms}^{-2}$, then its velocity is simply,

$$v = u + at$$
$$= 0 + 10t$$
$$= 10t \qquad (6)$$

So Figure 2.5 represents a curve for $v = 10t$. If our gannet falls for 2 s how far will it have fallen? Well, this is given by the area beneath the curve. We can calculate this area with ease, for the shaded area is simply the area of a triangle with base t and height v. The distance travelled,

$$s = \tfrac{1}{2}(t \times v)$$

$$= \frac{(t \times v)}{2}$$

And since $v = 10t$ then

$$s = \frac{(t \times 10t)}{2}$$
$$= 5t^2 \qquad (7)$$

So the distance travelled in 2 s,

$$s(2) = 5 \times 2^2$$
$$= 20\,\text{m}$$

Notice that if we differentiate equation (7) then if $s = 5t^2$,

$$ds/dt = 10t$$

(see section 2.2 above). Given a relationship between distance and time we can calculate velocity by differentiation. Conversely, given a relationship between velocity and time we calculate distances by integration.

Now look at Figure 2.6. Here, $y = f(x)$, and we want to know the area beneath the curve between $x_1 = a$ and $x_2 = b$. Consider two points x and $(x + \delta x)$. What is the area underneath the curve between these two points? Well the area of the thin rectangle (ABCD) is simply its height (CD) multiplied by its width (AB). That is $f(x) \times \delta x$. This is *almost* the same as the area beneath the curve, but it misses out the little shaded portion. However, if δx is *very* small the area of this little shaded portion becomes negligible and $f(x) \times \delta x = f(x)dx$ approaches the true area beneath the curve at point x.

Now pretend that we have a whole series of such little rectangular strips running side by side from $x_1 = a$ to $x_2 = b$. Then the area beneath the curve between a and b will be the sum of those little rectangular strips. That is,

$$\int_a^b f(x)dx$$

The function $f(x)$ is known as the *integrand* and the numbers a and b are the *lower* and *upper limits* of integration. Sometimes the limits are not specified and we have the *indefinite integral* so,

$$\int f(x)dx$$

(see section 2.5 for instance).

Certain standard functions have known integrals. For instance, the integral,

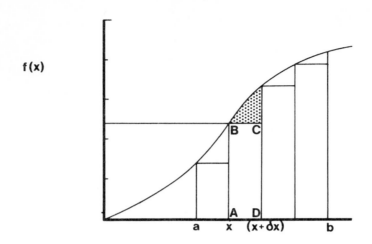

f(x)

B C

A D

a   x   (x+δx)   b

Figure 2.6: Integration: The area beneath the curve between a and b is approximated by a series of narrow oblong strips. As δx tends to 0 then the shaded area becomes negligible, and approximates the true area beneath the curve.

$$\int (1/x)dx = \ln x + C$$

where C is an arbitrary constant (the *constant of integration*). This is an important result which we shall use in section 2.5 and in Chapter 6. However, most of the integration in this book consists of using a frequency distribution as an approximation to a *probability density function*, deriving the *cumulative distribution function*, and then using this to calculate the probabilities of certain events. In order to illustrate the way in which 'integration' is used in this book we will look at the diving behaviour of the eider duck (*Somateria molissima*).

Example 3
Figure 2.7 is a frequency distribution of dive duration in the eider duck. It shows the relative frequency of dive durations. These data were obtained from adult females with chicks. These chicks are very vulnerable to predation by gulls (especially *Larus fuscus*; Mendenhall and Milne, 1985). Whilst diving the adults are unlikely to spot a gull attack, so the duration of a dive is extremely important: the longer a dive the greater the chances of losing a chick.

Suppose we are interested in the probability of a dive lasting between 2.0 and 4.9s. How could we use Figure 2.7 to obtain this probability? Well we simply calculate the area under the 'curve' between dives of 2.0 and 4.9s. In this example, we find that 60 per cent of dives are between 2.0 and 4.9s giving us a probability of 0.60. In other words, the probability of a dive lasting

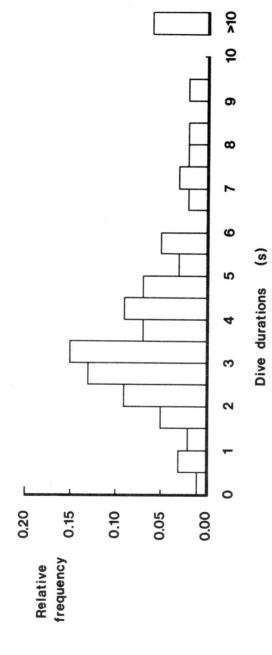

Figure 2.7: Relative frequency of dives of various durations for adult female eiders (Somateria molissima) with chicks. (Cyrus, R., Goodman, S., Hutchinson, J., and Neems, R., unpublished data) Most dives lasted between 3 and 3.5 s. Such frequency histograms provide us with a useful approximation to the probability density function.

between 2.0 and 4.9s is 0.60. Now the more and more dive durations we record, the closer the histogram comes to resemble a smooth curve. With a very large number of observations the histogram would be indistinguishable from a curve. We could then fit a function to this curve. This function is called the *probability density function* (or, p.d.f.). Integrating the probability density function between the limits 2.0 and 4.9 gives us the probability of a dive of between 2.0 and 4.9s,

$$p(2.0 < x < 4.9) = \int_{2.0}^{4.9} f(x).dx$$

We can replot Figure 2.7 to give the *cumulative* frequency of dives of various durations (Figure 2.8). Once again, if we collected many observations of dive durations this would come to approximate a smooth function. This function is called the *cumulative distribution function* (or, c.d.f.). We can derive the cumulative distribution function by integrating the probability density function. In this book we will use histograms of relative frequency as approximations to the p.d.f. and cumulative frequency histograms as approximations to the c.d.f.

In Chapter 4 we use the p.d.f. of the standard normal distribution to calculate the probability of an animal starving to death, and in Chapter 5 we use relative frequency histograms as an approximation to a p.d.f. in order to calculate the probability of predator detection.

2.5 Differential Equations

A differential equation is one which contains one or more *derivatives* of x and y and we are attempting to solve for y. For example,

$$dy/dx = 3x^2y$$

contains a first derivative (dy/dx) and is called a *first order differential equation.*

In order to solve for y we must first *separate* the variables x and y. We can do this by multiplying through by dx/y. So,

$$\frac{dy}{dx}\frac{dx}{y} = 3x^2y\frac{dx}{y}$$

Cancelling,

$$dy/y = 3x^2 dx$$

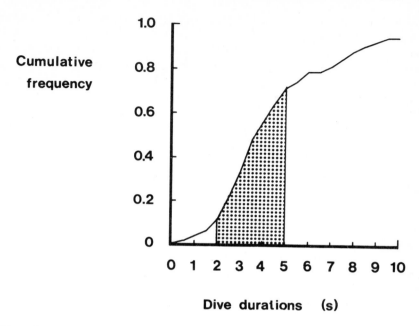

Figure 2.8: Cumulative frequency of dives of various durations (from Figure 2.7). This provides an approximation to the cumulative distribution function (see text). The probability of a dive lasting between 2.0 and 4.9 s is given by the area beneath the curve between 2.0 and 4.9 s.

And we can solve for *y* by integrating both sides of this equation. Remembering that $dy/y = (1/y)dy$ and that the integral of $1/y$ is *ln y* (see section 2.4 above),

$$\int 1/y\, dy = \int 3x^2\, dx$$

Then,

$$\ln y = x^3 + c$$

So,

$$y = e^{x^3 + c}$$
$$= e^c e^{x^3}$$

But $e^c = k$ (see Appendix 2) so

$$y = k e^{x^3}$$

which is what we wanted to know! This kind of approach can be applied to the classical model of population growth in an unrestricted environment. Although this example is lifted straight from ecology it will be all the more useful for our purposes (since it is probably already familiar).

Example 4

The classic model of unlimited population growth states that the rate of population growth is a function of population size. That is,

$$\text{rate of increase} = \text{constant} \times \text{size of population}$$

We can write this as,

$$dP/dt = kP$$

where P is the population size at any time t, and k is a constant. This equation contains a first derivative (dP/dt) and so it is a *first order* differential equation. This time we want to solve for P: we want to know the size of a population at time t.

As above we start by separating the variables P and t. We multiply through by dt/P. This gives us,

$$dP/P = kdt \tag{8}$$

Rembering that $dP/P = (1/P)dP$ and integrating equation (8),

$$\int (1/P)dP = k \int 1\, dt$$

$$\ln P = kt + c$$

Therefore,

$$P = e^{(kt+c)}$$

Now, when $t = 0$ then $P = e^c$ and so e^c is the initial size of the population. If we denote the initial size of the population by P_0 then this becomes,

$$P = P_0 e^{kt}$$

That is the population size, P, at time t is a function of the initial population size, P_0.

In Chapter 6 we solve a rather more complex *second order* differential equation to model an animal feeding to satiation. As the name implies, second order differential equations contain *second* derivatives,

$$\frac{d^2y}{dx^2} + b\frac{dy}{dx} + c\,y = 0 \qquad (9)$$

If b and c are constants then the solution takes the form of a simple exponential,

$$y = e^{kx}$$
$$dy/dx = ke^{kx}$$
$$d^2y/dx^2 = k^2 e^{kx}$$

And if we substitute these values into equation (9) this gives us,

$$k^2 e^{kx} + bke^{kx} + ce^{kx} = 0$$

which simplifies to,

$$k^2 + bk + c = 0$$

This is known as the *auxiliary quadratic equation*. Quadratic equations of this sort have two solutions, $k = k_1$ and $k = k_2$. In general then we have two complementary functions

$$y_1 = e^{k_1 x}, \text{ and } y_2 = e^{k_2 x}$$

where k_1 and k_2 are the two distinct solutions to the auxiliary quadratic equation.

The general solution to such an equation is obtained by forming a linear combination of the two complementary functions. That is an expression of the form,

$$y = Ae^{k_1 x} + Be^{k_2 x} \qquad (10)$$

where A and B are constants (see Newby, 1980).

This becomes clearer if we consider a simple example. Consider the second order differential equation,

$$d^2y/dx^2 + 7\,dy/dx - 8y = 0$$

Then the auxiliary quadratic equation is simply,

$$k^2 + 7k - 8 = 0$$

And there are two solutions $k = k_1$ and $k = k_2$ and these are given by,

$$k = \frac{-b \pm (b^2 - 4ac)^{1/2}}{2a}$$

where a, b and c are the three constants in the auxiliary quadratic equation (Newby (1980).
   In this example: $a = 1$; $b = 7$; and $c = -8$. So,

$$k = \frac{-7 + (7^2 - 4(1)(-8))^{1/2}}{2(1)}$$
$$= \frac{-7 \pm (81)^{1/2}}{2}$$

Giving,

$$k_1 = (-7 + 9)/2 = +1, \text{ and}$$
$$k_2 = (-7 - 9)/2 = -8$$

Therefore the solution is

$$y = Ae^x + Be^{-8x}$$

In Chapter 6 we encounter a second order differential of the form,

$$\frac{d^2y}{dx^2} - k^2y = 0$$

and the general solution to such an equation is,

$$y = Ae^{-kx} + Be^{+kx} \tag{11}$$

(Newby, 1980). In Chapter 6, we use this result to determine the optimal balance between feeding and vigilance for an animal feeding to satiation.

2.6 Geometric Progression

In Chapter 9 we use the sum of a geometric series to calculate the expected number of encounters between two animals. The general equation for such a geometric *progression* or *series* is given by,

$$k + kp + kp^2 + \ldots + kp^{n-1}$$

where p is called the *common ratio* and k is a constant.
The sum of such a series, S_n, is obtained as follows:

$$S_n = k + kp + kp^2 + \ldots + kp^{n-1} \tag{11}$$

Multiply through by p and we get,

$$pS_n = kp + kp^2 + kp^3 + \ldots + kp^n \tag{12}$$

Subtract equation (12) from equation (11) and this leaves,

$$S_n - pS_n = k - kp^n$$

since all the other terms cancel out!
Taking S_n and k outside of brackets gives us,

$$(1 - p)S_n = k(1 - p^n)$$

Therefore,

$$S_n = k\frac{(1 - p^n)}{(1 - p)}$$

Now, if we have an infinite geometric series such that n tends to infinity (and if $0 < p < 1.0$) then p^n tends to zero and can be ignored. This leaves us with,

$$S_n = k/(1 - p)$$

And it is this result that we put to such good use when evaluating the payoffs in the reiterated prisoner's dilemma game in Chapter 9.

2.7 Poisson Processes

A Poisson process is one in which events occur at random in time. The event might be the emission of an electron from a radioactive sample, the arrival of a customer in a queue, or a fatal kick from a mule (see Weaver, 1977 for a list of amusing examples). In Chapter 5 the event to be modelled is the interruption of feeding with a scan for predators. The characteristic feature of all these processes is their unpredictability; the events are said to occur 'at random'. How are we to formalise such a random process?

Poisson processes must meet three conditions.

1. The probability of an event occurring in a small time interval $[t, t+\delta t]$ is equal to $\lambda \delta t$ where λ is the rate of the Poisson process and δt is that small time interval.
2. The probability that two or more events occur in this small time interval $[t, t+\delta t]$ is zero.
3. The occurrence of events after time t is independent of (unaffected by) events before time t.

(NOTE: A purist would find room for $o(\delta t)$. However, I am not a purist!)

We can use these three axioms to calculate the probability of an event occurring within time t (that is, during time $[0, t]$).

First of all let us calculate the probability of no events occurring up to time $[t+\delta t]$. The probability of no events occurring before time $[t+\delta t]$ will be denoted $P_0([0, t+\delta t])$ and this is equal to,

$$P_0([0, t+\delta t]) = P(\text{no events in time } [0, t]) \times$$
$$P(\text{no events in time } [t, t+\delta t])$$

Now the probability of no events in time $[t, t+\delta t]$ is *one* minus the probability of *one or more* events in time $[t, t+\delta t]$. That is,

$$P_0([t, t+\delta t]) = 1 - P(\text{one event in time } [t, t+\delta t])$$
$$- P(\text{two or more events in time } [t, t+\delta t])$$

By Axiom (1) the probability of one event in time $[t, t+\delta t]$ is simply $\lambda \delta t$. And by Axiom (2), the probability of two or more events occurring in time $[t, t+\delta t]$ is zero. So,

$$P_0([t, t+\delta t]) = P_0([0, t]) \times (1 - \lambda \delta t)$$

If we multiply out the right hand side of the equation, then,

$$P_0([t, t+\delta t]) = P_0([0, t]) - \lambda \delta t P_0([0, t])$$

Rearranging,

$$P_0([0, t+\delta t]) - P_0([0, t]) = -\lambda \delta t P_0([0, t])$$

And,

$$\frac{P_0([t+\delta t]) - P_0([0,\ t])}{\delta t} = -\lambda P_0([0,\ t])$$

Now, as δt tends to zero then the left-hand side tends to the derivative of $P_0([0,\ t])$ (see section 2.3 above), and so,

$$\frac{dP_0([0,\ t])}{dt} = -\lambda P_0([0,\ t]) \tag{13}$$

And the general solution to this kind of differential equation is,

$$P_0([0,\ t]) = Ae^{kt} \tag{14}$$

(see section 2.5).

All we need to do now is to specify the constants A and k. Differentiating this equation (section 2.2 above) we get,

$$\frac{dP_0([0,\ t])}{dt} = kAe^{kt} \tag{15}$$

Substituting equations (14) and (15) into equation (13) we get,

$$Ake^{kt} = -\lambda Ae^{kt}$$

And A and e^{kt} cancel leaving,

$$k = -\lambda \tag{16}$$

Now, when $t = 0$ we know that the probability of no events occurring in time [0, 0] is 1. That is $P_0([0,\ 0]) = 1$. We can use this to calculate the constant A. When $t = 0$,

$$P_0([0,\ 0]) = Ae^0 = 1$$

That is,

$$A = 1 \tag{17}$$

Substituting for A and k (equations (16) and (17)) in the general equation (equation (14)) we get:

$$P_0([0,\ t]) = e^{-\lambda t} \tag{18}$$

And so the probability of one or more events occurring in time t is simply,

$$p = 1 - e^{-\lambda t} \tag{19}$$

In Chapter 5 this result is used to model the probability of a bird scanning in time t.

And what happens if we have two independent Poisson processes?

Let us say that our two Poisson processes generate inter-event intervals of length t_1 and t_2. We are interested in the event $[t' > t]$. This is the event that the smaller of t_1 and t_2 is *greater* than some interval t. If the *smaller* of the two events (t_1 and t_2) is greater than t then *both* the events $[t_1 > t]$ *and* $[t_2 > t]$ must occur. That is,

$$
\begin{aligned}
P[t' > t] &= P([t_1 > t] \text{ and } [t_2 > t]) \\
&= P(t_1 > t) \times P(t_2 > t) \qquad \text{(since } t_1 \text{ and } t_2 \text{ are independent)} \\
&= e^{-\lambda t} e^{-\lambda t} \\
&= e^{-2\lambda t}
\end{aligned}
$$

And so,

$$P[t' < t] = 1 - e^{-2\lambda t}$$

And we can use the same argument to show that if we have n independent processes then,

$$P[t' < t] = 1 - e^{-n\lambda t} \tag{20}$$

In Chapter 5 we use this result to calculate the probability that a flock of n birds will detect a predator, but Poisson processes have wider applications.

Example 5

A territorial male butterfly sits in a sunspot waiting for the arrival of a female. Let us assume that females arrive at random with a mean arrival rate of two butterflies/hour. Suppose our butterfly leaves his territory for 6 min in order to feed. What is the probability he *does not* miss the arrival of a female? In this case an event is the arrival of a female and we assume that these events occur at random according to a Poisson process (λ = two butterflies/hour). So, according to equation (18), the probability of no events occurring in 6 min ($t = 6/60$ hours = 0.1 hours) is,

$$
\begin{aligned}
p &= e^{-\lambda t} \\
&= e^{-2(0.1)} \\
&= e^{-0.2} \\
&= 0.819
\end{aligned}
$$

If the cost of feeding is simply a lost opportunity to copulate with a female then the probability that our hungry butterfly will have to pay this cost is simply $(1 - 0.819) = 0.181$.

Example 6

Suppose our territorial butterfly is now interested in two kinds of significant biological event: one is the arrival of a female (λ_f = two/hour); and the second is the arrival of a rival male (λ_m = two/hour). If a female arrives our male copulates with the female, and if a male arrives they contest the territory. Our butterfly slips away for 6 min. What is the probability that either a female or a rival male arrives in that time? Assuming that the two processes are independent and since both are occurring at the same rate ($\lambda_m = \lambda_f$), then from equation (20), the probability that one or more of these events will occur in 6 minutes ($t = 0.1$ hours) is simply,

$$p = 1 - e^{-n\lambda t}$$
$$= 1 - e^{-(2)(2)(0.1)}$$
$$= 0.330$$

So, if our male slips away for 6 min there is about a 1 in 3 chance that he misses an important biological event (a female or rival male).

Poisson processes can be used in this way to model (very simply) the cost of switching from one activity to another. In these examples we have considered a butterfly switching from territorial defence to feeding. And in Chapter 5 we look at the switch from scanning for predators to feeding. In both cases we are interested in the detection of a random event. In this example that event is the arrival of a female or rival male. In Chapter 5 we are interested in the arrival of a predator.

2.8 Summary

In this Chapter I have introduced the mathematics used in this book. In addition, I hope that the examples show how the mathematics can be used to model behaviour.

The flight speed and sleeping time examples illustrate most of the important steps in the development of optimality models in behavioural ecology. The first stage involves identifying the costs and benefits of a behaviour. The second stage involves specifying the relationship between those costs and benefits and, say, the duration (Example 1) or rate (Example 2) of the behaviour. These costs and benefits are then combined to obtain the *net* benefit. This assumes of course that the two are measured in the same currency.

Problems arise when costs and benefits are measured in different currencies. In Chapter 5 we look at the conflict between feeding and vigilance. Time spent feeding occurs at the expense of time spent looking for predators. We can measure feeding benefit fairly easily (see Chapters 3 and 4), and we can measure the cost of feeding in terms of a fall in vigilance (and so an increase in predation risk, Chapter 5). But how do we combine the two? We cannot subtract predation risk (a probability) from the feeding benefit (perhaps an energetic value). Much of the manipulation we see in this book involves juggling the costs and benefits so that they are expressed in the same currency.

Another important point is that the models often contain arbitrary parameters. In Example 1 we were uncertain about the parameter k. As a first guess we let $k = 2$. However, we found that our predicted sleeping times were very sensitive to this parameter. When this happens we have two options, both requiring *independent* corroboration of the arbitrary parameter. Either we select that value of k which gives us the closest approximation to observed sleeping times *and then* seek corroboration of this value either by experiment or with a fresh data set. (This is the *inverse optimality* approach (McFarland, 1977), so called because we infer cost functions from the animal's behaviour rather than predict the behaviour from a cost function.) Alternatively, we can estimate this parameter (by observation or experiment) and insert it directly into the model. The main point is that where our model is sensitive to such parameters we require more information about those parameters.

Another general point to be made is that there is no such thing as *the* optimal solution. The optimal solution depends upon our optimisation criteria. If our criterion is cost minimisation, then our prediction will be different from one maximising net benefits. In Example 2 we calculated the optimal flight speed *assuming* that birds minimise their energetic costs. However, McNeill Alexander (1982) predicts a quite different optimal speed assuming that birds minimise the total power. We have to state in what sense our model is the optimal solution.

Finally, we can see that in order to use mathematics to model behaviour we have to make certain assumptions about that behaviour. In Example 6 we assumed that the arrival rates of male and female butterflies are independent. However, if males pursue females then the arrival of a female is likely to be followed by the arrival of a rival male, and arrival rates will not be independent as the model assumes. Assuming that they are will give us an incorrect value for the probability of missing a significant biological event, and so an incorrect value for the cost of feeding.

Without even looking at any models we have identified some of the important issues in modelling in behavioural ecology: identifying costs and benefits; deriving cost-benefit functions; translating costs and benefits into the same currency; identifying important parameters; specifying optimisation criteria; and identifying (and verifying) model assumptions. In the next chapter we see how these general points are realised in some 'real' models.

Chapter 3

Optimising a Single Behaviour 1: Optimal Foraging Theory

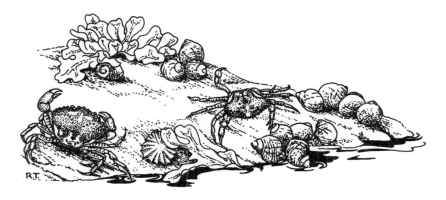

3.1 Introduction

In Example 1 in Chapter 2 I outlined a very simple model of sleeping behaviour in mammals. This model tackled the question of how long an animal should sleep once it has fallen asleep. In this chapter we shall look at some 'real' models which tackle similar questions. These models tackle questions about how an animal should perform a behaviour given that it is maximising some simple optimality criterion — models involving optimisation of a single behaviour. As it happens most of the models in this chapter are about foraging behaviour, and this particular branch of behavioural ecology is known as *optimal foraging theory*.

Models of optimal foraging are perhaps the best known group of models in behavioural ecology. They have already been described in some detail by a number of authors (see Krebs, 1978; Krebs and Davies, 1981; Krebs, Stephens and Sutherland, 1983; Krebs and McCleery, 1984). What I want to do in this chapter is to outline these models, giving a brief account of prey selection, optimal diets and the Marginal Value Theorem, before alighting upon a worked example — a detailed account of central place foraging theory.

It seems reasonable to assume that natural selection has produced efficient, economic animals (see Chapter 1). One way that animals might evaluate prey items is according to their profitabilities. The more profitable the prey, the more highly preferred is that prey. Size is an important index of profitability since large prey tend to be of higher energetic value — they contain more food. However, larger prey are not always the most profitable. They may be more difficult to catch or take longer to eat. An animal might eat two or three small prey in the time taken to tackle a single large one. This means that an animal should take both the food content (energetic returns) and the time taken to handle the prey into account when deciding which is its preferred prey. One way of combining the two is to choose prey which maximise the *rate* of energetic return, that is, the energetic returns per unit time spent handling prey (*profitability*).

In 1978, Bob Elner and Roger Hughes of the University College of North Wales, undertook their classic study of optimal prey choice in the shore crab (*Carcinus maenas*). Common throughout the length of Britain's coastline, the shore crab feeds voraciously on mussels (*Mytilus edulis*) breaking them open with its powerful pincers. However, shore crabs are pretty fussy about what they eat. They do not take any old mussel! They avoid small mussels because these are relatively low in calorific (energetic) value; and they avoid large mussels because they take too long to open. (They can open two or three small mussels in the time taken to open a single, large mussel.) In fact shore crabs prefer mussels of intermediate size, between 20 and 25 mm long. By so doing they maximise their energetic returns per unit time spent handling a mussel (that is, the profitability). In other words, crabs maximise the ratio of the net energetic yield to the time spent handling their prey (Figure 3.1).

Note that in Figure 3.1 the crabs do not only select the mussels of the optimal size. They usually select mussels between 15 and 25 mm but sometimes they take smaller mussels ($<$ 10 mm) and sometimes very large mussels ($>$ 30 mm). Why should this be? One possibility is that if mussels of the optimal size are scarce it may pay a crab to take suboptimal prey. Our crab might obtain a higher overall rate of energy intake by taking suboptimal mussels. There is no point in waiting for a mussel of the optimal size to come along if a crab encounters that particular size just once or twice in a lifetime.

3.2 The Classical Model of Prey Choice

In order to calculate how many different sizes should be eaten one must take into account the amount of time spent searching for mussels as well as their profitabilities. Let the amount of time spent searching for prey be T_s s. Our predator encounters two types of prey at rates λ_1 and λ_2 prey/s. These prey types contain E_1 and E_2 calories and take h_1 and h_2 s to handle. Thus the profitabilities of the two prey types are E_1/h_1 and E_2/h_2 respectively.

Now, if the predator spends T_s s searching for prey it will encounter

$$n_1 = T_s \lambda_1, \text{ type 1 prey}$$

and

$$n_2 = T_s \lambda_2, \text{ type 2 prey}$$

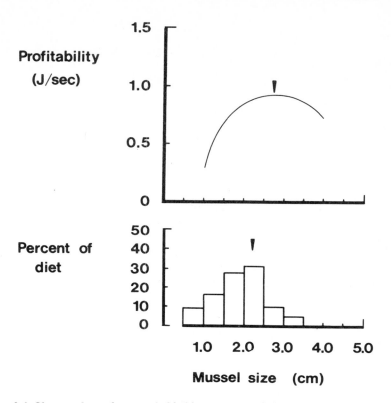

Figure 3.1: Shore crabs prefer mussels 20–30 mm long. This is the most profitable mussel size, giving the highest energetic return per unit time. (After Elner and Hughes, 1978.)

The total energetic return, E, will be equal to the number of encounters multiplied by their respective energetic values. That is,

$$E = n_1 E_1 + n_2 E_2 \qquad (1)$$

And the total time spent handling these prey will equal the number of encounters multiplied by their handling times. That is,

$$T_h = n_1 h_1 + n_2 h_2 \qquad (2)$$

To put this in conventional terms we must first substitute for n_1 and n_2 in equations (1) and (2). Thus the energetic returns,

$$E = T_s \lambda_1 E_1 + T_s \lambda_2 E_2$$

or,

$$E = T_s(\lambda_1 E_1 + \lambda_2 E_2) \tag{3}$$

And the total time spent handling prey, T_h, is given by

$$T_h = T_s\lambda_1 h_1 + T_s\lambda_2 h_2$$

or,

$$T_h = T_s(\lambda_1 h_1 + \lambda_2 h_2)$$

So the total time, T, spent searching for and handling prey will be,

$$\begin{aligned} T &= T_s + T_h \\ &= T_s + T_s(\lambda_1 h_1 + \lambda_2 h_2) \end{aligned} \tag{4}$$

And so the energetic return per unit time spent searching for and handling prey (E/T) is simply equation (3) divided by equation (4). That is,

$$E/T = \frac{T_s(\lambda_1 E_1 + \lambda_2 E_2)}{T_s + T_s(\lambda_1 h_1 + \lambda_2 h_2)} \tag{5}$$

And the searching time, T_s, cancels out leaving

$$E/T = \frac{\lambda_1 E_1 + \lambda_2 E_2}{1 + \lambda_1 h_1 + \lambda_2 h_2} \tag{6}$$

Example 1
Suppose our optimal forager sets aside 100 s to search for prey. He encounters prey type 1 at rate 0.10 prey/s, and prey type 2 at 0.01 prey/s ($\lambda_1 = 0.10$; $\lambda_2 = 0.01$). Prey type 1 contains 10 calories and takes 5 s to handle ($E_1 = 10$; $h_1 = 5$). Prey type 2 contains 10 calories and takes 10 s to handle ($E_2 = 10$; $h_2 = 10$). What is the rate of energetic return if our predator takes *both* prey types?

Well, in T_s s our predator will encounter $n_1 = (T_s\lambda_1)$ prey of type 1, and $n_2 = (T_s\lambda_2)$ prey of type 2. That is,

$$100 \times 0.10 = 10 \quad \text{type 1 prey, and}$$
$$100 \times 0.01 = 1 \quad \text{type 2 prey}$$

From the former (type 1) he will obtain ($n_1 E_1$) calories and from the latter (type 2) he will obtain (n_2E_2) calories. That is,

$$10 \times 10 = 100 \text{ calories from type 1 prey, and}$$
$$1 \times 10 = 10 \text{ calories from type 2 prey.}$$

So his total energetic return, $E = (100 + 10) = 110$ calories.

Now the total time spent searching for prey is only 100 s. However, our predator must also handle his prey. The total time spent handling his prey will be equal to the number of encounters with each prey type (10 and 1 respectively) multiplied by their handling times (5 s and 10 s respectively). So the total time spent handling prey will be,

$$T_h = (n_1 h_1) + (n_2 h_2)$$

or,

$$T_h = (10 \times 5) + (1 \times 10)$$
$$= 60 \text{ s}$$

And the total time spent searching for and handling prey, T, will be given by,

$$T = T_s + T_h$$
$$= 100 + 60$$
$$= 160 \text{ s}$$

And so the rate of energetic return E/T for a predator taking *both* prey types will be

$$E/T = 110/160$$
$$= 0.6875 \text{ calories/s}$$

The same result is obtained using equation (6). Thus,

$$E/T = \frac{\lambda_1 E_1 + \lambda_2 E_2}{1 + \lambda_1 h_1 + \lambda_2 h_2}$$
$$= \frac{(0.1 \times 10) + (0.01 \times 10)}{1 + (0.1 \times 5) + (0.01 \times 10)}$$
$$= 1.1/1.6$$
$$= 0.6875 \text{ calories/s}$$

So equation (6) gives us the rate of energetic return if the animal is taking both prey types, in other words, *generalising*. What happens if it *specialises* on one prey type? For the sake of argument let prey type 1 be the more profitable prey (as it was in Example 1). Thus,

$$E_1/h_1 = 10/5 = 2 \text{ calories/s}$$
$$E_2/h_2 = 10/10 = 1 \text{ calorie/s}$$

And this means that $E_1/h_1 > E_2/h_2$ so type 1 prey are more profitable than type 2 prey.

What we want to know is at what point should an animal drop prey type 2 from its diet and specialise on prey type 1? If our animal specialises on prey type 1 then it will obtain

$$E = T_s(\lambda_1 E_1) \text{ calories} \tag{7}$$

and this will take,

$$T = T_s + T_s(\lambda_1 h_1) \text{ s} \tag{8}$$

since type 2 prey are always rejected (which we assume takes no time at all).

To calculate the profitability (E/T) of specialising on prey type 1 we simply divide equation (7) by equation (8). Thus,

$$E/T = \frac{T_s(\lambda_1 E_1)}{T_s + T_s(\lambda_1 h_1)}$$

And the searching times (T_s) cancel to give,

$$E/T = \frac{\lambda_1 E_1}{1 + \lambda_1 h_1} \tag{9}$$

Now if the profitability of specialising (equation 9) is greater than that of generalising (equation 6) then our optimal forager should specialise. That is, if

$$\frac{\lambda_1 E_1}{1 + \lambda_1 h_1} > \frac{\lambda_1 E_1 + \lambda_2 E_2}{1 + \lambda_1 h_1 + \lambda_2 h_2} \tag{10}$$

then our predator should specialise on prey type 1.

In our Example 1, if our predator specialises on prey type 1 then his energetic returns per unit time will be,

$$E/T = \frac{\lambda_1 E_1}{1 + \lambda_1 h_1}$$

$$= \frac{(0.1 \times 10)}{1 + (0.1 \times 5)}$$

$$= 1/1.5$$

$$= 0.6667 \text{ calories/s.}$$

This is less than the energetic returns from generalising (0.6875 calories/s) and so in this instance our optimal forager should not specialise on type 1 prey.

Another way of looking at this problem is to calculate the threshold encounter rate λ_1 at which our optimal forager should specialise on prey type 1. Or, put another way, what is the expected time to find the next item of prey type 1 (that is, $1/\lambda_1$) at which our predator should specialise? Rearranging equation (10) (see Appendix 3.1) we find that when the expected time to the next item of prey type 1 is

$$1/\lambda_1 < \frac{E_1 h_2}{E_2} - h_1 \qquad (11)$$

then our optimal forager should specialise on type 1 prey.

Returning to Example 1, our predator should only specialise when the expected waiting time to the next type 1 item is

$$1/\lambda_1 < \frac{10.10}{10} - 5$$

$$< 5 \text{ s.}$$

Or, in other words, our predator should not specialise until the encounter rate with type 1 prey, λ_1, exceeds $1/5 = 0.20$ prey/s. In our example the encounter rate is 0.10 and so our predator should generalise.

This simple model can also be extended to other, rather more complex, optimal diet problems. Given a choice of, say, three prey types we can ask if our optimal forager should take one, two or all three types? The energetic returns (E/T) from taking all three prey types will be

$$\frac{\lambda_1 E_1 + \lambda_2 E_2 + \lambda_3 E_3}{1 + \lambda_1 h_1 + \lambda_2 h_2 + \lambda_3 h_3} \qquad (12)$$

And if equation (6) < equation (12) > equation (9) then our optimal forager should take all three prey types.

In fact Thompson and Barnard (1984) and Barnard and Thompson (1985) have extended the model in this way to predict the optimal diet of lapwings (*Vanellus vanellus*) and golden plovers (*Pluvialis apricaria*) taking earthworms of *six* different size classes (see also Thompson, 1986). Using a sophisticated measure of *net* energetic intake (which takes into account the probability of an earthworm being stolen by blackheaded gulls (*Larus ridibundus*) associated with the flock, see Chapter 5), Thompson and Barnard calculated the expected energetic returns from: specialising solely on the most profitable size class; generalising to the second most profitable size class; the third most profitable size class; fourth; fifth, and finally taking all six size classes. This model predicts that plovers will maximise their mean rate of energy intake by taking only the *three most profitable* size classes, and this is precisely what the birds do (Figure 3.2).

The optimal diet model has been tested in the laboratory in what has become a classic of optimal foraging lore. John Krebs and colleagues trained great tits to select mealworms from a conveyor belt. The conveyor belt allowed the encounter rates of two prey types to be varied precisely. The prey

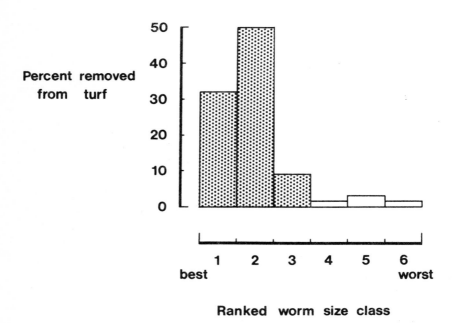

Figure 3.2: Plovers and earthworms: as predicted, plovers feed almost exclusively on worms from the three most profitable size classes.

used in the experiments were mealworms in drinking straws. One prey type was twice as long as the other and so contained twice the calorific value. Handling times were calculated by direct observation. As predicted great tits specialised on the larger mealworms once the encounter rate λ exceeded a threshold value calculated from the model (Figure 3.3; Krebs *et al.*, 1977).

3.2 Marginal Value Theorem (MVT)

Sadly, most great tits do not have their mealworms delivered on a conveyor belt. Instead they usually encounter their prey in discrete patches, and much of the day is spent travelling between such patches. Worse still, the longer a great tit spends in a patch the harder and harder it becomes to find or catch prey. Either it begins to deplete the food patch as time passes, or the prey

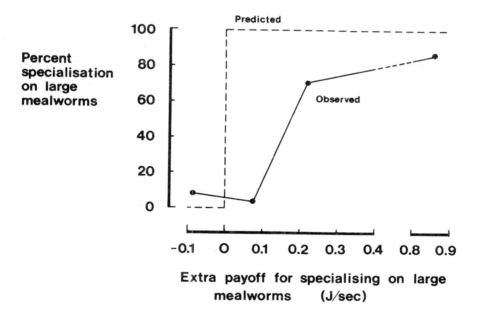

Figure 3.3: Great tits and mealworms. (After Krebs et al., 1977.) When the payoff for specialising exceeds that of generalising, great tits switch to a specialist diet. The switch is not quite the all-or-nothing affair predicted by optimal foraging theory; great tits show partial preferences. Only when the extra payoff from specialising is very large do they specialise almost exclusively on the more profitable prey.

The extra payoff is simply, $\quad \dfrac{\lambda_1 E_1}{1 + \lambda_1 h_1} - \dfrac{\lambda_1 E_1 + \lambda_2 E_2}{1 + \lambda_1 h_1 + \lambda_2 h_2}$

(rather unsportingly) move away to avoid being eaten. The question our optimal forager must ask is how long should he stay in a patch? If he leaves too early he passes up an excellent opportunity for further feeding. If he stays too long it becomes harder and harder to find food and he wastes valuable time which could be spent in a fresh patch.

In 1976, Ric Charnov of the University of British Columbia lifted the solution to this problem straight from economic theory. According to his Marginal Value Theorem (MVT) an animal should stay in a patch until its rate of food intake drops to a level equal to the average for the environment as a whole (Charnov, 1976). That is, the average amount of food per patch divided by the time spent in a patch plus the time taken to travel between patches.

The optimal patch residence time, T_p, is that which maximises the net rate of energy intake, R, where R is given by,

$$R = E(T_p)/(T_t + T_p) \qquad (13)$$

where T_t is the average time taken to travel between patches. $E(T_p)$ simply means that the energetic returns, E, are a function of the time spent in the patch, T_p. If we know the relationship between $E(T_p)$ and T_p we can simply differentiate R with respect to T_p, set the first derivative equal to zero, solve for T_p, and check that this is a maximum by differentiating again to obtain the second derivative (see section 2.3 in Chapter 2). However, we can also solve this problem graphically.

This graphical solution is probably familiar to most behavioural ecologists (though the reasoning behind it may be less familiar!). Figure 3.4 shows a hypothetical intake curve for a predator feeding in a patch. At point A our predator leaves a patch and travels for T_ts until it reaches a second patch at point B. It starts to feed. At first the rate of energetic gain (food intake) is high, but it soon begins to fall off.

If we draw a line from point A to the curve (point C) then we can draw a right angled triangle ACO. The gradient of the line AC is CO/AO. Note that CO is the energetic return, $E(T_p)$. Note also that $AO = T_t + T_p$. So the gradient $AC = E(T_p)/(T_t + T_p)$. Now note the uncanny resemblance between this equation and equation (13). If our predator is to maximise its net rate of energy intake, R, then it must maximise the gradient of the line AC. This gradient is at its greatest when it is at a tangent to the curve. If we then drop a perpendicular from that tangent we have the optimal patch time, T_p.

An important corollary of the marginal value theorem is that as the time taken to travel between patches increases then the average intake for the environment as a whole decreases so we would expect to see animals spending longer in patches. It pays to stay longer as travel times increase because the expected returns from moving on are that much lower. Figure 3.5 uses the graphical solution illustrated above to show that the optimal patch residence time T_p does indeed increase with increasing travel time, T_t.

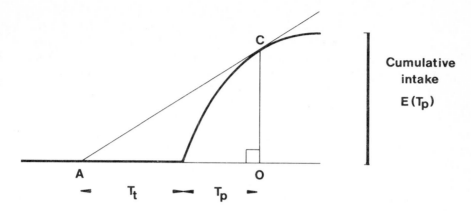

Figure 3.4: Graphical solution to the marginal value problem. At point A our optimal forager leaves one patch and travels to the next. The line AC is at a tangent to the cumulative food intake curve for a patch. CO is the perpendicular from the curve. The gradient of the curve = CO/AO (see text).

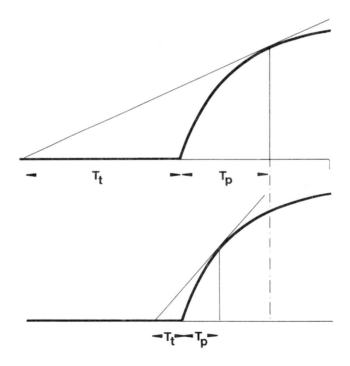

Figure 3.5: Travel time and optimal patch times; the optimal patch residence time (T_p) increases with travel time (T_t). Long travel times mean longer optimal patch times.

In an extremely elegant test of this prediction, Robin Cook and Barbara Cockerell at the Hope Department of Entomology in Oxford, recorded the behaviour of waterboatmen (large insects often found on ponds and ditches) feeding on mosquito larvae (Cook and Cockerell, 1978). To a waterboatman each mosquito larva represents an individual patch. Upon capturing a mosquito, this voracious little predator sucks out the insides of its hapless victim. By interrupting waterboatmen as they fed, Cook and Cockerell were able to show that the rate of food extraction decreased with time spent feeding (Figure 3.6). They calculated the exact form of the intake curve for their waterboatmen and then manipulated travelling times by changing prey density. They argued that the higher the prey density the shorter the inter-catch interval and so the shorter the travel times (T_t). They then used the marginal value theorem to calculate the optimal patch times at each prey density and compared them with the observed values (Figure 3.7). They found a close match between observed and predicted patch times.

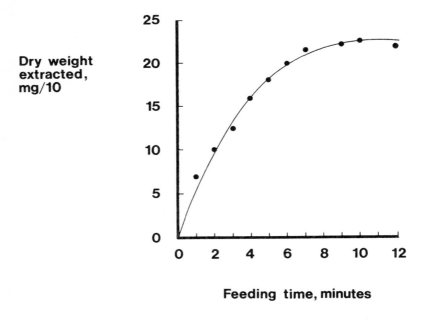

Figure 3.6: Cumulative intake curve for Notonecta *(waterboatman). The more time spent feeding the lower the rate at which food is extracted from prey. (After Cook and Cockerell, 1978.)*

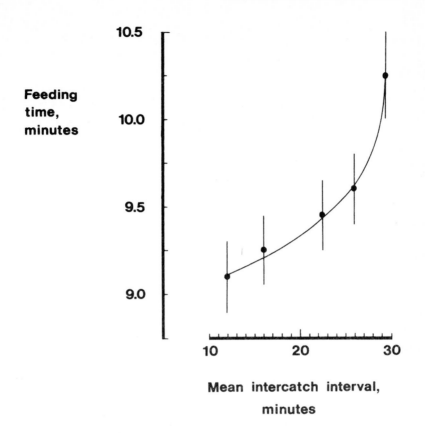

Figure 3.7: Optimal patch time for Notonecta: *as predicted from the marginal value theorem, the feeding time* (T_p) *increases with the mean intercatch interval* (T_i).

3.3 Central Place Foraging

One important application of the marginal value theorem has been its extension to the special case of central place foraging in animals. Many animals make repeated trips to a feeding site and then bring back a load of food to a central place such as a nest or food store. Suppose our central place forager arrives at a feeding site and decides to take a number of prey back to the nest. He starts to load up. At first he is able to load up with ease, but as the numbers of prey captured increase it becomes more and more difficult to find further prey. Each capture takes longer. At some point our central place forager is better off leaving the patch and returning to the nest rather than trying to make another capture. But how big a load should he carry?

Gordon Orians and N. Pearson (1979) pointed out that we can extend the Charnov model to answer this question. They showed that the optimal load size depends upon the average quality of patches in the habitat. The better the environment the shorter the patch residence time, and so the smaller the optimal load (Figure 3.8). Only when the environment is very poor should our forager struggle to make additional captures. And, once again, as the travel time increases the optimal patch time increases and so the optimal load increases.

This general prediction has been supported by a large number of studies. However, in the next section I want to turn our attention to one particular study and one particular group of central place foraging models.

3.4 The Starling's Dilemma

Alecjandro Kacelnik developed a number of models of central place foraging in the starling (*Sturnus vulgaris*) whilst a research fellow at Groningen University in the Netherlands (Kacelnik, 1984). Kacelnik was intimately involved in the development and application of optimal foraging models in the mid-70s while a graduate student of John Krebs.

The field experiments to test the models were carried out on the island of Schiermonnikoog in the Dutch Wadden Sea. For some years members of the Department of Zoology at Groningen University had been engaged in behavioural and physiological work with the starling. Starlings are fairly

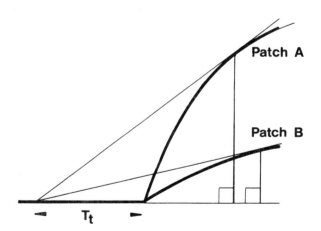

Figure 3.8: Central place foraging. The optimal patch time (and hence the optimal load size) depends upon patch quality. If the average patch quality is high (patch A) then the optimal patch time is relatively short. If the average patch quality is low (patch B) then the optimal patch time is relatively long.

common on Schiermonnikoog and had taken to using nest boxes established by members of the university's field station.

During the breeding season these starlings lay between four and six eggs. Upon hatching, the parent birds must collect food and deliver it to their young in the central place (the nest box). The parents carry out a fairly regular cycle of behaviour, visiting the nest and feeding the young before flying to a feeding site, collecting prey and returning to the nest box, where the cycle starts once again. The problem facing the starling is how many prey should be collected before returning to the nest box?

Kacelnik trained two male starlings to collect food from an artificial patch. This 'patch' consisted of a raised platform in front of a hide in which Kacelnik sat with an assistant. Once a bird landed on the platform, he delivered mealworms to the starling via a plastic pipe. The number of worms delivered in a single visit, N, was a function of time spent in the patch, T_p,

$$N(T_p) = 1.52 \ln T_p \qquad (14)$$

This schedule simulates patch depletion; at first the rate of prey 'capture' is quite high but as time on the platform, T_p, increases so the rate of delivery decreases.

By varying the distance between the 'patch' and the starling's nest box Kacelnik could manipulate the travelling time, T_t. The problem facing the starling was how many prey should be take back to the nest?

3.4.1 Model Solutions

In our discussion of optimal foraging theory and the marginal value theorem we assumed that animals attempt to maximise their net energetic returns per unit time. Kacelnik considered three such *rate* maximising models. These three models required estimates of the total time for a full cycle, T. One cycle is the time from nest to patch and back again, and,

$$T = T_f + T_p + T_n \qquad (15)$$

where T_f is the round trip flight time in both directions, T_p is the time in the patch, and T_n is the time in the nest.

Model 1: YIELD

According to this model, starlings should maximise,

$$\text{YIELD} = (NV)/T \qquad (16)$$

where N is the number of prey obtained, and V is the *metabolisable* energy value of each prey (in joules). The metabolisable energy value is the energy content of each prey multiplied by the predator's digestive efficiency. Using metabolisable energy rather than the straight energetic value means that we are taking into account the fact that not all of that energy is available to the predator. Basically this YIELD model is the straight *energetic-returns-per-unit-time* model that we encountered in our discussion of optimal foraging and marginal value theorem, and the model assumes that starlings will *maximise* their YIELD.

Model 2: DELIVERY
This model is similar to the first but it assumes that the starling takes into account its own energy expenditure in each cycle. Thus,

$$\text{DELIVERY} = \text{YIELD} - E_p \qquad (17)$$

where E_p is the energy expenditure by the parent. E_p is a function of patch residence time, according to the equation,

$$E_p = (M_f T_f + M_n T_n + M_p T_p)/T \qquad (18)$$

where M_f, M_n and M_p are the metabolic rates (in watts) while the parent is flying, in the nest and in the patch respectively, and again this model assumes that starlings *maximise* their DELIVERY.

Model 3: FAMILY GAIN
This is the most sophisticated of the rate maximising models. This model predicts the optimal patch time if the parent is maximising the energy available for chick growth. The model supposes that a parent will take into account the energy expenditure of its chicks as well as its own energy expenditure (the significance of this assumption will become clear in a minute).

$$\text{FAMILY GAIN} = \text{DELIVERY} - E_c N_c \qquad (19)$$

where N_c is the number of chicks in the brood and E_c is the average metabolic rate of each chick. In order to estimate E_c Kacelnik assumed that chicks had two major metabolic states, resting and begging. Normally a chick sits quietly in the nest. However, when the parent arrives with a beakful of juicy mealworms the chicks beg frantically for their share. Begging is very important since each chick is in competition with its brothers and sisters. If it fails to obtain food from its parents then it will simply die. However the metabolic cost of begging is much greater than for resting. So,

$$E_c = [M_{cb} T_n + M_{cr}(T_f + T_p)]/T \qquad (20)$$

where M_{cb} and M_{cr} are the metabolic rates of the chicks while begging and resting respectively. In other words the energy expenditure of the chick is M_{cb}

while the parent is in the nest for time, T_n, but much lower, M_{cr}, during the remaining time, $(T_f + T_p)$. So according to this model it may actually pay a starling to spend longer in a patch and so reduce the energetic costs to the chicks. When $(T_f + T_p)$ is small then the energetic cost of begging must be paid many times. By staying 'too long' in a patch, the chicks gain by paying the cost of begging less often.

M_f, M_n, M_p and V were all estimated from other metabolic data. However the metabolic rates of resting (M_{cr}) and begging (M_{cb}) were guessed from the adult data. Kacelnik assumed that begging has the same metabolic rate as an intermediate level of work in an adult and that a chick is at its basal metabolic rate while resting. One question we might ask is how such estimates affect the model's predictions. This is a topic to which we will return in section 3.5.

Model 4: ENERGETIC EFFICIENCY

This model is rather different from the other models. It is based on the possibility that feeding may be constrained by thermodynamic efficiency. The argument is that spending energy while foraging may itself be highly costly. For example if heat dissipation is constrained a starling may have to take time out from foraging in order to cool down. When this cost is important animals may choose to maximise thermodynamic efficiency (the energy collected/unit energy spent). Clearly this kind of model owes little to optimal foraging theory. Instead it stems from the metabolic work that was in progress at Groningen University where the study was carried out. This model did not produce a terribly close fit to the data and we shall not discuss it any further (see Kacelnik, 1984 for details).

3.4.2 Testing the Models

Two points must be clarified before we discuss the predictions of the models. The first point to note is that rather than compare patch residence times Kacelnik examined the number of prey items for which the bird should wait. The reason for this is fairly obvious. If a starling catches its fourth prey after, say, 45 s and the next prey will not be delivered for a further 45 s it is a waste of time to hang around for an extra 5 s just to make sure he stays for the predicted *time* of, say, 50 s.

The second point is that Kacelnik was compelled to estimate a large number of parameters — mainly metabolic rates. One question which we might ask is how do such estimates affect the models' predictions? One way of finding out is to allow these estimates to take a range of values within reasonable limits. We then look at the effect of these estimates on our model predictions. In other words we carry out a *sensitivity analysis*. With luck the predictions will be less sensitive to variation in these parameters than they are to the differences between the models (as in this case). Of course it is very much up to the modeller to decide upon the 'reasonable limits'. Although this may sound like fudging this is one of those areas where we become biologists and not mathematicians. It is usually pretty clear what is and is not a 'reasonable estimate'.

All three models produced the same qualitative predictions. All three predict that as the distance between the nest and the patch increases the optimal number of prey N^* also increases. Figure 3.9 shows the optimal predictions for the FAMILY GAIN model. With very short round trip flight times the optimal prey load is only three mealworms. As flight times increase this rises to six mealworms.

So how well did the models do?

FAMILY GAIN produced the highest proportion of identical observed and predicted visit lengths (N^*). The predicted visit lengths were confirmed by the birds on 63 per cent of tests and were never out by more than a single prey item.

Figure 3.10 shows the observed prey loads for one of the starlings and com-

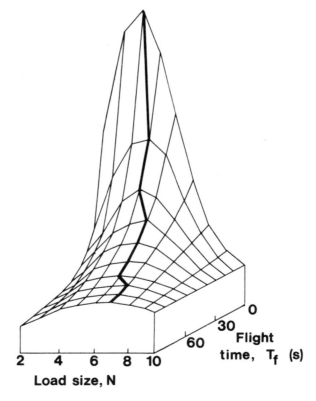

Figure 3.9: FAMILY GAIN (1). Profitability (J/s) as a function of load size and flight time (T_f); as the flight time increases, the load size maximising profitability (bold line) increases. (After Kacelnik, 1984.)

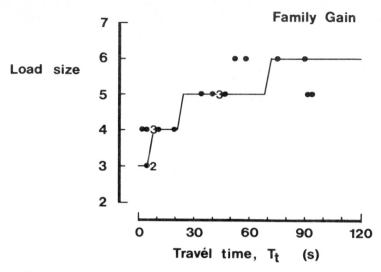

Figure 3.10: FAMILY GAIN (2). Observed and predicted load sizes for an individual male starling; as travel time increases the optimal load size (number of mealworms) increases.

pares these with those predicted by the FAMILY GAIN model. But how do we compare the fit of these data to the model predictions? One way is to look at the points where the models and the data part company — the 'errors'. Both the YIELD and the DELIVERY models consistently predicted smaller optimal N^* than observed. Only the FAMILY GAIN model showed no systematic bias for either short or long visits (Figure 3.11).

3.5 Conclusions

Optimal foraging models arose from economic approaches to the study of animal behaviour. Early models of optimal foraging assumed that foragers attempt to maximise their mean net rate of energy intake. These models attempted to predict optimal prey choice and optimal patch times on the basis of this assumption.

Central place foraging is a branch of optimal foraging theory concerned with animals collecting food and returning to a more or less fixed point (the central place) such as a nest box or food cache. Central place foraging theory has attracted a great deal of attention in recent years. Kacelnik (1984) identifies three reasons for this interest. Firstly, tests of optimal foraging models require measurements (travel times, patch times, intake curves) which can be made much more readily on central place foragers than itinerant foragers. In addition, the quality of the data is often better since observations

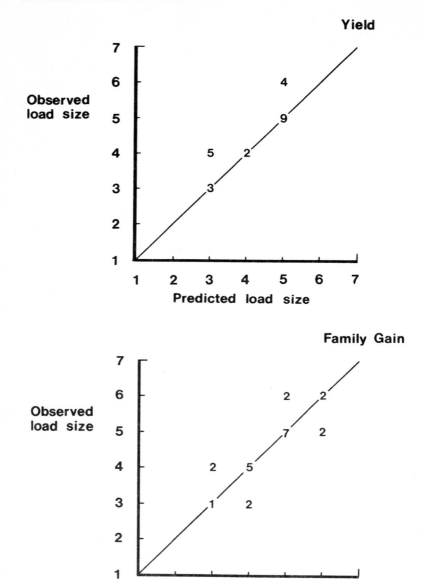

Figure 3.11: Observed and predicted load sizes for the Yield and the Family Gain models. Observed load sizes showed no systematic departures from the predictions of the family gain model. In contrast, the yield model consistently underestimated the observed load sizes.

can be made over long periods and can be aided by instruments in the central place (balances, video-cameras). And finally, central place foragers are often gathering food for their offspring, so that there is a direct link between foraging efficiency and reproductive success.

It was for these reasons that Kacelnik decided to carry out a study of central place foraging in the starling. The three 'rate' models were each refinements of a straight central place model predicting that central place foragers should maximise their mean rate of energetic return. The first model (YIELD) looks at metabolisable energy; the second model (DELIVERY) takes into account the energy expenditure of the parent bird; and the third model (FAMILY GAIN) also accounts for the energy expenditure of the chicks.

Each model was thought of in the field while running the experiments. The third model (FAMILY GAIN) was stimulated by a short film of the view from the inside of the nest box which Kacelnik saw part way through the study. He was deeply impressed by the chicks' efforts to outbeg their siblings. It was clear that this begging would have enormous energetic repercussions. It was a natural step to carry this through and realise these costs as model 3.

Each of the three models produces the same broad prediction; as the travel time (round trip flight time) increases so a starling should stay longer in a patch and collect more prey. However, the FAMILY GAIN model scored the highest proportion of identical observed and predicted visit lengths, and this was the only model not to show systematic errors. Both the YIELD and DELIVERY models consistently underestimate patch times.

It is fairly clear that all the models discussed in this chapter belong to the same family. Although they tackle different questions about foraging behaviour (Which prey to choose? How many prey types? How long to stay in a patch?), each assumes that animals maximise the mean rate at which they obtain energy. The only difference between the models is that they either redefine the time period over which maximisation occurs (T_h, $T_h + T_s$, $T_t + T_p$), or (as in the case of the various central place foraging models) we observe increasing refinement of the *net* energetic returns to include parental costs (DELIVERY) and then the energetic costs of the chicks (FAMILY GAIN).

Although we have confined this chapter to models of optimal foraging, similar models have been applied to other behaviours. Copulation in the dung-fly (*Scatophaga stercoraria*) is perhaps the best-known example (Parker, 1984; Houston and McNamara, 1985). These models also assume rate-maximisation, but this time the assumption is that males are maximising the rate at which they fertilise female eggs. In the next chapter we move away from rate-maximisation and take a look at a risk minimisation.

Appendix 3.1

We want to calculate the critical encounter rate at which our predator should specialise on prey type 1. This occurs when,

$$\frac{\lambda_1 E_1}{1 + \lambda_1 h_1} = \frac{\lambda_1 E_1 + \lambda_2 E_2}{1 + \lambda_1 h_1 + \lambda_2 h_2}$$

Rearranging,

$$(\lambda_1 E_1)(1 + \lambda_1 h_1 + \lambda_2 h_2) = (1 + \lambda_1 h_1)(\lambda_1 E_1 + \lambda_2 E_2)$$

And if we multiply out the brackets we get,

$$\lambda_1 E_1 + \lambda_1 E_1 \, \lambda_1 h_1 + \lambda_1 E_1 \, \lambda_2 h_2 = \lambda_1 E_1 + \lambda_2 E_2 + \lambda_1 E_1 \, \lambda_1 h_1 + \lambda_1 h_1 \, \lambda_2 E_2$$

Cancelling $\lambda_1 E_1$ and $\lambda_1 E_1 \, \lambda_1 h_1$ leaves us with,

$$\lambda_1 E_1 \, \lambda_2 h_2 = \lambda_1 h_1 \, \lambda_2 E_2 + \lambda_2 E_2$$

And λ_2 also cancels leaving

$$\lambda_1 E_1 h_2 = \lambda_1 h_1 E_2 + E_2$$

Removing E_2 on the right hand side to brackets gives us,

$$\lambda_1 E_1 h_2 = (\lambda_1 h_1 + 1) E_2$$

And, if we rearrange this we get,

$$\frac{\lambda_1 E_1 h_2}{E_2} = \lambda_1 h_1 + 1$$

We then remove λ_1 on the right-hand side to brackets, which gives us,

$$\frac{\lambda_1 E_1 h_2}{E_2} = \lambda_1 (h_1 + 1/\lambda_1)$$

And λ_1 cancels leaving

$$\frac{E_1 h_2}{E_2} = h_1 + 1/\lambda_1$$

Rearranging,

$$1/\lambda_1 = \frac{E_1 h_2}{E_2} - h_1$$

We could rearrange this to give us the encounter rate λ_1 at which our optimal forager should specialise solely on prey type 1. However this is a very useful form of the equation since it gives us the critical time $1/\lambda_1$ at which our optimal forager should specialise on prey type 1.

Chapter 4
Optimising a Single Behaviour 2: Stochastic Models of Foraging Behaviour

4.1 Introduction

In the previous chapter we looked at a group of models which assume that animals maximise their *mean* rate of return. However, there are situations when it is not enough to know the *mean* return. In Chapter 3 we assumed that the energetic return from a prey of type 1 was always E_1; we assumed that the return from staying in a patch for T_1 s was always $E(T_1)$; and we assumed that travel times (T_t) were constant. As a result the models in Chapter 3 are all *deterministic* models: once we knew the patch time, we knew the energetic return; once we knew the prey type, we knew its energetic value. In real life it is never quite that easy: the energetic value of a prey type varies from one item to the next; no patch is the same as the next and each offers a different return for a given patch time; and, of course, travel times vary — one patch may be a stone's throw away, another several miles.

This variability introduces a probabilistic element to behaviour. If an animal stays for T_p s in a patch then *on average* it may well obtain $E(T_p)$ calories. But there is also a chance that it gets more or less than this amount. In this chapter we are going to look at how this kind of statistical variation or *stochasticity* effects our predictions; in other words, we shall look at *stochastic* models of behaviour.

Once again most of the examples are confined to studies of foraging behaviour (but in principle the arguments can be applied to many other behaviours; see later). In this chapter we are going to look at a series of optimality models which assume that animals minimise the probability of starvation rather than maximise energetic returns.

This account of *risk-sensitive foraging theory* begins with two experiments by Tom Caraco and co-workers (Steve Martindale and Tom Whitham) in Tucson, Arizona. Caraco developed an interest in optimality and applied probability while a graduate student with Larry Wolf at Syracuse in New York.

It is a standard result from economic studies of decision-making that people are not only sensitive to the mean reward, but also the variability (*risk*) about that mean. Caraco reasoned that if this holds good for people it probably holds for other animals too. He offered yellow-eyed juncos (*Junco phaeonotus*) a choice between two feeding stations. One station always provided a constant number of seeds, while the alternative station provided a variable number of seeds. The number of seeds at the constant station was equal to the expected (average) number at the variable station. For instance, in one experiment juncos were offered a choice between a feeding station which always delivered two seeds and a second station which delivered four seeds on half of all trials and none at all in the other half. The expected value of the two feeding stations is given by the value of the reward multiplied by the probability of its occurrence. That is,

$$(2 \times 1.0) = 2.0 \text{ seeds}$$

for the constant station, and,

$$[(0 \times 0.5) + (4 \times 0.5)] = 2.0 \text{ seeds}$$

for the variable station.

What Caraco found was that juncos usually preferred the constant station to the variable station — they preferred a dead certainty to a gamble; in other words they were *risk-averse*. However, if a junco's expected daily energy expenditure was greater than its expected intake then it would opt for the variable station! That is, when the going got tough and it looked as though they would not get enough food from the constant station to meet their metabolic requirements, the juncos took a gamble and switched to the variable patch. They became *risk-prone*. Caraco suggested that such risk-sensitive behaviour would be predicted by a model minimising the probability of starvation. In the following section the development of such a model is outlined.

4.2 Risk Sensitivity

To emphasise the difference between animals minimising the probability of starvation and animals maximising their mean returns I will call the former 'risk-sensitive foragers' and contrast their behaviour with 'optimal foragers'. Indeed I will pit optimal foragers against their risk-sensitive cousins. Do not forget that when we come to reject optimal foraging models in favour of risk-sensitive models we are not rejecting optimality, but simply disputing the optimality criterion (minimising the probability of starvation as opposed to maximising energetic returns).

It is a cold, dark day in winter. In a corner of the wood a bird is about to make its last foraging decision of the day. This decision is a matter of life or death. In a few seconds it will be too dark to forage. It requires 50 units of food to survive the cold night and it has only 46 units in reserve. To make up the shortfall it needs to find four units of food. Our bird is confronted by two food patches, A and B (Figure 4.1). Patch A produces three units of food at every visit. Patch B produces five units of food on 50 per cent of visits and nothing at all the rest of the time.

The expected returns from patch A are actually greater than those from patch B; on average our bird can expect three units of food from patch A and only $[(0 \times 0.5) + (5 \times 0.5)] = 2.5$ units from patch B. And so it is that our optimal forager maximising his mean energetic returns opts for patch A with monotonous regularity and (with equally monotonous regularity) starves to death the following night. In contrast our risk-sensitive forager minimises the risk of starvation by opting for patch B. He has a 50:50 chance of obtaining nothing at all and so starving to death. On the other hand he has a 50:50 chance of obtaining five units of food and surviving the night. By opting for patch B he risks getting nothing at all, but if by chance he does manage to

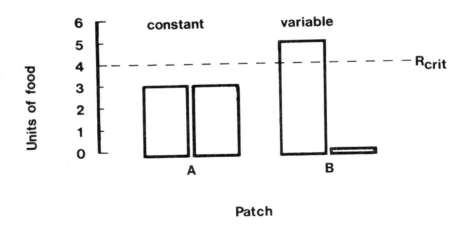

Figure 4.1: A foraging bird is confronted by two patches. Patch A gives 3 units of food on every visit (the constant patch); patch B gives five units of food on half of all visits, and nothing on the other half (the variable patch). Our bird will obtain enough food to survive the night (R_{crit}) only if it opts for the variable patch (even though the mean return from the variable patch is lower than that from the constant patch).

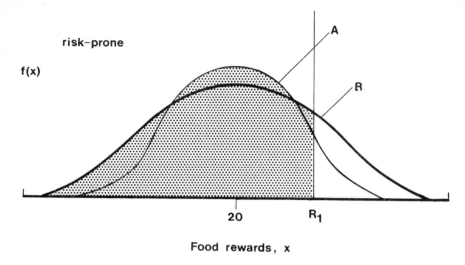

Figure 4.2: Risk-prone choices: the frequency distribution of food rewards in two patches A and B. Each has the same mean, but patch B shows greater variance than patch A. If our forager needs R_1 units of food then he maximises his chances of surviving the night by minimising the shaded area beneath the curves — by opting for patch B — and the animal is said to be risk-prone.

obtain five units of food then this is greater than the shortfall and he will survive the night. Opting for the variable patch increases his chances of surviving the night. Clearly risk-sensitive foraging makes sense.

Here is another example: Figure 4.2 shows the distribution of food rewards in two patches A and B. Each distribution has the same mean expectation; on average each animal can expect 20 units of food. However the variance in patch B is greater than in patch A.

Let R_1 be the animal's overnight requirement. What is the probability of starvation? In other words what is the probability of our animal obtaining a food reward less than his requirements? The shaded area beneath the two curves represents the proportion of visits on which our forager can expect to obtain less than his requirements: in other words, the probability of starvation. In this case our bird will minimise the risk of starvation by opting for the patch with higher variance — patch B; he is *risk-prone*. But this is only true when the requirement R is greater than the animal's mean expectation. Look what happens when R is less than the mean (Figure 4.3).

In Figure 4.3 we have the same two patches as in Figure 4.2. This time his requirements (R_2) are rather less than the amount he can expect to obtain. So this time our risk-sensitive forager minimises the risk of starvation by opting for the patch with the lower variance in the distribution of food rewards — patch A; he is *risk-averse*.

This is the kind of logic that David Stephens of Oxford University used to

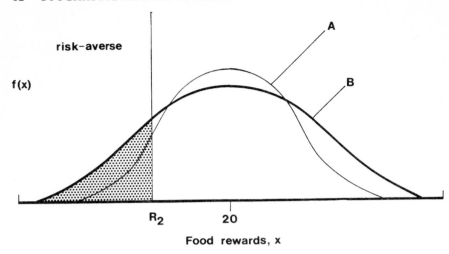

Figure 4.3: Risk-averse choices: this time the animal's requirement (R_2) is less than the mean expectation. On this occasion our forager minimises the probability of starvation by opting for patch A — the patch with low variance — and the animal is said to be risk-averse.

describe the behaviour of Tom Caraco's juncos (Stephens, 1981). Their behaviour follows the simple rule:

> be risk-averse if your expectation is greater than your requirements, and
> be risk-prone if your requirement is greater than your expected returns.

Barnard and Brown (1984) tested this simple prediction in a study of the foraging behaviour of the common shrew (*Sorex araneus*). They presented hungry shrews with a choice between a constant and a variable food station. They then manipulated the animal's expected returns (intake rate) relative to its requirements and recorded the number of visits to the variable station. As predicted, when very hungry (intake < requirement) shrews preferred the variable stations (they were *risk-prone*). However, when their requirements were less than their expected returns they were *risk-averse* (Figure 4.4).

Clearly this model shows why animals should be risk-sensitive. It also highlights the dependence of risk-sensitivity on an animal's food reserves. This explains why juncos and shrews are risk-prone only when they expect to be in negative energy balance (requirement greater than expectation) at the end of the day.

4.3 Mean and Variance

The two patches in Figures 4.2 and 4.3 have the same mean but different

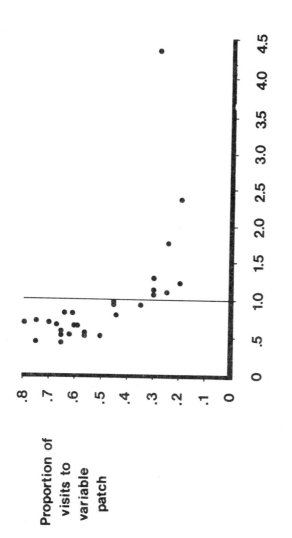

Figure 4.4: Risk-sensitivity in the shrew: when a shrew's expected intake is less than its requirements (intake : requirement < 1) they tend to opt for the variable patch (risk-prone). When the expected intake is greater than the requirement (intake : requirement > 1) the animals opt for the constant patch (risk-averse). Pooled data for all shrews (adapted from Barnard and Brown, 1984).

variances. In the real world foragers will probably be faced with a variety of patches each offering different combinations of mean and variance. Which one should a risk-sensitive forager choose? This is one of the questions tackled by the following model.

Assume that throughout the day our risk-sensitive forager makes decisions about how to forage, and let n be the number of decisions left in the day, R the amount of food an animal requires to survive the night, and S the variable describing the animal's energy supply when it must stop foraging for the night. The probability of starvation is equivalent to the probability that the bird's reserves are less than its requirements, or $P(S < R)$.

Now then, let X_i be the net amount of food gained in the ith interval, where X_i is a variable with a mean μ_i and variance σ_i^2. Furthermore let us assume that the X_i are independently and identically distributed — the size of a reward in one interval does not affect the size of reward in the next.

At the end of the day the bird will starve if the sum of all the food gained following the n foraging decisions (S) is less than its requirements. That is,

$$P(S < R) = P(\sum_{i=1}^{n} X_i < R) \tag{1}$$

Now providing the number of foraging intervals, n, is large we can use the *central limit theorem* to find the distribution of the sum of variables

$$\sum_{i=1}^{n} X_i.$$

The central limit theorem tells us that as our sample size (n) increases, so the distribution of $\sum X_i$ approaches a normal distribution. In other words the sum of food rewards obtained in all the foraging intervals is normally distributed.

(In general, the central limit theorem states that the distribution of means of samples taken from any population will tend towards the normal distribution as the size of the samples taken increases. So, as our sample size increases the means of samples (size N) drawn from a population (mean μ and variance σ^2) *with any distribution* approaches a normal distribution (with mean μ and variance σ^2/N). Therefore the distribution of the sum (S) will be normally distributed with mean $N\mu$ and variance σ^2. The important point for our purposes is that it does not matter what the actual distribution of food rewards is since their sum (and thus the animal's reserves) will be normally distributed).

To make things easier we will call the mean and standard deviation of this distribution μ_T and σ_T respectively, where μ_T is the expected mean return from decisions made in foraging time, T,

$$\mu_T = \sum_{i=1}^{n} \mu_i$$

and, σ_T, is the standard deviation of food rewards in the foraging time, T,

$$\sigma_T = \left[\sum_{i=1}^{n} \sigma_i^2 \right]^{1/2}$$

Now,

$$Z = [\sum_{i=1}^{n} X_i - \mu_T] / \sigma_T \tag{2}$$

has an approximately normal distribution with mean zero and variance one (the standard normal).

If we rearrange equation (2) we find that,

$$\sum_{i=1}^{n} X_i = \mu_T + \sigma_T.Z \tag{3}$$

And if we substitute for

$$\sum_{i=1}^{n} X_i$$

in equation (1):

$$P(S < R) = P(\mu_T + \sigma_T.Z < R) \tag{4}$$

And this is equivalent to

$$P(S < R) = P(Z < (R - \mu_T)/\sigma_T) \tag{5}$$

And so the probability of starvation is given by the area beneath the curve of this standard normal distribution (Figure 4.5; and see section 2.6 in Chapter 2). That is,

$$P(S < R) = \Phi[(R - \mu_T)/\sigma_T] \tag{6}$$

where $\Phi[\ ]$ is the cumulative distribution function (c.d.f.) of a normally distributed variable (Stephens, 1981; Krebs, Stephens and Sutherland, 1983).

$\Phi[\ ]$ can be found in the following way. Suppose, for example, that we have a distribution of food rewards with a mean, μ_T, of 20 units and standard devi-

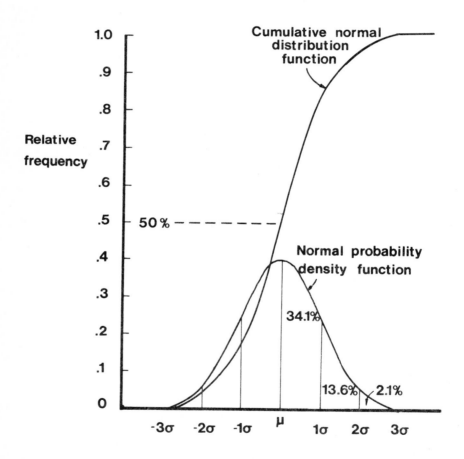

Figure 4.5: The normal distribution and the cumulative area beneath the normal distribution. If $z = 1.0$ then statistical tables tell us that the shaded area beneath the normal distribution curve is 84.1% of the total area. So, in the worked example, the proportion of rewards less than $z = 1.0$ is 0.841. That is, on 84.1% of visits our forager will obtain less than its requirement and so starve to death. (See text.)

ation, σ_T of five units. If the animal's requirement, R, is 25 units then we know from equation (5) that,

$$Z_1 = (R - \mu_T)/\sigma_T = (25 - 20)/5 = 1.0$$

If we consult a table of standardised scores (Z scores) for the normal distribution (see, for example, Neave, 1981) and look up the value $Z = 1.0$ then we find that the area beneath the standard normal to 1.0 is 0.841. This means that the probability of starvation is 0.841 (see Figure 4.5).

We would have obtained exactly the same probability of starvation had the mean been 15 units and the standard deviation 10 units:

$$Z_2 = (R - \mu_T)/\sigma_T = (25 - 15)/10 = 1.0$$

What this means is that for any value of Z there is a range of various combinations of means and standard deviations for which the probabilities of starvation are equal.

Now, if we take a value of Z, say Z', then

$$Z' = (R - \mu_T)/\sigma_T$$

And if we rearrange this then,

$$\mu_T = R - \sigma_T . Z' \qquad (7)$$

which is the familiar slope–intercept equation ($y = a + b.x$) for a straight line in μ_T, σ_T space.

Rather than calculate the probability of starvation for every combination of mean and variance offered by the environment, we can use equation (7) to determine which of a number of patches offering a combination of means and variances an animal should choose. By maximising the slope of the line from R to the feasible set (that is, the means and variances offered by the environment) in μ_T, σ_T space we minimise Z and thus the probability of starvation. We can see how this works in the following examples.

In Figure 4.6 we have two patches A and B: patch A offers a mean of ten units and a standard deviation of one unit, and patch B offers a mean of ten units and a standard deviation of five units. If the animal's requirement is for five units which patch should it choose? By maximising the slope of the line from the requirement R to the patches A and B our risk-sensitive forager minimises Z and thus the probability of starvation. In other words it should opt for patch A. We can see that this is true by calculating the Z scores for the two patches. For patch A,

$$Z_a = (5 - 10)/1 = -5$$

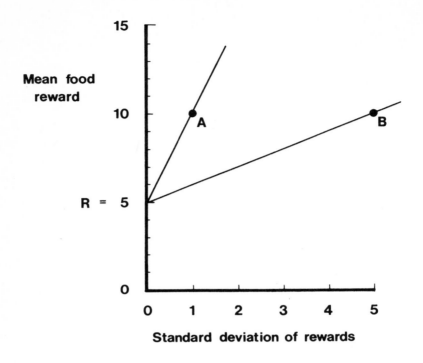

Figure 4.6: Patches A and B give the same mean reward but different standard deviations. Our risk-sensitive forager minimises the probability of starvation by maximising the slope of the line from R to the feasible set. In this case the feasible set consists of only two patches. R is less than the mean reward so our forager minimises the probability of starvation (maximises the slope of the line) by opting for patch A (risk-averse choice).

And for patch B,

$$Z_b = (5 - 10)/5 = -1$$

Thus $Z_a < Z_b$ and so our risk-sensitive forager minimises the probability of starvation by opting for patch A.

In Figure 4.7 we have the same two patches but the animal's requirement R, is 15 units. According to our graphical method our risk-sensitive forager minimises his probability of starvation by maximising the slope of the line from R to the two patches A and B. This time the slope is maximised by opting for patch B (the *risk-prone* choice). And this is exactly what we would predict if we calculated the respective Z values for each patch. In patch A,

$$Z_a = (15 - 10)/1 = +5$$

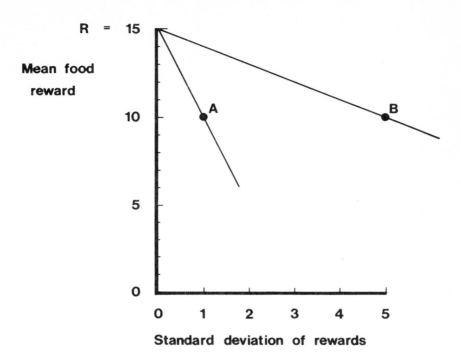

Figure 4.7: As for Figure 4.6 except that this time the requirement, R, is greater than the mean reward and so the probability of starvation is minimised (slope maximised) by opting for patch B (risk-prone choice).

And in patch B,

$$Z_b = (15 - 10)/5 = +1$$

This time $Z_b < Z_a$ and so our forager minimises his risk of starvation by opting for patch B (as we found using the graphical method).

Figure 4.8 shows the set of feasible alternatives for patches with different means μ and standard deviations σ. It follows from equation (7) above that our risk-sensitive forager minimises Z, and so the probability of starvation by maximising the slope of the line from the intercept, R, to the feasible set of means and variances offered by patches within the environment. In Figure 4.8 this means that our risk-sensitive forager minimises the probability of starvation by opting for patch A. Note that our forager could actually increase its mean returns by opting for patch B. However, this is only the optimal solution for an animal maximising its mean energetic returns. This would not be the optimal solution for an animal minimising its probability of starvation since it would also mean an increase in variance.

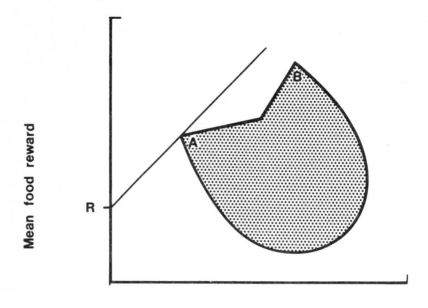

Standard deviation of food rewards

Figure 4.8: Feasible set (shaded area) of combinations of μ *and* σ *offered by a hypothetical environment. The probability of starvation is minimised by maximising the slope of the line from R to the feasible set (point A). Note that in this example our forager could actually increase its* mean *intake by opting for patch B.*

Indeed our early examples are simply special cases of this method (Figure 4.9). When R is less than the animal's expected returns then a risk-sensitive forager minimises its probability of starvation by opting for patch A, the patch with low variance — the *risk-averse* choice. When R is greater than the animal's expected returns then it minimises the probability of starvation by opting for patch B, the patch with high variance — the *risk-prone* choice.

Caraco and Lima (1985) and Barnard and Brown (in press) have looked at mean-variance trade-offs in juncos and shrews respectively. Both groups report the predicted trade-offs. Given a choice between a constant and a variable patch animals are generally risk-averse unless the mean reward at the variable station is greater than the mean reward at the constant station (Figure 4.10). Increasing the variability can mean that the variable station is visited less frequently than the constant station even when the latter offers a lower mean reward.

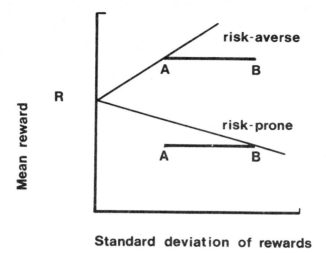

Standard deviation of rewards

Figure 4.9: Given a choice between two patches, A and B, offering the same mean reward, our risk-sensitive forager should opt for the patch offering lower variance (patch A) if the expected mean return is greater than the animal's requirement (risk-averse). If the requirements are greater than the expected returns then the animal maximises the slope of the line (and so minimises the probability of starvation) by opting for patch B (risk-prone).

4.4 Patches and Risk

One of the most interesting applications of risk-sensitive foraging theory has been to the problem of choosing optimal patch residence times. You may recall from Chapter 3 that the optimal patch residence time T_p is derived from the equation for the rate of energetic return, R:

$$R = E(T_p)/(T_p + T_t) \tag{8}$$

where T_t is the average time taken to travel between patches and $E(T_p)$ is the net energetic returns from staying in the patch for time T_p.

This is a purely deterministic model — it takes no account of the variability in time taken to travel between patches. In real life we know that travel times vary. Sometimes an animal may have to travel a considerable distance before stumbling upon a fresh patch. At other times he may find a new patch virtually next door. What is the effect of variability in travel times on the optimal residence time of a risk-sensitive forager? Given that travel times (T_t) are variable, what is the patch residence time (T_p) which minimises the probability of starvation? David Stephens collaborated with his former supervisor Ric Charnov on this problem (Stephens and Charnov, 1982).

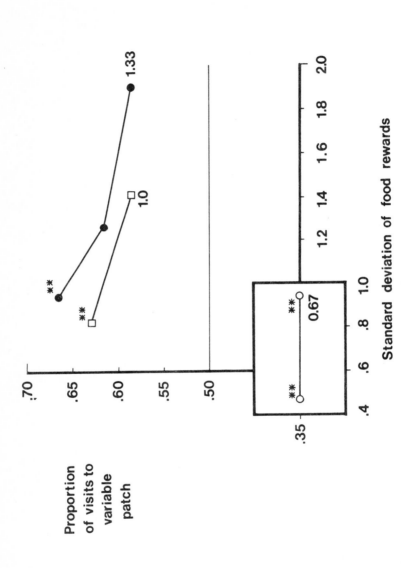

Figure 4.10: Mean-variance trade-offs in the common shrew. When the mean reward at the variable station was greater than or equal to the mean reward at the constant station (1.33 or 1.0 units) then shrews preferred the variable patch provided that the variance (and so the standard deviation) in rewards was not too great. When the mean reward at the variable station was less than that at the constant station (0.67 units), shrews preferred the constant station. Asterisks indicate significant departures from risk-indifference. (Modified from Barnard and Brown, in press.)

Let us start by assuming that patches are identical and that the patch residence time T_p completely specifies the net returns from each patch. $E(T_p)$ is identical for each patch. What is the value of T_p which minimises the risk of starvation? Well, before we can answer that question we have to specify how the mean and variance of energetic returns from each patch changes with T_p. The following account gives a feel for what is going on.

Take a look at Figure 4.11(a). Here we have an animal feeding in an environment with three patches. This animal spends 10 s in each patch and obtains 12 g of food in each. The travel time to the first patch is 30 s; to the second 20 s; and to the third 10 s. Thus the returns from each patch are,

$$
\begin{array}{lll}
\text{patch 1} & E/(T_t + T_p) = 12/(30 + 10) = 0.3\,\text{g/s} \\
\text{patch 2} & = 12/(20 + 10) = 0.4\,\text{g/s} \\
\text{patch 3} & = 12/(10 + 10) = 0.6\,\text{g/s}
\end{array}
$$

And the mean return from the three patches is,

$$
\begin{aligned}
R_{\text{mean}} &= (0.3 + 0.4 + 0.6)/3 \\
&= 0.433\,\text{g/s}
\end{aligned}
$$

Using standard methods (obtainable from any elementary statistical text and many pocket calculators) we can calculate the standard deviation of net returns,

$$
\text{standard deviation} = 0.125.
$$

In Figure 4.11(b) we have the same three patches and the same three travel times. However, this time our forager spends 20 s in each patch, and obtains 20 units of food from each visit. Now what is the mean return and the standard deviation? Well, the rate of return, R, from each patch is

$$
\begin{array}{lll}
\text{patch 1} & R_1 = 20/(30 + 20) = 0.4\,\text{g/s} \\
\text{patch 2} & R_2 = 20/(20 + 20) = 0.5\,\text{g/s} \\
\text{patch 3} & R_3 = 20/(10 + 20) = 0.67\,\text{g/s}
\end{array}
$$

Thus the mean and standard deviation of energetic returns from each of the three patches is now,

$$
\begin{aligned}
R_{\text{mean}} &= (0.4 + 0.5 + 0.67)/3 \\
&= 0.523\,\text{g/s}
\end{aligned}
$$

$$
\text{standard deviation} = 0.112\,\text{g/s}
$$

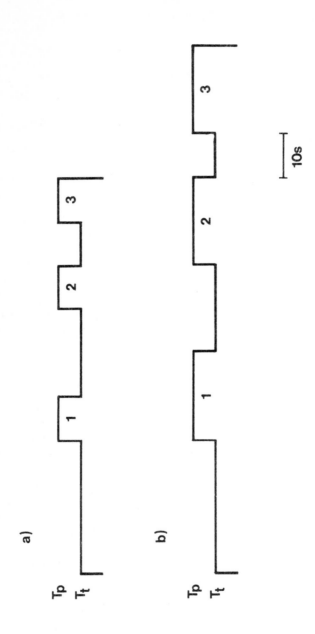

Figure 4.11: Patch use and risk. Our forager moves between three patches (1, 2 and 3). The travel times between the three patches are 30, 20 and 10 s respectively. In (a) the animal stays in each patch for 10 s and obtains 12 g of food. This means that the rate of return from each patch is 0.3, 0.4 and 0.6 g/s respectively. Thus for a patch time (T_p) of 10 s the mean rate of return is $(0.3 + 0.4 + 0.6)/3 = 0.433\,g/s$ and the standard deviation is 0.125 g/s. In (b) our forager spends 20 s in each of our three patches, and obtains 20 g of food from each of those patches. This time the mean rate of return from each patch is 0.4, 0.5 and 0.67 g/s, giving a mean rate of return of $(0.4 + 0.5 + 0.67)/3 = 0.523\,g/s$ and standard deviation of 0.112 g/s. (See text for details.)

We could do this for a variety of patch times, T_p, and in each case the mean and variance of returns would change. We could then draw a graph of how μ and σ change with patch times. Then we could draw a line in μ,σ space and use our graphical method to calculate the optimal patch time T_p — that which minimises the risk of starvation.

Stephens and Charnov (1982) have done just this (but rather more formally) for an environment in which the travel times, T_t, are randomly distributed (Figure 4.12). At first both the mean and standard deviation of food rewards increase with patch times. At time t_1 the standard deviation of food rewards reaches a maximum and begins to fall. However, the mean food reward continues to increase reaching a maximum after time t_2. Thereafter, both the mean and standard deviation of food rewards fall.

We can now use our graphical method to calculate the optimal patch time.

Once again we simply draw the line passing from the animal's requirement (R) to the feasible set in such a way as to maximise the slope of that line (and so minimise the probability of starvation). This time our 'feasible set' is a curve. Figure 4.13 gives the optimal patch time with two requirements, one in which the requirements are greater than the mean expectation, and one in which the requirements are lower. Note that the traditional mean-maximising optimal forager always stays for t_1s. It can also be seen that if the expected returns are greater than the animal's net requirements (which will usually be the case) then risk-sensitive foragers 'overstay' in a patch.

4.5 Skew

It is clear that animals should be sensitive both to the mean and variance (= standard deviation[2]) of food rewards. However, in the Stephens and Charnov model outlined in section 4.4 we assumed that the number of foraging intervals, n, is large and therefore that the distribution of rewards in those intervals (spanning the remaining time, T) is close to a normal distribution. Ideally we might like to see a general model which caters for deviations from the assumptions of normality. Tom Caraco and Paul Chasin have devised such a model (Caraco and Chasin, 1984).

Let X be the food rewards and let the probability distribution of X (which we can think of as equivalent to the frequency distribution; see section 2.4 in Chapter 2) be $f(X)$. As in the previous section let R be the forager's overnight requirement — the amount of food needed to survive the night. Then the probability of starvation is equivalent to the probability of obtaining fewer than R rewards.

$$P(X < R) = \int_0^R f(X) \, . \, dX \tag{11}$$

(see section 2.6 of Chapter 2).

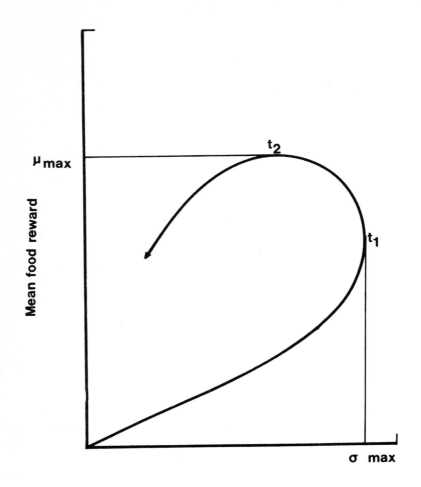

Figure 4.12: Patch use and risk: The mean and standard deviation of feeding returns change as patch time increases. Note that the standard deviation of rewards reaches a maximum (t_1) before the mean reaches a maximum (t_2).

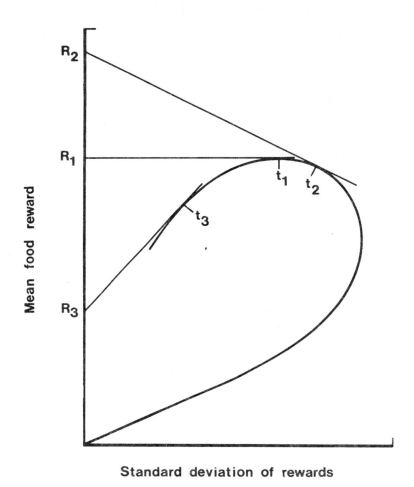

Figure 4.13: Optimal patch times: the patch time at which the probability of starvation is minimised depends upon our forager's requirements. If the requirements are less than our forager's expectation (R_3) then the slope of the line to the feasible set is maximised (and the probability of starvation minimised) by staying until time t_3. However, if the requirements are greater than the expectation (R_2) the slope is maximised (and probability of starvation minimised) by staying until time t_2. Only when the expectation equals the requirements (R_1) does the optimal patch time (t_1) correspond to the optimal patch time for a mean-maximising forager following the marginal value theorem prediction. (After Stephens and Charnov, 1982.)

This is equivalent to the proportion of rewards, X, less than the requirement, R. In other words the cumulative frequency of rewards up to R. For example in Figure 4.14 we have a hypothetical frequency distribution of food rewards. If the overnight requirement, R, is 30 units of food then in this patch the animal is unlikely to survive; only 15 per cent of visits produce more than 30 units.

Say that our risk-sensitive forager is faced with a choice between two patches, A and B, and the probability densities of food rewards are $f(x_a)$ and $f(x_b)$ respectively. If our forager visits patch A then the probability of starvation is given by the probability that x_a is less than the requirement R, or $P(x_a < R)$. And if it visits patch B then the probability of starvation is $P(x_b < R)$. Faced with a choice between two such patches (and assuming that it has complete knowledge about the reward distributions) our forager should opt for whichever patch gives the smallest probability of starvation.

Our forager should follow the simple decision rule: if $P(x_a < R) < P(x_b < R)$ then opt for patch A, otherwise opt for patch B.

Take a look at the two distributions in Figure 4.15. Each represents the distribution of rewards in two patches, A and B. Each patch has the same mean, the same variance, and the same skew. However, patch A is positively skewed, and patch B is negatively skewed. It is clear that in some situations (for example, $R = R_1$) a risk-sensitive forager minimises the risk of starvation (the shaded areas beneath the two curves) by opting for patch A. In other situations (for example, $R = R_2$ in Figure 4.16) a risk-sensitive forager minimises the risk of starvation by opting for patch B.

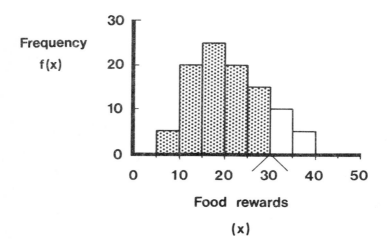

Figure 4.14: Hypothetical frequency distribution of food rewards. The animal requires 30 units of food to survive the night. This hypothetical patch produces 30 units or more on only 15% of all visits. So the probability of starvation is 0.85.

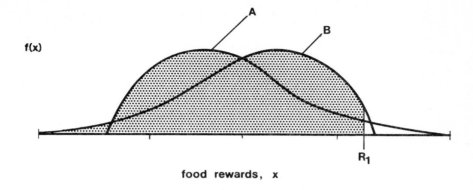

Figure 4.15: Skew: Two distributions of food rewards with equal means and equal variances. However each patch is skewed in opposite directions. Patch A is positively skewed. Patch B is negatively skewed. If the animal's net food requirement is R_1 then our risk-sensitive forager minimises its probability of starvation (given by the shaded area beneath the curves) by opting for patch A.

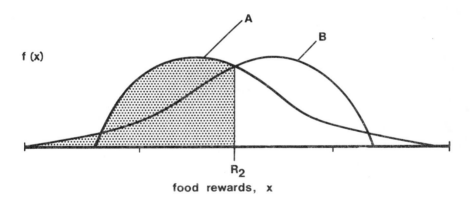

Figure 4.16: Skew: This time our risk-sensitive forager minimises the probability of starvation (given by the shaded area beneath the curves) by opting for patch B. (See text.)

Clearly a risk-sensitive forager should be sensitive to the skew of a distribution.

Caraco and Chasin (1984) carried out an experimental test of the responses of white-crowned sparrows (*Zonotrichia leucophrys*) to reward skew. They manipulated energy budgets so that the mean reward from two feeding stations (with the same mean and the same variances) were in excess of their daily requirements — region PQ of Figure 4.17. They predicted that their

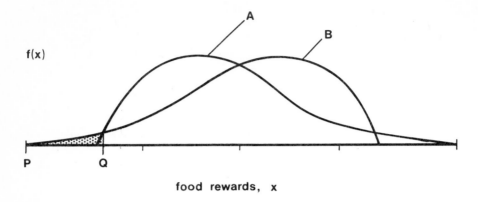

Figure 4.17: Sparrows with a requirement in the region PQ minimise their risk of starvation (given by the shaded area beneath the curves) by opting for patch A — a preference for positively skewed rewards.

sparrows should show a preference for the positively skewed patch — patch A. They did! Sparrows showed a significant preference for the positively skewed feeding station in 41 of 72 (57 per cent) experiments. They were indifferent in 23 experiments (32 per cent) and preferred the negatively skewed station in only eight experiments (11 per cent). Under these experimental conditions sparrows showed a significant preference for a positively skewed reward schedule.

4.6 Summary

Models of risk-sensitive foraging owe their origin to psychological and economic models of choice behaviour in people. In translating these models to animal behaviour we assume that natural selection has favoured efficient, economic animals. We assume that risk-sensitive foragers are more likely to survive cold, winter nights.

Tom Caraco made the first important step in modelling risk-sensitive foraging by recognising that means are incomplete descriptions of reward schedules. This recognition was in part attributable to the application of psychological and economic thinking to the problem of optimal foraging. Variance and mean-variance relationships are thoroughly worked problems in psychological circles, but it needed someone with a background in these areas to recognise their importance for optimality models. This led directly to the junco experiments (see section 4.2).

In these experiments, Tom Caraco, Steve Martindale and Tom Whitham looked for evidence of risk-sensitivity in captive juncos. They offered juncos the choice of two feeding stations each with the same mean reward but different variances. They found that juncos were risk-averse providing that their expected energetic requirements were less than the expected returns from the two feeding stations. However, if the birds expected to be in negative energy balance at the end of the day then the birds were risk-prone.

This finding stimulated David Stephens (also with a background in applied probability) to develop his model of risk-sensitive foraging. He demonstrated that Caraco's '24-hour expected energy balance rule' would be predicted if juncos were minimising their probability of starvation.

The simple model of risk-sensitive foraging outlined in section 4.2 looked only at choices between patches offering the same mean but different variances. Its extension to cover differing mean-variance combinations was a natural step. The central limit theorem was an obvious candidate for combining different means and variances (see section 4.3). Stephens and Charnov (1982) also extended their model to consider its implications for classical patch-use theory (see section 4.4). Finally Tom Caraco formulated the general model accommodating reward schedules deviating from normality (see section 4.5).

Inevitably, this account of risk-sensitive foraging omits some of the models. In particular, I have said little about *variance-discounting models* (Caraco, 1981; Real, 1980, 1981). These suggest that animals maximise the mean (μ) discounted by a certain amount (k) of the variance (σ). That is, they maximise ($\mu - k\sigma$). If an animal is risk-averse, then k is positive; and if it is risk prone then k is negative. Unlike the *z-score* models, *variance-discounting* models cannot predict the direction of risk sensitivity on *a priori* grounds. I find the *z*-score models intuitively more appealing. Regelmann (1984) discusses the relationship between *z*-score and variance-discounting models and derives conditions under which the two models actually make rather different predictions.

One problem for *z*-score models is that for an animal to be risk-prone the probability of starvation must be greater than 0.50 (Krebs, Stephens and Sutherland, 1983). This suggests massive mortality amongst small passerines, small mammals and other risk-prone foragers. However, the *z*-score models assume that a forager makes only one decision about whether to choose high or low variance. This underestimates the probability of survival because it ignores the possibility that a risk-prone choice will result in a gain large enough to allow the forager to become risk-averse (Houston and McNamara, 1982).

Perhaps the most interesting point to arise out of this description is the interdisciplinary background to risk-sensitive models. Mathematical models from one discipline (in this case economics/psychology) are readily adapted to a second (behavioural ecology). Once we find a mathematical framework for our problem, we can use the known properties of the mathematics to make interesting predictions. And the original discipline of the problem is irrelevant.

Although I have confined this chapter to a discussion of foraging behaviour, we can apply the same general principles to other behaviours. Wherever you get variability in returns then animals are likely to be risk-sensitive. For instance, two breeding areas may have exactly the same average return (in terms of offspring produced) but the variation in returns between those two areas may be very different. One area may offer a relatively constant return; the other may offer bumper prospects in good seasons, but complete failure in others. Which should our breeder choose? Or two females may be equally fecund but one may show considerable variation in seasonal production while the other is relatively constant. The problem of risk-sensitivity is not confined to feeding behaviour!

In the following chapter we are going to look at another example where the variability may be a matter of life or death: how do scanning patterns affect the probability of an animal detecting a predator? At first this sounds completely unrelated to the problem of risk-sensitive foraging, but we shall see that they have a great deal in common.

Chapter 5
Temporal Patterns: Vigilance in Birds

5.1 Introduction

So far we have confined our discussion to how animals behave once they have decided to forage, copulate, or whatever. However, in this and the following chapter, we look at how an animal decides which behaviour to perform next. Should an animal torn between hunger and thirst feed first or drink first? The answer will depend upon how hungry or how thirsty it is. Should it feed in one long bout and then drink? Or should it alternate between the two? These questions about optimal behaviour sequences are the kinds of questions tackled in the next chapter. However, in this chapter we start by asking some questions about the functional significance of certain behavioural sequences. Do *temporal patterns* really matter? Do such patterns affect survival value? In this chapter I am going to show how important they are by considering some simple models of vigilance in birds.

If you watch a blue tit on a peanut feeder you will notice that it interrupts feeding with short intervals in which it appears to look around. How, we might ask, does such scanning behaviour affect the probability of predator detection? At an intuitive level it seems pretty obvious that the more often an animal looks up, or the more time spent scanning, the more likely it is to detect a predator. However, we had to wait until 1973 before Ron Pulliam of the University of Arizona came up with a formal model of the relationship between scanning rate and predator detection (Pulliam, 1973).

In fact Pulliam was not interested in vigilance *per se*. His main interest was in flocking in birds. In particular he was interested in the benefits which birds might derive from joining flocks. Increased vigilance might be one such benefit; a flock of birds might be expected to be more likely to detect predators than solitary individuals. By developing a formal model of such an advantage Pulliam hoped that this idea would gain wider credence (at the time there was a fierce debate about the significance of predator avoidance for avian flocking (see Lazarus, 1972)).

5.2 Pulliam's Model

At first glance modelling the probability of predator detection seems an impossible task. Whether an animal spots a predator will depend on the predator's behaviour, its direction of attack, the availability of cover and a host of other variables. Pulliam (1973) chose to ignore most of these variables. Instead he made a powerful, simplifying assumption — that predator detection depends upon an animal looking up during a critical period lasting Ts. This critical period is the time taken for a predator to complete its final uncovered dash. Before a predator breaks cover we simply assume that it cannot be detected and once it breaks cover the predator will always be detected providing the animal looks up in time. More about T later!

By introducing the theoretical construct, T, we turn the question 'How does scanning rate affect the probability of predator detection?' into 'Given a scanning rate, λ, what is the probability of a bird looking up in an interval lasting Ts?' This is a much easier question to answer, one with an instantly recognisable mathematical solution. What we want to know is the probability of an interscan interval (the time between two consecutive scans) shorter than the predator approach time, T.

To calculate this probability we need to make one or two assumptions about the behaviour of birds and their prey. First, we need to assume that attacks are randomly timed (see later). The next step is to make some assumptions about the process *generating* scanning events. Pulliam asked us to assume that the process generating scanning events is a *Poisson process* (see section 2.7 in Chapter 2). Given that this is the case then the probability of a scanning event occurring in time t is given by,

$$p = 1 - e^{-\lambda t} \tag{1}$$

where λ is the rate at which the Poisson process generates scanning events (see section 2.7, Chapter 2).

Now, if we let t equal the predator approach time, T, then we have the probability of a scanning event occurring during the predator approach time. That is we have the probability of a bird detecting an attack of duration T,

$$p = 1 - e^{-\lambda T} \tag{2}$$

where λ is the mean scanning rate (in scans/min) and T is the attack time (in minutes).

Example 1
If a bird is scanning at a rate of 10 scans/min, then the probability that it will detect an attack of length 6 s is

$$p = 1 - e^{-\lambda T}$$
$$= 1 - e^{-10.6/60}$$
$$= 1 - 0.368$$
$$= 0.632$$

And with a higher scanning rate (say 15 scans/min) the probability of predator detection is considerably higher,

$$p = 1 - e^{-\lambda T}$$
$$= 1 - e^{-15.6/60}$$
$$= 1 - 0.223$$
$$= 0.777$$

The important step in developing the model was to introduce a critical period (the predator approach time) over which detection could occur. Once this critical period was identified, it was simply a case of tailoring the problem to fit the mathematics and this was achieved by assuming a Poisson process.

You will remember that the purpose of this model was to look at the effects of flock size on predator detection. To do this we simply consider a flock of birds, size N, in which each individual bird is generating scanning events at rate λ. In other words, we have N independent Poisson processes. The probability of at least one of those processes generating an event in time T is simply,

$$p = 1 - e^{-N\lambda T}$$

In other words the probability, P_g, of at least one member of a flock scanning in the interval T is equal to one minus the probability of all birds failing to make a scan, or,

$$P_g = 1 - e^{-N\lambda T} \tag{2}$$

Which is simply the probability of a flock (size N) with a mean scanning rate for each individual (λ) detecting an attack of length T. P_g is the group's 'corporate vigilance' (Bertram, 1980).

Example 2

We saw earlier (Example 1) that the probability of a bird scanning at 10 scans/min detecting an attack of length 6 s was 0.632. What happens if we have *two* such birds scanning independently of each other. Then, by equation (2), the probability that at least one of them will scan in time $T = 6$ s is simply,

$$P_g = 1 - e^{-N\lambda T}$$

$$= 1 - e^{-2.10.6/60}$$

$$= 1 - 0.135$$

$$= 0.865$$

It is clear from Examples 1 and 2 that as flock size, N, or scanning rate, λ, increase so the probability of predator detection increases (Figure 5.1). Alternatively, as flock size increases birds can afford to lower their scanning rates without suffering a fall in corporate vigilance (Figure 5.2).

In the decade following the publication of Pulliam's model there has been a

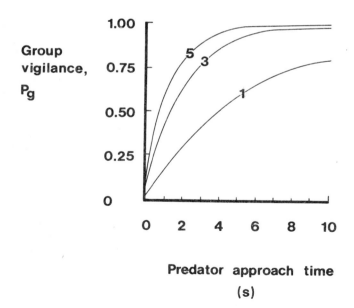

Figure 5.1: Predator detection and flock size. As flock size increases, from one to five individuals, so the probability of predator detection increases for a range of predator approach times, T.

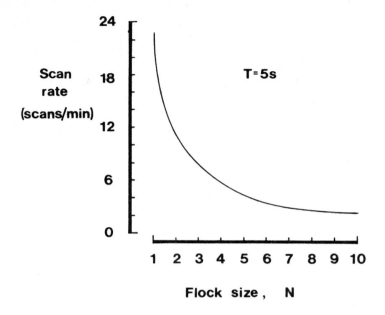

Figure 5.2: Scanning rates and flock size. Scanning rate falls with increasing flock size, N, whilst maintaining a constant level of corporate vigilance ($P_g = 0.85$).

spate of papers supporting one or both of the above predictions. However, in a direct test of the model Mark Elgar and Carla Catterall of Griffith University, Brisbane found consistent departures from Pulliam's model when they compared the scanning rates of flock-feeding sparrows (*Passer domesticus*) with those predicted by the model.

Elgar and Catterall (1981) rearranged Pulliam's original model (equation (2)) to predict the relationship between scanning rate, λ, and flock size, N. Thus,

$$\lambda = -\ln{(1 - P_g)}/NT \qquad (3)$$

They assumed that birds attempt to maintain a constant probability of predator detection, P_g. Since P_g and T are unknown, they allowed these to vary and then predicted scanning rates as a function of flock size. They then selected the values of P_g and T giving the closest fit to their observed values (Figure 5.3). As you can see they found departures from the predicted scanning rates especially in small flocks. Why does the Pulliam model break down?

In order to qualify as a Poisson process the Poisson events must be instantaneous. In this case, scans are modelled as Poisson events, and so this means that Pulliam's model assumes that scans are instantaneous. However,

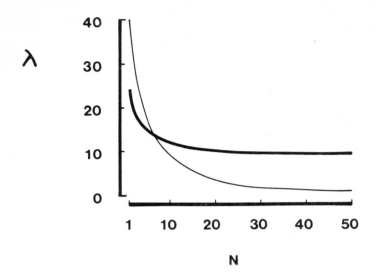

Figure 5.3: A test of the Pulliam (1973) model. Observed (bold curve) and predicted (feint curve) scanning rates (λ) for flocking house sparrows. In small flocks the model consistently overestimates, and in large flocks underestimates, observed scanning rates.

scans are *not* instantaneous so they place a limiting constraint on scanning rates. If a bird has a scan duration of 1 s it cannot (with the best will in the world) attain scanning rates greater than 60 scans/min! Elgar and Catterall attributed the failure of the model to a failure of this assumption. (Note that although this explains the departures from the model in small flocks, it does not explain why birds in large flocks have consistently *higher* scanning rates than the model predicts.)

Two other findings brought Pulliam's model into question. If the process generating scanning events is a Poisson process then we would expect the intervals between these events to follow an exponential distribution (see section 2.8 in Chapter 2). For scanning behaviour this means that the *inter-scan intervals* should be exponentially distributed. Unfortunately, this is not the case. Instead birds seem to avoid very short and very long interscan intervals (Elcavage and Caraco, 1983; Hart and Lendrem, 1984; Lendrem, 1982, 1983; Lendrem *et al.*, in press; Sullivan, 1985). The second big problem is that birds show some temporal or spatial synchrony of scanning behaviour — they do not scan independently of each other. If one individual looks up, its companion is more likely to look up (to see what his companion is looking at?). This means that their levels of vigilance are usually much lower than would be predicted if they were scanning independently of each other (Lazarus, 1979).

Such findings contributed to a feeling of unease about Pulliam's model. It was against this background that the next generation of vigilance models was developed.

5.3 Scanning Patterns

An important corollary of Pulliam's model is that scanning rates provide an adequate description of vigilance behaviour in birds. In this section I hope to demonstrate that scanning rates alone do not provide an adequate description of vigilance behaviour and that scanning patterns are just as important.

Figure 5.4 shows hypothetical frequency distributions of interscan intervals for two birds. If you refer back to Chapter 3 then you will notice a more than superficial resemblance to Figure 4.3. This is no accident! The author developed the following arguments in parallel with David Stephens' work on risk-sensitive foraging. The author applied the same logic to avian vigilance as Stephens had applied to risk-sensitive foraging theory.

In Figure 5.4 each bird has the same average scanning rate and so the same mean interscan interval. According to Pulliam then each has the same likelihood of detecting an approaching predator. However, one bird (the bold curve) shows greater variation — greater variance — in its interscan intervals. The two birds have different *scanning patterns*. Do these scanning patterns affect the probability of predator detection?

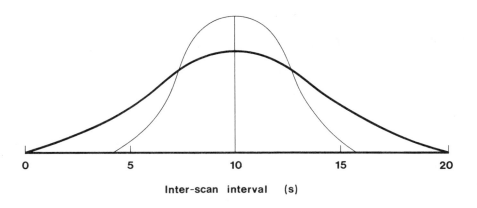

0   5   10   15   20

Inter-scan interval (s)

Figure 5.4: Hypothetical frequency distributions of interscan intervals for two birds. Both birds share the same mean scanning rate and so the same mean interscan interval. However, one bird (the bold curve) shows greater variance in interscan intervals than the other (the feint curve). If the predator approach time, T, equals 15 s then the area beneath the two curves gives the probability of a bird making a scan before the predator completes its final uncovered dash. This area is much greater (and so the probability of predator detection is much higher) for the bird showing low variance (feint curve). (See text.)

Instead of considering a randomly attacking predator let us assume that we have a 'wait and see' predator — one which waits for prey to stop scanning and start feeding before it makes an attack. This is not as unrealistic as it first sounds. Many ground predators, such as cats, are known to use prey behaviour when stalking prey, and lions often wait for prey to start feeding before making an attack (Schaller, 1972).

Let the time taken for the predator to make an attack — the predator approach time — equal 15 s. What is the probability of the two birds detecting such an attack? Once again we are simply asking 'What is the probability of an interscan interval being shorter than the predator approach time?'. For a predator that attacks at the start of an interscan interval ($t = 0$ s) and finishes at $t = T = 15$ s this is simply equivalent to the area beneath the curve between 0 and 15 s (Figure 5.4).

We can see straight away that this area is greater for the feint curve than for the bold curve. That is, the feint bird is more likely to make a scan than the bold bird. It is more likely to detect an attack length 15 s than the bold bird. Clearly the probability of predator detection depends upon the distribution of interscan intervals as well as the scanning rate.

To give another example (this time with real data): Figure 5.5 shows the frequency distributions of interscan intervals for individual ostriches in 'groups' of one (feint curve) and in groups of three and four birds (bold curve). What is the probability of *individuals* in each group detecting a predator, such as a lion, with an attack time of 40 s?

Once again we simply calculate the area under each curve. In this case this area is simply the proportion of interscan intervals less than 40 s. In fact we find that solitary birds are *more* likely to detect our predator than *individuals* in groups of three and four ostriches. But is this still true for other values of *T*? We can allow *T* to take any value we like and calculate the respective probabilities to produce a 'vigilance curve' (Lendrem, 1982, 1983, 1984; Hart and Lendrem, 1984). If we do this for our ostriches we find that solitary birds are consistently more vigilant than birds in groups of three and four (Figure 5.6).

The important step in developing upon Pulliam's model has been to focus on the interscan interval as the vigilance parameter of special interest (rather than scanning rate). By so doing the problem of scan duration does not arise and we make no assumption about the pattern of scanning behaviour. However, the major drawback of this method is that we have slipped in a major assumption about predator behaviour — that predators cue an attack on prey behaviour. Although some predators do wait for an animal to start feeding before launching an attack many predators do not. We must modify the model so that it can handle randomly attacking predators. This is slightly tricky!

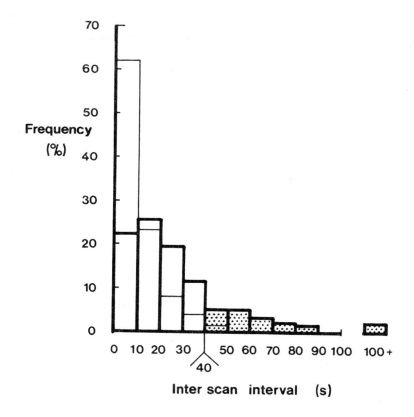

Figure 5.5: Vigilance in ostriches: Frequency distributions of interscan intervals for solitary ostriches (feint curve) and individuals in groups of three and four ostriches (bold curve). In this example the predator approach time, T = 40 s. The shaded areas are the probabilities of individuals failing to detect such attacks. The probability of birds detecting such attacks is 0.98 for solitary birds and 0.84 for individuals in groups of three and four ostriches. (After Hart and Lendrem, 1984.)

5.4 Random Attacks

The following model was a joint effort by a number of people. Alan Grafen of Oxford University and Rob Kirkwood of Nottingham University came up with the solution independently of each other. Andy Hart of Oxford University did the hard work of working out what Grafen and Kirkwood had both said.

To calculate the probability of detecting a randomly attacking predator we need to know the proportion of time spent scanning by the prey and the frequency distribution (roughly equivalent to the probability density; see

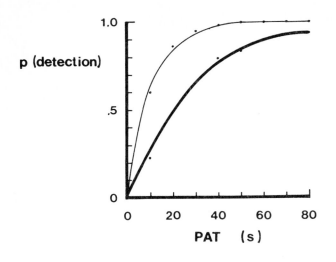

Figure 5.6: Vigilance in ostriches: Vigilance curves for solitary birds (feint curve) and individuals in groups of three and four ostriches (bold curve). For a wide range of predator approach times (PAT), solitary individuals are more vigilant than individuals in groups. (See text.)

Lendrem, 1984; Hart and Lendrem, 1984, and section 2.5 in Chapter 2) of interscan intervals. Let p_s be the proportion of time spent scanning and $f(t)$ the frequency distribution of interscan intervals.

Now, if a predator attacks randomly then on a proportion $(1 - p_s)$ of occasions the bird will be feeding and the start of the attack will be undetected. How long will it be before the bird makes a scan and detects our random predator?

The first thing which we have to take into account is that a randomly attacking predator is more likely to arrive during a long interscan interval than a short interscan interval. For example a randomly timed attack is twice as likely to fall into a 2s interscan interval as a 1s interval. The second thing to take into account is that randomly attacking predators are more likely to turn up during frequent interscan intervals. For example, if an interval lasting 2s appears once every ten interscan intervals then a randomly timed attack is ten times as likely to fall into such an interval than if it occurs only once in every 100 intervals.

In fact the proportion of all attacks which fall into intervals of length ts is given by the total time for all intervals of that length, as a proportion of all time. The total time in intervals of length ts is equal to $t \cdot f(t)$ (the duration of those intervals multiplied by their frequency). Therefore the probability of attacks falling into intervals of this length is,

$$g(t) = \frac{t \cdot f(t)}{\int\limits_0^\infty t \cdot f(t) \cdot dt} \tag{4}$$

The denominator is simply the sum of all the products of all intervals and their frequencies. So $g(t)$ is a probability density function approximated by the frequency distribution of randomly interrupted interscan intervals (see section 2.4 in Chapter 2).

Now the probability of detection depends upon the length of the interrupted interval (Figure 5.7). If the interrupted interval is less than the predator approach time, T, then the bird will always make a scan before the predator completes its final dash and will always detect the predator. However, if the interval is greater than T s then detection depends upon the point of interruption (Figure 5.8). On T/t occasions the attack will begin less than T s before the next scan and the attack will be detected. For example if T is 5 s long and the interrupted interval is 10 s long then there is a 50 : 50 chance that a randomly timed attack will fall in the second half of the interval and the predator will be detected.

To calculate the probability of detecting an attack started at random within

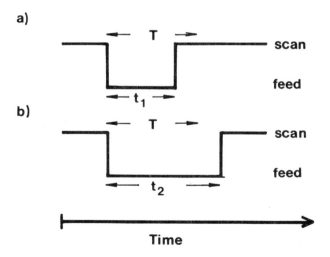

Figure 5.7: *Random attacks: This figure shows an interscan interval sandwiched between two scans. The predator approach time* $= T$ *s. An attack falling into the interval* t_1 *will never be successful because* $t_1 < T$ *and so the bird will always make a scan before the predator completes its final uncovered dash. However,* $t_2 > T$, *and so an attack falling into interval* t_2 *may be successful.*

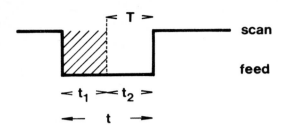

Figure 5.8: Random attacks: Here we have an interscan interval, t, lasting 10 s. The predator approach time, T = 5 s. t > T so an attack falling into this interval may be successful. Attacks which begin less than T s before the end of the interval (t₂) will be detected. However, attacks which begin more than T s before the end of the interscan interval (t₂) will pass undetected. In this case the probability of predator detection will be T/t = 5/10 = 0.50.

an interscan interval we effectively calculate T/t for every randomly interrupted interval greater than T. More formally, the probability of detecting an attack started at random within an interscan interval is given by

$$G(T) = \int_0^T g(t) \cdot dt + \int_T^\infty T/t \cdot g(t) \cdot dt \qquad (5)$$

The first half of the equation represents the proportion of interrupted intervals shorter than the attack time. The second half of the equation is the proportion of intervals for which the attack begins less than Ts before the end of an interscan interval (for those intervals longer than Ts).

However, this is the probability of detection only on those $(1 - p_s)$ occasions when an attack falls into an interscan interval. On a proportion, p_s, of occasions a bird will be scanning when an attack begins. Such attacks will be detected immediately, and so the overall probability of detecting an attack by a random predator, p_d, is simply,

$$p_d = p_s + (1 - p_s) \cdot G(T) \qquad (6)$$

(compare Lendrem, 1984).

Figure 5.9 shows vigilance curves for solitary ostriches calculated according to equation (6). The second curve shows the same curve for solitary birds assuming 'wait and see' rather than random attacks.

So here we have a model of vigilance in birds which does not assume that birds scan randomly (according to a Poisson process) or that scans are instantaneous, but which does cater for randomly attacking predators. However, so far, we have said nothing about corporate levels of vigilance in

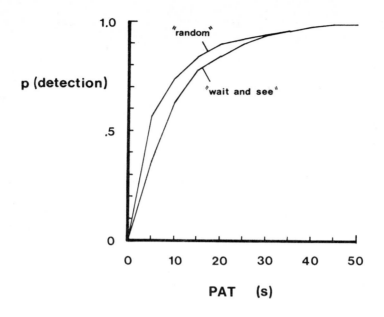

Figure 5.9: Vigilance curves for solitary ostriches attacked by 'random' and 'wait-and-see' predators; the latter predators do better than 'random' predators for a variety of attack times, T.

groups of animals. To do that we must turn to the problem of independent scanning.

5.5 The Independence Problem

If, like Pulliam, we assume that birds scan independently of each other then the probability of at least one member of a flock detecting a randomly attacking predator is simply one minus the probability of all birds failing to detect that predator.

If p_d is the probability of a bird detecting a predator then $(1 - p_d)$ is the probability of that bird failing to detect that predator. If birds scan independently of each other then the probability of two birds failing to detect a predator is simply the probability of the first bird failing to detect a predator multiplied by the probability of the second bird failing to detect a predator. If both birds have the same level of vigilance (p_d) then this is simply $(1 - p_d)(1 - p_d)$, or $(1 - p_d)^2$. The probability of three birds failing to detect a predator is $(1 - p_d)^3$, and of N birds is $(1 - pd)^N$. Now the probability, P_g, of a flock of birds size N detecting a predator is simply one *minus* the probability of all birds *failing* to detect that predator. In other words,

$$P_g = 1 - (1 - p_d)^N \tag{7}$$

(see Lendrem, 1983, 1984).

However, ideally, we would like to drop the independence assumption altogether. Hart and Lendrem (1984) present some solutions to this problem. The simplest way is to treat the flock as a unit and ask directly what is the probability of the group detecting an approaching predator. To do this we need to know the frequency distribution of intervals when all birds have their heads down feeding and the proportion of time for which one or more birds is scanning. These then take the values of $f(t)$ (the frequency distribution of interscan intervals) and p_s (the proportion of time spent scanning) and we simply calculate levels of vigilance as if flocks were individuals (see section 5.4).

Figure 5.10(a) shows the frequency distribution of intervals when all heads were down for ostriches in groups of three and four birds. From this distribution the corporate levels of vigilance (illustrated in Figure 5.10(b)) were calculated. Note that groups of ostriches are more likely to detect predators than solitary ostriches even though *individuals* in groups are less vigilant (see section 5.3).

5.6 Testing the Model

Throughout this book a certain amount of emphasis is placed on testing models. However, a model need not be testable for it to be interesting. In sections 5.4 and 5.5 we have seen how a more general model of avian vigilance has been developed by sidestepping the assumptions of the Pulliam (1973) model. Assumption reduction can be an end in itself. The best model is that which gives the closest fit to the data whilst minimising the number of assumptions upon which the model is based (McCleery's (1977) parsimony principle). However, as it happens, Thompson and Lendrem (1985) have tested the above model, not with ostriches, but with plovers.

Throughout the British winter, lapwings (*Vanellus vanellus*) and golden plovers (*Pluvialis apricaria*) make a living by hunting for worms in agricultural pastureland. Worm capture requires prey location (using visual and auditory cues) during which plovers adopt a characteristic 'crouching' posture (the 'crouching time'). Once located the worm is extracted, mandibulated and swallowed (the 'handling time'). Thompson and Lendrem assumed that crouching and handling are periods of reduced vigilance equivalent to the interscan intervals observed in blue tits, ostriches and other animals.

Associated with these plovers are blackheaded gulls (*Larus ridibundus*). These make a living from stealing worms from the plovers (Thompson, 1984,

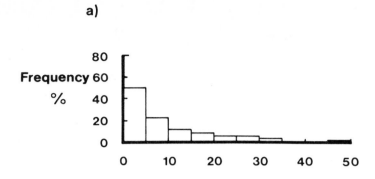

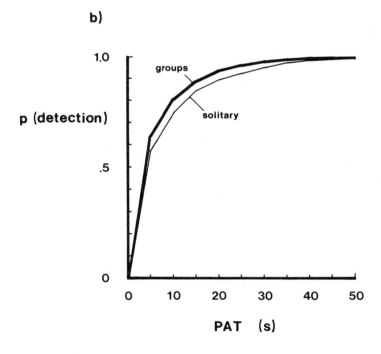

Figure 5.10: Ostrich vigilance: (a) frequency distribution of intervals when all ostriches were feeding in groups of three and four birds; (b) vigilance curves for solitary ostriches (feint curve) and corporate vigilance for groups of three and four ostriches (bold curve) attacked by 'random' predators. These curves calculated without assuming independent scanning. Note that groups of three and four ostriches are consistently more vigilant than solitary ostriches even though *individual levels of vigilance are lower (see Figure 5.6).*

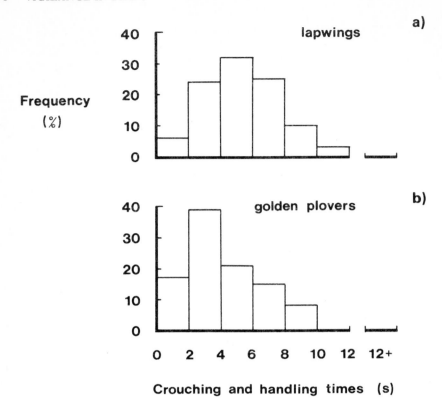

Figure 5.11: Frequency distributions of crouching and handling times for (a) lapwings (n = 107) and (b) golden plovers (n = 409).

1986; Barnard and Thompson, 1985). During the crouching and handling episodes blackheaded gulls can approach unseen. If a plover fails to make a scan before the gull completes its approach then the attack is successful and the gull steals the plover's worm. This means that kleptoparasitic attacks are analogous to predatory attacks. Since kleptoparasitic attacks are relatively frequent (about 2 attacks/min/flock) we can use them to test vigilance models.

Of course losing a worm is hardly comparable with the lost reproductive success that follows a successful predation (unless you happen to be the worm). However this should not affect the basic model. There may be differences in the scanning patterns of plovers on the lookout for predators and those on the lookout for kleptoparasitic gulls. However, this just changes the distribution of interscan intervals (crouching and handling times) upon which we base our vigilance predictions.

Thompson and Lendrem used the distribution of combined crouching and handling durations to predict the probability of gull detection. At first they used crouching and handling times for all members of a plover flock. However, most members of a plover flock are not attacked by gulls. Only those taking large worms (> 32mm) are attacked because these yield the highest energetic returns (Thompson, 1986). So, effectively, the first model was based on the wrong distribution of interscan intervals. The second version of the model used the frequency distribution of crouching and handling durations for plovers taking large worms (see Figure 5.11).

It is worth noting that a third version of the model looked at what happens when a gull launches an attack at the start of the handling time rather than the crouch. This version uses the frequency distribution of handling times alone to calculate detection probabilities. It consistently overestimated the probability of gull detection (Thompson and Lendrem, 1985).

The model assumes that gulls launch an attack at the start of a crouch. So this corresponds to the ostrich model developed in section 5.3 (see Hart and Lendrem, 1984, and their equation (4)). If $f(t)$ is the frequency distribution of combined crouching and handling durations, and T is the gull's flight attack time (FAT), then the probability of gull detection is equivalent to the probability of a combined crouching and handling time $(c + h)$ shorter than the FAT.

$$p(t < T) = \int_{0}^{T} f(t) \cdot dt \tag{8}$$

which is equivalent to the proportion of intervals shorter than T, where $t = (c + h)$. Turning to Figure 5.12, if the flight attack time, T, is 4s then 30% of combined crouching and handling durations (the shaded area) are shorter than the flight attack time and the probability of gull detection is therefore 0.30. And if $T = 6$s then 62% of combined crouching and handling times are shorter than T and so the probability of gull detection is 0.62. In this way we can construct vigilance curves for our plovers as outlined in section 5.3.

We can now compare these predicted detection probabilities with those observed in the field. These observed probabilities were obtained in the following way. Thompson and Lendrem assumed that if a gull caught a plover with a worm then the attack had not been detected. If plovers detected an attack they either dumped the worm on the turf and took flight, or, if they had time, took flight still clutching the worm (with the gull in hot pursuit!). The observed vigilance curves are thus the proportion of detected attacks for attacks of 1, 2, 3 ... etc.s. For example, Thompson and Lendrem observed 16 gull attacks lasting 2s, and only eight were detected. The probability of gull detection for a FAT $= 2$s is therefore 0.50. The observed vigilance curves are compared with the expected curves in Figure 5.13.

There was no significant difference between observed and expected curves

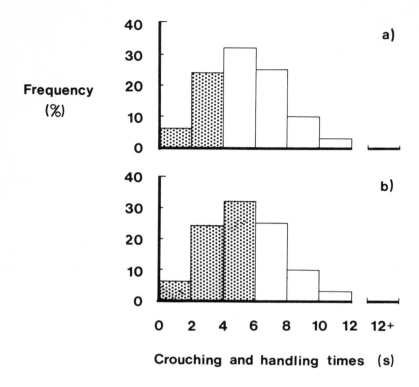

Figure 5.12: Calculating levels of vigilance for lapwings; 30% of crouching and handling times are less than 4 s (a), and 62% of crouching and handling times are less than 6 s (b). The predicted detection probabilities are 0.30 and 0.62 for attacks lasting 4 s and 6 s respectively. (See text.)

either for lapwings or for golden plovers. However, an even closer fit was obtained when an arbitrary constraint of a 1 s delay between the start of a crouch and the launch of an attack was introduced. This constraint means that gulls wait for 1 s before launching an attack. Such a delay makes good sense, 25% of all crouches are aborted — probably false alarms, the mean duration of such aborted crouches was 0.5 s. By waiting for 1 s a gull ensures that a plover really has detected a worm.

5.7 Summary

Our starting point was the question 'How does scanning behaviour affect levels of vigilance?' The big step forward was taken by Ron Pulliam in introducing the theoretical construct, T, the predator approach time. This trans-

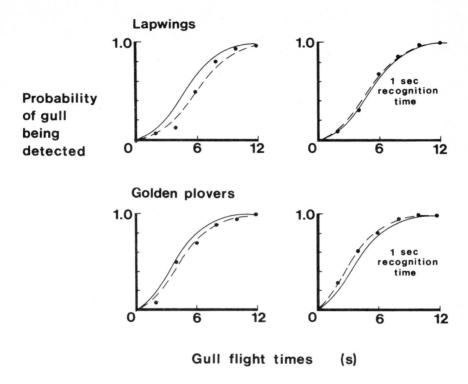

Figure 5.13: Observed (broken curve) and predicted (smooth curve) levels of vigilance for lapwings and golden plovers, with and without the 1 s recognition time constraint. Observed curves are based on 194 and 101 gull attacks for lapwings and golden plovers respectively. (After Thompson and Lendrem, 1985.)

formed our original question into 'What is the probability of a bird looking up in an interval *T*?' or 'What is the probability of an interscan interval shorter than *T*?'. And if we assume that birds scan according to a Poisson process then we have a piece of instantly recognisable mathematics to fit the situation.

Pulliam's model is a nice example of 'off-the-peg' modelling. Once the right question had been asked the appropriate mathematics was instantly recognisable. All that was left to do was to tailor the behaviour to fit the mathematics. However, in tailoring the behaviour to fit the mathematics we are required to make three rather unrealistic assumptions (random, instantaneous and independent scanning). 'Off-the-peg' models do not always fit! Later models attempted to sidestep these assumptions.

The first crucial step was to make an assumption about predator behaviour — that predators attack at the start of a feeding bout (an interscan interval). This vital first step was suggested by parallel developments in risk-sensitive foraging theory (see Chapter 4). Making this assumption allowed two of

Pulliam's assumptions (random and instantaneous scanning) to be dropped. However, this was achieved at a price, and that price was to restrict the model to cases where predators waited for prey to begin feeding (to start an interscan interval) before making an attack.

The next step was to develop a more general model which catered for randomly attacking predators. This was relatively straightforward (see section 5.4) once it was recognised that a bird would only fail to detect a predator if that randomly arriving predator arrived during an interscan interval longer than the predator approach time, T, and more than Ts before the end of such an interval. All that remained was to put this in mathematical notation.

With random and instantaneous scanning out of the way, this left only the problem of independent scanning to be solved. The solution was obvious — to treat a flock of birds as a unit and calculate levels of vigilance as if that unit were an individual.

At the end of the day what we have is a model of vigilance in birds which does not assume that birds scan randomly, instantaneously or independently of each other. In developing this model we have illustrated the importance of assumption reduction in behavioural ecology. In this case by reducing the assumptions upon which the original model relied we have produced a model which resembles more closely the behaviour of real birds — the model has greater *ecological validity*. However, this is only a starting point for yet more realistic models.

Perhaps, the most important message to be gleaned from this chapter is that temporal patterns are important. In the next chapter we look at temporal patterns in more detail, and we begin to look at ways of combining two or more behaviours in an optimality model.

Chapter 6
Behaviour Sequences: Feeding and Vigilance

6.1 Introduction

In Chapter 5 we began to look at what happens when a conflict arises between two behaviours. In particular we were interested in the conflict between feeding and scanning for predators. Time spent feeding occurs at the expense of time spent scanning for predators; and time spent scanning for predators occurs at the expense of time spent feeding. There are costs and benefits to both behaviours. What is the optimal way in which to alternate between the two? This is a question about optimal behaviour sequences. In this chapter we are going to look at the optimal way in which to switch between two conflicting behaviours. Although we will be discussing models of feeding and vigilance the same general principles can be applied to any two behaviours. We must start by identifying the costs and benefits of the two behaviours.

If the *benefit* of feeding is some function of time spent feeding then we can think of time spent not feeding as the *cost* of scanning for predators. We could then use our models in Chapter 5 to measure the benefit of scanning for predators (as an increase in vigilance and so a fall in predation risk) and to specify the cost of feeding (in terms of a fall in vigilance, and so an increase in predation risk).

However, having specified the costs and benefits of our two behaviours, in order to predict the optimal way in which to alternate between the two we still have a problem. Feeding benefit and scanning costs may be measured in, say, grams of food. However, scanning benefits and feeding costs will be measured as changes in vigilance (and so predation risk). In this chapter we look at one way in which we can combine these two rather different currencies.

103

In Chapter 3 I presented some simple models of optimal foraging in animals. These models involved problems of *static* optimisation, problems in which the optimal solution did not change with time: our shore crab faced by the optimal mussel size problem, for instance; and the starling calculating the number of prey to take back to its young. However, many of the problems that animals encounter require optimisation over a period of time. And the optimal solution may change with time. In this chapter we are going to examine some simple, *dynamic* models which look at the balance between feeding and vigilance as an animal approaches satiation. This is an exercise in *dynamic optimisation*, and the technique we shall explore is that of Pontryagin's method.

6.2 Pontryagin's Maximisation Principle

The basic idea is very simple. We start by assuming that an animal is choosing its behaviour in such a way as to manipulate its internal state. Being in any state is assumed to carry with it certain costs. In this example, being hungry carries with it associated costs (such as an increase in the risk of starvation; see Chapter 4). Rather than pay the high cost of being hungry an animal might choose to reduce this cost by feeding. Although feeding reduces an animal's hunger level, it means that the animal incurs other costs. Feeding reduces the amount of time spent being vigilant and so increases our forager's predation risk (see Chapter 5). The hungry animal is caught in a Catch 22 situation. If it feeds it incurs costs associated with an increase in predation risk; if it does not feed it incurs costs associated with an increase in starvation risk. The optimal solution is to minimise the cost C which is a function both of motivational state x (being hungry), and the behaviour u (feeding). And the animal must minimise this cost from the start of feeding (0) to satiation (t). In other words it must minimise the integral,

$$\int_0^t C(u,x) \cdot dt$$

Pontryagin approached the optimal control problem by defining a state function (called the Pontryagin or Hamiltonian, H). *Pontryagin's maximisation principle (PMP)* states that the problem of finding the least cost is equivalent to instantaneously maximising H, where,

$$H = \lambda \dot{x} - C(u,x) \tag{1}$$

(which can be rewritten as an instantaneous minimisation).

That is, the animal should maximise the rate at which it reduces its hunger deficit ($\dot{x} = dx/dt$) whilst minimising the costs incurred: u is known as the *control* variable (the variable that allows the animal to *control* its internal state x). λ is called the *costate* variable. It tells us how a change in state, x, affects the Hamiltonian, H. So the costate variable changes at a rate $d\lambda/dt = -dH/dx$. And according to Pontryagin the rate at which the animal's state, x, changes is given by $dx/dt = dH/d\lambda$.

In the following section we shall take a look at a classic example of the application of the Pontryagin method.

6.3 Satiation Curves

In 1975 Richard Sibly and David McFarland of Oxford University applied dynamic optimisation methods to the problem of how an animal should feed in order to minimise the costs outlined in section 6.2 (Sibly and McFarland, 1976). They suggested that an appropriate cost function for an animal feeding to satiation might be a quadratic function (just as we did in our example (2) in Chapter 2), such that,

$$C(x,u) = k_1 x^2 + k_2 u^2 \qquad (2)$$

where k_1 and k_2 are constants that weight the relative importance of the costs associated with a particular state x (being hungry) and a behaviour u (feeding). Adopting a quadratic function means that a given reduction in x reduces the cost more when x is large, than when it is small. In other words, food is more valuable to a hungry animal than it is to a satiated animal. Similarly a given reduction in the feeding rate u leads to a large drop in costs when u is large, but a rather smaller drop when u is small. In other words, high feeding rates are much more costly than low feeding rates. Sibly and McFarland envisaged that one cost associated with feeding is a fall in vigilance; an animal feeding quickly is less likely to detect a predator than one feeding slowly.

Equation (2) can be reorganised to simplify the calculations. We can rescale k_1 relative to k_2. Then we set $k^2 = k_1/k_2$. This gives us,

$$C(x,u) = k^2 x^2 + u^2 \qquad (3)$$

(We use k^2 to simplify the calculus!)

Sibly and McFarland assumed that the rate at which a hungry animal can reduce its food deficit is given by,

$$dx/dt = \dot{x} = -ru \qquad (4)$$

where u is the feeding rate and r is the availability of food. If food is super-abundant then the rate at which an animal feeds is determined solely by the maximum rate at which it can feed.

We defined the Hamiltonian as,

$$H = \lambda \dot{x} - C(x,u) \qquad (1)$$

And the optimal strategy is to choose a feeding rate, u, so as to instantaneously minimise H (see section 6.2 above).

In other words, the optimal solution is for our hungry animal to reduce its food deficit as quickly as possible (maximise the absolute value of equation (4)) whilst minimising the various costs (equation (3)).

Substituting for $\dot{x}$ and $C(x,u)$ in equation (1) we find that the solution is to feed at an exponentially decreasing rate (equation (9)). Those prepared to believe this without working through the algebra might like to skip straight to equation (9)).

Substituting for $\dot{x}$ and $C(x,u)$:

$$\begin{aligned} H &= \lambda(-ru) - (k^2x^2 + u^2) \\ &= -\lambda ru - u^2 - k^2x^2 \end{aligned} \qquad (5)$$

Differentiating equation (5) with respect to u,

$$dH/du = -\lambda r - 2u$$

Now H is minimised when $dH/du = 0$. So,

$$dH/du = -\lambda r - 2u = 0$$

Rearranging,

$$-\lambda r - 2u = 0$$
$$-2u = \lambda r$$
$$u = -\lambda r/2$$

So our hungry animal minimises the Hamiltonian by choosing a feeding rate $u = -\lambda r/2$. Clearly it would be nice if we knew a little more about the costate variable, λ!

Now, substituting for u in equation (5) we get,

$$H = -\lambda r(-\lambda r/2) - (-\lambda r/2)^2 - k^2x^2$$

$$= \frac{\lambda^2 r^2}{2} - \frac{\lambda^2 r^2}{4} - k^2x^2$$

$$= \frac{\lambda^2 r^2}{4} - k^2 x^2 \tag{6}$$

And differentiating equation (6) with respect to x gives us,

$$dH/dx = -2k^2 x$$

Now, by definition,

$$d\lambda/dt = -dH/dx$$

(see section 6.2). So,

$$\begin{aligned} d\lambda/dt &= -dH/dx \\ &= -(-2k^2 x) \\ &= 2k^2 x \end{aligned} \tag{7}$$

Differentiating equation (6) with respect to λ gives us,

$$\begin{aligned} dH/d\lambda &= 2\,\lambda r^2/4 \\ &= \quad \lambda r^2/2 \end{aligned}$$

And, by definition,

$$dx/dt = dH/d\lambda$$

(see section 6.2 above). So,

$$\begin{aligned} dx/dt &= dH/d\lambda \\ &= \lambda r^2/2 \end{aligned} \tag{8}$$

And differentiation of this equation with respect to t gives us

$$d^2 x/dt^2 = \dot{\lambda} r^2/2$$

Now, we already know that $\dot{\lambda} = d\lambda/dt = 2k^2 x$ (equation (7)). By substitution,

$$\begin{aligned} d^2 x/dt^2 &= 2k^2 x r^2/2 \\ &= k^2 r^2 x \end{aligned}$$

So our forager minimises its costs when,

$$d^2x/dt^2 = k^2r^2x$$

Rearranging this we get the second order differential equation,

$$d^2x/dt^2 - k^2r^2x = 0$$

and the solution to a differential equation of this form is,

$$x(t) = Ae^{-krt} + Be^{+krt}$$

where A and B are constants (see section 2.5 in Chapter 2).

We need to know A and B. In order that the deficit x tends to zero as an animal approaches satiation then $B = 0$ (otherwise the animal never satiates). This means that the second term disappears, so that:

$$x(t) = Ae^{-krt}$$

Furthermore, when $t = 0$,

$$x(t) = Ae^0$$

so A must equal the initial deficit, x_0, and

$$x(t) = x_0e^{-krt}$$

This describes the optimal way for the state to change with time.

This means that the behaviour u should have a trajectory (through time) of the form,

$$u(t) = kx(t)$$
$$= kx_0e^{-krt} \tag{9}$$

In other words the animal should perform behaviour u at an exponentially decreasing rate. We can translate this into an expression for the cumulative food intake (the so-called 'satiation curve'). The cumulative amount of food eaten in time t ($N(t)$) equals the original deficit *minus* the present deficit. That is,

$$N(t) = x_0 - x(t)$$
$$= x_0 - x_0e^{-krt}$$
$$= x_0(1 - e^{-krt}) \tag{10}$$

So the predicted satiation curve is an exponential.

This prediction was tested by Robin McCleery (1977) also at Oxford University. He attempted to fit a variety of curves to observed feeding rate data for rats feeding in Skinner boxes (Figure 6.1). Although other functions (such as hyperbolas and parabolas) produced a close fit to the observed data the exponential curve left the smallest residual error.

Such a curve makes good functional sense. When x (the food deficit) is large it is worth feeding rapidly (large u) to reduce x, because a change in x reduces the cost substantially. However, as x gets smaller, the cost of feeding very quickly (large u) is not offset by the reduction in cost associated with u. The result is that u declines as the food deficit, x, is reduced (resulting in the exponential decline in feeding rate and the exponential satiation curve).

In the next section, we are going to look at a second application of dynamic optimisation methods. This time we shall examine the trade-off between feeding and *territorial* vigilance.

6.4 Feeding and Territoriality in the Great Tit

In this section we spell out a second application of the Pontryagin method, which involves a certain amount of algebra. This we have relegated to two Appendices (6.1 and 6.2), not because it is particularly difficult but because it

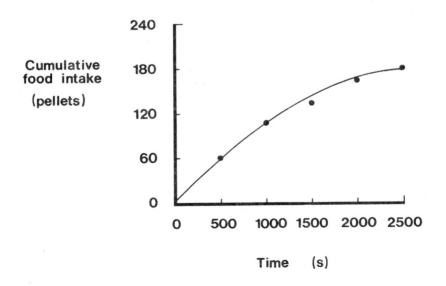

Figure 6.1: Satiation curve for rat feeding in a Skinner box. As predicted, the exponential curve shows a close fit to the observed intake curve. (After McCleery, 1977.)

makes the text easier to follow. Do not be alarmed by the algebra; it is more straightforward than it looks!

In spring, male great tits (*Parus major*) establish territories that they defend against intruders. These males alternate territorial defence with short visits to feeding sites on their territory. This defence consists of territorial singing and intruder chases. The problem facing a male great tit is how much time to devote to territorial defence and how much time to devote to feeding. If a male spends too long in a feeding patch then another male might enter his territory undetected. Experimental tests have shown that the more time the intruder spends on a territory the longer it takes to evict him: time in which the territory owner could be doing more useful things (such as feeding). At the same time if a great tit spends too long on territorial defence he has to go hungry, and so runs the risk of starvation. What is the optimal balance between feeding and territorial defence?

In 1982 Ron Ydenberg of Oxford University created a laboratory analogue of this situation at the university's field station in Wytham Wood. Great tits were kept in outdoor flight cages, but had access to an indoor arena where they could feed from an operant patch (Figure 6.2). By hopping on a perch a great tit could get this device to dispense fly pupae. In order to simulate the diminishing returns from feeding in a patch, Ydenberg arranged that the probability of a reward declined for each successive hop on the perch. In fact the schedule meant that the expected number of pupae gained after B hops was $\sqrt{B}$. For example, a great tit had to make four hops on the perch to obtain two pupae. However, it required a total of 16 hops to obtain the fourth pupa (Figure 6.3).

The birds were given the option of resetting the operant device at any time by flying to a perch located across the arena. While in the patch, a bird's view of the arena was obstructed by an opaque screen. This meant that great tits could only monitor the arena for intruders when flying to the reset perch. They could not see intruders while feeding in the patch.

Our hungry territory owner faces a sticky problem. He can feed by spending time at the operant device, but he cannot monitor his 'territory' for intruders while feeding. If he spends too long in the feeding patch then he must spend a lot of valuable feeding time evicting an intruder. And if the worst came to the worst he might lose his territory altogether — much too costly. On the other hand he cannot afford to spend all day monitoring intruders. How can an owner best allocate his time to meet these two conflicting demands? How can he strike a balance between feeding and territorial vigilance?

6.4.1 Solution to the Great Tit's Dilemma

Clearly our territory owner needs to alternate between the two behaviours (feeding and defence). The ideal solution is to adjust his time in the patch (B) and the time between the patch and the reset device and back (T) (during which he can monitor his territory) in such a way as to minimise the total cost incurred as he steadily reduces his hunger deficit. This is clearly an exercise in dynamic optimisation, and once again we shall apply Pontryagin's method. This allows us to predict the optimal way for B and T to change as our hungry great tit reduces his food deficit.

Ydenberg took this problem to Alasdair Houston (also at Oxford University) and together they developed the following model.

In their experiments the rate at which great tits were able to reduce their food deficits, dx/dt (written $\dot{x}$) was determined by the reward schedule,

$$\dot{x} = -\sqrt{B/(Bh + T)} \qquad (11)$$

where B is the number of hops whilst in the patch and h is the average amount of time taken to make a single hop. In other words, it is a function of the

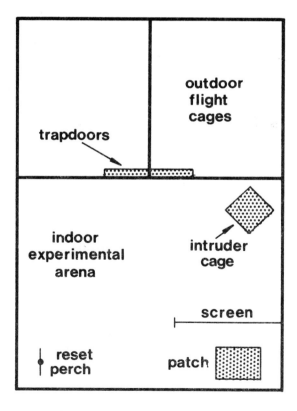

Figure 6.2: Feeding and territoriality in the great tit: experimental set-up for the great tit experiments. The screen prevents great tits from monitoring the arena for intruders while feeding in the patch.

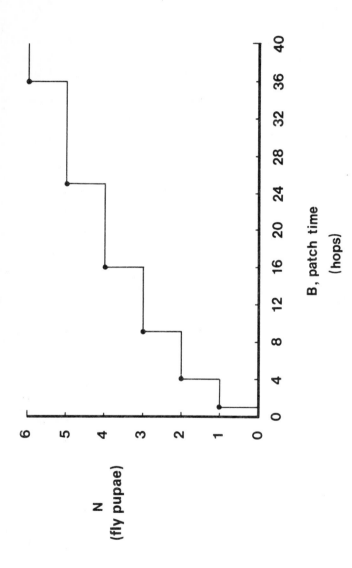

Figure 6.3: Cumulative food intake 'curve' for the Ydenberg and Houston great tit experiments. A single hop is sufficient to dispense the first pupae. However, the second requires three further hops (making four hops altogether), the third requires eight hops, the fourth 16, and so on. This reward schedule simulates patch depletion (see Chapter 3).

amount of time spent in the patch (time in the patch $= Bh$). (For example, if $h = 0.5s$ and $T = 10s$, then if our territory owner makes four hops he will obtain two pupae and spend $4 \times 0.5s$ in the patch. So the rate at which he is reducing his food deficit is $2/(2 + 10) = 1/6$ pupae/s.)

Now according to PMP (section 6.2 above) the hunger and intrusion costs, C, are minimised by minimising the Hamiltonian H, where,

$$H = \lambda \dot{x} - C(u,x) \qquad (1)$$

As in section 6.3 the cost function (C) is a complex function of the food deficit (x) and the control variable (u). However, this time the control variable (u) is a function of both B and T. The animal can control its costs by manipulating both B and T. Moreover, as we shall see, the state cost is not explicit in this model.

Now the Hamiltonian, H, is minimised when the rate of change of H (dH/dt) is zero (see section 2.3 in Chapter 2). However, we have to consider changes along two time dimensions; time in the patch (B) and time between the patch and the reset perch (T). So the Hamiltonian is minimised when both dH/dB and dH/dt are zero. So we start by differentiating H with respect to B and T. Thus (from equation (1)):

$$dH/dB = \lambda d\dot{x}/dB - dC/dB \qquad (12)$$

and,

$$dH/dT = \lambda d\dot{x}/dT - dC/dT \qquad (13)$$

Now, we already know from equation (11) that,

$$\dot{x} = - \sqrt{B}/(Bh + T)$$
$$= -B^{1/2}(Bh + T)^{-1}$$

Differentiating $\dot{x}$ with respect to T,

$$d\dot{x}/dT = -B^{1/2}/(Bh + T)^2 \qquad (14)$$

And if we differentiate with respect to B (see Appendix 6.1) then,

$$d\dot{x}/dB = (T - Bh)/2B^{1/2}(Bh + T)^2 \qquad (15)$$

Now we know that H is minimised when dH/dB and dH/dT are equal to zero. At this point the right-hand side of equations (12) and (13) will be equal. So,

$$\lambda d\dot{x}/dB - dC/dB = \lambda d\dot{x}/dT - dC/dT \qquad (16)$$

And if we substitute for $d\dot{x}/dT$ and $d\dot{x}/dB$ (equations (14) and (15)) and eliminate λ (see Appendix 6.2) this yields,

$$dC/dT[(Bh - T)/2B] = dC/dB \qquad (17)$$

And this will hold when H is minimised. So, in order to find the optimal relationship between B and T we need only to specify how the cost function, C, changes with T and B. That is we need to specify dC/dT and dC/dB.

6.4.2 Choosing the Cost Function

In order to put values into equation (17) we need to know the costs associated with patch residence time (B) and the travel time (T). We know that intrusion costs increase with B; the longer an intruder spends in a territory the more time taken to evict him and the greater the probability that he will take over that territory. This means that long patch times $(B$, during which an intruder can pass undetected) are more costly. We do not know the exact relationship between patch residence time, B, and cost. However, it seems reasonable to assume that this cost increases with patch time. Perhaps, the simplest relationship we can think of is a straightforward linear relationship. So,

$$C(B) = k_1B$$

In other words the cost, C, is some linear function of patch time, B. And, if we differentiate with respect to B then,

$$dC/dB = k_1 \qquad (18)$$

What this means is that costs increase with patch time B, and that the rate of increase depends upon the constant k_1. This constant is a measure of intrusion rate.

Now all we need to know is how the cost C changes with travel time T (that is, dC/dT). We know that intrusion costs fall with increasing travel time. That is, longer travel times are better for intruder detection. The more time spent travelling between the patch and the reset perch the more likely that an intruder will be detected and the smaller the eviction costs. (Remember that travel time is not fixed; by pausing to sing or to scan his territory from the reset perch, our great tit can increase his travel time between the patch and the reset device and back again.)

This time we want to choose a cost function which allows costs to fall with increasing travel time, T. A simple inverse function does the trick:

$$C(T) = k_2/T$$
$$= k_2T^{-1}$$

And differentiating with respect to T this gives us

$$dC/dT = -1 \cdot k_2 \cdot T^{-2}$$
$$= -k_2/T^2 \tag{19}$$

And k_2 is another constant representing the intrusion rate.

Note that both costs are in terms of intrusion risk. Intrusion risk increases with patch time (B) and decreases with travel time (T). So, although we are modelling a trade-off between feeding and vigilance, our earlier manipulation has actually eliminated the state costs (that is, the hunger costs).

We can now substitute for dC/dB and dC/dT (equations (18) and (19)) in equation (17):

$$-k_2/T^2[(Bh - T)/2B] = k_1$$

Rearranging,

$$(-k_1/k_2)T^2 = [(Bh - T)/2B]$$

And,

$$(-k_1/k_2)T^2 2B = Bh - T$$

Or,

$$T = Bh + (2k_1/k_2)BT^2$$

We can call $2k_1/k_2$ a single constant K which is an index of intrusion rate. The larger the value of K the higher the intrusion rate. (Intrusion rates are known to show both daily and seasonal variation; see Ydenberg, 1982). This then simplifies to,

$$T = Bh + KBT^2$$
$$= B(KT^2 + h)$$

And so,

$$B = T/(KT^2 + h) \tag{20}$$

Which specifies the optimal patch time, B, for values of T chosen by the great tit. Note that in eliminating the costate variable (λ) the hunger costs are no longer explicit in the model, though it is a change in this cost which is presumably responsible for changes in B and T. Using equation (20) we can now calculate exactly how they should change as a great tit approaches satiation.

6.4.3 The Optimal Trajectory

From equation (20) above we can calculate the optimal relationship between B and T. That is, we can plot the optimal trajectory through B, T space. When constructing the model it was known from a crude analysis of earlier data that travel time (T) increased as great tits fed, and that patch times tended to decrease following intrusions (Ydenberg, 1982). However, the exact shape of the optimal trajectory was completely unexpected. Figure 6.4 shows that as the travel time (T) increases the patch times (B) first increase and then decrease. The effect is to produce a bow in the trajectory.

Ydenberg and Houston (in press) explain this peculiar bow as follows (see also Krebs and McCleery, 1984). They argue that when a hungry great tit leaves his roosting hole first thing in the morning, the need to keep an eye open for intruders causes travel time (T) to increase immediately. However, the costs of a large food deficit mean that patch times must also increase at first in order to reduce that deficit. As this deficit is reduced, the hunger cost

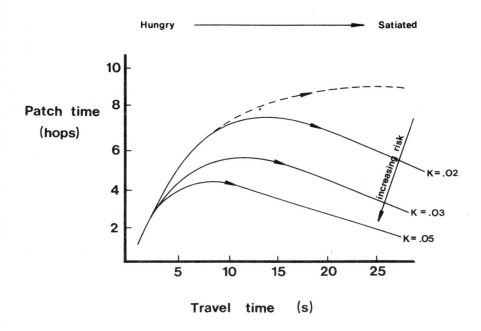

Figure 6.4: Predicted trajectories. At first the optimal patch time increases with increasing travel time, but as a great tit approaches satiation the optimal patch time decreases. Increasing intrusion risk leads to a fall in patch residence time.

(not explicit) begins to shrink; but the intrusion cost continues to be substantial, and so patch times (B) begin to decrease allowing an increase in travel times (T) during which a tit can stay on the watch for intruders. It is this shift in the balance of costs that causes the trajectory to reverse direction.

6.4.4 A Test of the Model

The predictions of the above model were tested by depriving great tits of food for 1 hour and then allowing them to feed in the experimental arena (see Figure 6.2). As described above, great tits had been trained to obtain fly pupae from the operant device in the experimental 'patch'. Birds obtained their fly pupae by hopping on the perch. The number of hops required to obtain pupae increased with patch time (B). Thus very few hops were required to obtain one or two pupae, but many hops were required to obtain a third or a fourth. At any point a great tit could reset the operant device by flying from the patch to the reset perch. This perch set the operant device back to square one, and on its return to the 'patch' the bird could obtain one or two pupae with very few hops. Ydenberg and Houston manipulated the bird's assessment of intrusion risk by simulating a territorial intrusion prior to two of the trials.

During a trial the length of each patch visit (B) and the time taken to travel to the reset perch and back (T) were recorded. They then split each trial into five successive 'quintiles' (in which the amount of food eaten was the same in each quintile). They then calculated the mean patch time (B) and travel time (T) for each quintile. The results are shown in Figure 6.5.

There is a broad agreement between these results and the predictions in Figure 6.4. As predicted the travel times (T) increased throughout a trial. The patch times (B) showed an initial rise rapidly reaching a peak before falling steadily during the remainder of the trial. Finally, the entire trajectory is shifted downwards following a simulated intrusion.

In spite of the large variation the results are in broad, qualitative agreement with the predictions of the model.

However, the results do not show a close match to the predicted trajectory. In particular, the model consistently underestimates the patch times (B). Although it incurs intrusion costs while in a patch it looks as though a great tit is willing to suffer such costs in order to reduce his food deficit.

6.5 Summary

In this chapter, we have seen how dynamic optimisation methods can be used to solve some interesting problems. The particular method employed was Pontryagin's maximisation principle. The important step was to think of behaviour as a means of manipulating internal state. Any state is considered

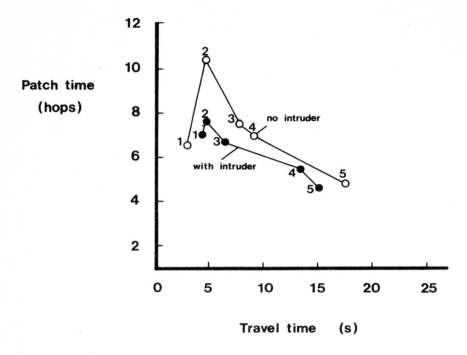

Figure 6.5: Observed trajectories. The results are in broad agreement with the predicted trajectories (see Figure 6.4). Great tits show the characteristic bowed trajectory; and simulating an intrusion shifts the trajectory. However, the model consistently underestimates patch times.

to carry with it certain costs. We then simply specify how an animal (our *control system*) should manipulate its internal state in order to minimise those costs.

The two models discussed in this chapter are *control* models. And the approach is adopted from *control theory* — a theory more usually associated with engineering. Indeed Pontryagin was a rocket engineer, not a behavioural ecologist. However, the principles remain the same whether we are modelling the behaviour of a great tit or a rocket. The trick is to identify the costs, state how they change with time and then manipulate the equations to eliminate the costate variable. The algebra may make us feel a little queasy, but it is not desperately difficult to follow.

And the same methods can be applied equally well to other aspects of an animal's behavioural ecology. McNeill Alexander (1982) gives an account of three applications of PMP to life history tactics (see also Sibly, Calow and Nichols, 1985, for another recent application).

Of course the match between prediction and observation is not all we might hope for. The Ydenberg and Houston model, for instance, consistently underestimates patch times. These shortcomings can, perhaps, be traced to the rather simple cost functions. In choosing a cost function no attempt was made to obtain a 'realistic' function. However, we do not need to specify the exact cost function to obtain some interesting predictions. The model is reasonably *robust*; as long as the cost function increases with patch time and decreases with travel time then we will get a bowed trajectory. (In fact the choice of a linear cost function was guided as much by its mathematical tractability as its ecological validity!)

Of course, it is possible (at least in principle) to work backwards from the observed data to specify a cost function which could have produced the observed results (the so-called *inverse optimality* approach; see McFarland, 1977, and section 2.8 in Chapter 2). For instance, given that satiation curves are exponential we might have worked backwards to deduce that the cost functions are quadratic (though this is not as straightforward as it sounds; see McFarland and Houston, 1981, pp. 154–5). The resulting model is *not* simply a redescription of the observed data (Krebs and McCleery, 1984). Once identified, the derived cost function can be tested in further experiments or with additional data. There is nothing particularly fishy about inverse optimality, though there are practical limitations to how far you can go in specifying all the relevant costs (McFarland and Houston, 1981).

In the next chapter we stay with the problem of feeding and territorial defence, but move on to some rather different behavioural questions. In the process we look at a rather different way of combining various currencies.

Appendix 6.1

Remembering the rule for the differentiation of a product (section 2.2 in Chapter 2), if we differentiate $\dot{x}$ with respect to B,

$$d\dot{x}/dB = (1/2)B^{-1/2}(Bh + T)^{-1} + B^{1/2}(-1 \cdot h(Bh + T)^{-2})$$

$$= \frac{(1/2)B^{-1/2}}{(Bh + T)} - \frac{h \cdot B^{1/2}}{(Bh + T)^2}$$

Multiplying the first term by $(Bh + T)/(Bh + T) = 1$:

$$d\dot{x}/dB = \frac{(Bh + T)((1/2)B^{-1/2})}{(Bh + T)(Bh + T)} - \frac{hB^{1/2}}{(Bh + T)^2}$$

$$= \frac{(Bh + T)((1/2)B^{-1/2}) - hB^{1/2}}{(Bh + T)^2}$$

And if we multiply out the terms in brackets we get,

$$d\dot{x}/dB = \frac{(1/2)B^{-1/2} \cdot Bh + (1/2)B^{-1/2}T - hB^{1/2}}{(Bh + T)^2}$$

$$= \frac{((1/2)hB^{1/2} - hB^{1/2} + (1/2)TB^{-1/2})}{(Bh + T)^2}$$

$$= \frac{((1/2)TB^{-1/2} - (1/2)hB^{1/2})}{(Bh + T)^2}$$

Now, $B^{1/2} = B \cdot B^{-1/2}$ (Appendix 6.2). So,

$$d\dot{x}/dB = \frac{((1/2)TB^{-1/2} - (1/2)hB \cdot B^{-1/2})}{(Bh + T)^2}$$

$$= \frac{(1/2)B^{-1/2}(T - hB)}{(Bh + T)^2}$$

$$= \frac{(T - Bh)}{2B^{1/2}(Bh + T)^2}$$

Appendix 6.2

Substituting for $d\dot{x}/dT$ and $d\dot{x}/dB$ in equation (16) allows us to eliminate the costate variable λ. From equations (12) and (13),

$$dH/dB = \lambda d\dot{x}/dB - dC/dB, \text{ and}$$

$$dH/dT = \lambda d\dot{x}/dT - dC/dT$$

Now, H is at a minimum when $dH/dB = dH/dT = 0$, and so both these equations will be equal to 0. That is,

$$0 = \lambda d\dot{x}/dB - dC/dB, \text{ and}$$

$$0 = \lambda d\dot{x}/dT - dC/dT$$

Rearranging,

$$dC/dB = \lambda d\dot{x}/dB, \text{ and}$$
$$dC/dT = \lambda d\dot{x}/dT$$

Now we already know that,

$$d\dot{x}/dB = (T - Bh)/(2B^{1/2}(Bh + T)^2) \qquad (16)$$

And,

$$d\dot{x}/dT = -B^{1/2}/(Bh + T)^2 \qquad (15)$$

So, substituting for $d\dot{x}/dB$ and $d\dot{x}/dT$ gives us,

$$\frac{dC}{dB} = \lambda \frac{(T - Bh)}{2B^{1/2}(Bh + T)^2}$$

And,

$$\frac{dC}{dT} = -\lambda \frac{B^{1/2}}{(Bh + T)^2}$$

Solving for λ,

$$\lambda = \frac{dC}{dB} \times \frac{2B^{1/2}(Bh + T)^2}{(T - Bh)}, \text{ and}$$

$$\lambda = \frac{-dC}{dT} \times \frac{(Bh + T)^2}{B^{1/2}}$$

This manoeuvre allows us to eliminate the costate variable, λ:

$$\frac{dC}{dB} \times \frac{2B^{1/2}(Bh + T)^2}{(T - Bh)} = \frac{-dC}{dT} \times \frac{(Bh + T)^2}{B^{1/2}}$$

And $(Bh + T)^2$ is common to both sides so cancels leaving,

$$\frac{dC}{dB} \times \frac{2B^{1/2}}{(T-Bh)} = \frac{-dC}{dT} \times \frac{1}{B^{1/2}}$$

And rearranging,

$$\frac{dC}{dB} = \frac{-dC}{dT} \times \frac{[1 \times (T-Bh)]}{[B^{1/2} 2B^{1/2}]}$$

$$= \frac{-dC}{dT} \times \frac{[(T-Bh)]}{[2B]}$$

$$= \frac{+dC}{dT} \frac{[(Bh-T)]}{[2B]}$$

Chapter 7

Short-term and Long-term Optimality Models: Territoriality

7.1 Introduction

So far in this book we have looked at models that optimise behaviours or behaviour sequences over relatively short time periods. In Chapter 3, our starling maximises energetic returns per round-trip flight time; and in Chapter 6 our great tit optimises behaviour from the start of a feeding bout until satiation. One problem with such *short-term* optimality models is that optimisation may take place over a rather longer time period. In this chapter we will look at both short-term and long-term optimality models of territorial behaviour. I shall break away from presenting an historical introduction (the interested reader is referred to the very clear account by Krebs and Davies, 1981). Instead, I shall explain the main ideas by introducing a very simple model outlined by McNeill Alexander (1982).

7.2 Optimal Territory Size: A Simple Model

Many animals maintain territories in order to defend feeding areas. The bigger the territory the more food secured. However, as territory size increases the costs of defending that territory increases. This results in a trade-off between feeding benefit and defence costs. The obvious question is 'What is the optimal territory size?' The answer depends, of course, upon the costs and benefits involved.

McNeill Alexander (1982) considers an animal feeding exclusively on its territory and excluding all competitors (we shall consider a model of territory-sharing in section 7.5). He assumes that the territory owner attempts to maximise the number of prey collected in each day. Let us assume that the owner defends a circular territory of area A. Then the number of prey available in a territory of area A is simply,

$$N = dA \qquad (1)$$

where d is the density of prey in the territory. This model assumes that the owner does not deplete its territory — by the following day we assume that all the prey have been replaced, so that the density is constant.

The territory owner defends its territory by patrolling the perimeter. We can assume that the proportion of time spent in territorial defence increases with the circumference of the territory. If the territory is circular then the circumference,

$$C = 2\pi R$$

where R is the radius of the territory. In other words, the circumference of the territory (and so the perimeter to be patrolled) is proportional to the radius (R).

In addition, the *area* of the territory,

$$A = \pi R^2$$

So, the area (A) is proportional to R^2, or, conversely, the radius (R) is proportional to the square root of the area. Since the circumference C is proportional to the radius, and the radius is proportional to the square root of the area, then the circumference (C) must be proportional to the square root of the area $(A^{1/2})$.

And if the time spent in territorial defence is proportional to the length of the perimeter (that is, the circumference) then it follows that it will be proportional to the square root of the territory size. That is:

$$T_d = kA^{1/2} \qquad (2)$$

where T_d is the proportion of time spent in territorial defence, and k is some constant of proportionality.

If an animal spends a proportion of time T_d in territorial defence, then this leaves a proportion $(1 - T_d)$ of its time for feeding. That is,

$$T_f = (1 - kA^{1/2}) \qquad (3)$$

where T_f is the proportion of time left available for feeding.

The total amount of food collected in this time will depend upon the rate at which food can be collected, r. Thus the number of prey collected in time T_f is

$$N = r(T_f)$$
$$= r(1 - kA^{1/2}) \tag{4}$$

where r is the feeding rate.

Now we will assume that our model owner is in equilibrium with its food supply. In other words it does not eat more food than is available, nor does it defend a territory bigger than absolutely necessary to meet its daily requirements. If this holds (and it seems sensible) then the optimal territory size is that in which the number of available prey (equation (1)) equals the number which can be collected in the time available for feeding (equation (4)). That is, when,

$$dA = r(1 - kA^{1/2}) \tag{5}$$

We can see this graphically in Figure 7.1. Note that if the territory size is too

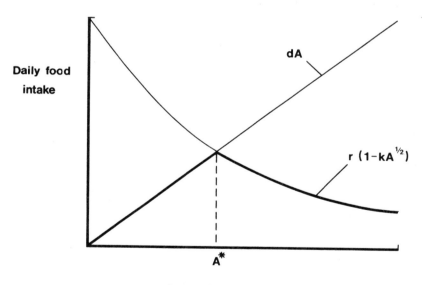

Figure 7.1: Optimal territory size. The number of prey available to the territory owner increases with territory size. However, the time spent in territorial defence increases with territory size leading to a reduction in the time available for collecting available prey. If an animal is in equilibrium with its food supply then the optimal territory size is A^*. The owner's daily food intake increases up to A^*. Thereafter it declines. (See text.)

small ($< A^\star$) then the territory owner has plenty of time in which to feed, but the prey are simply not available. On the other hand, if the territory is too big ($> A^\star$) then it spends a large proportion of its time in territorial defence and daily intake falls. The bold curve shows the observed intake rate as a function of territory size. At first, intake increases with territory size. However, once we reach the optimum ($A^\star$) there follows a slow decline in intake with increasing territory size.

This simple general model does lead to some interesting predictions. For instance, as the quality of the territory (d) increases, the slope of the line (representing prey availability) becomes steeper, and the optimal territory size shrinks (Figure 7.2).

McNeill Alexander would be the first to admit that the model is too simple to be true. But it does capture the essence of the territory owner's dilemma. In the next section we are going to look at a rather more ambitious model. This attempts to predict both the optimal territory size and time budgets for the golden-winged sunbird (*Nectarinia reichenowi*).

7.3 Costs and Benefits of Territoriality in the Golden-winged Sunbird

Nectarinia is a nectar-feeding bird which lives in East Africa. Outside of the breeding season *Nectarinia* defend patches of *Leonotis nepetefolia* flowers from

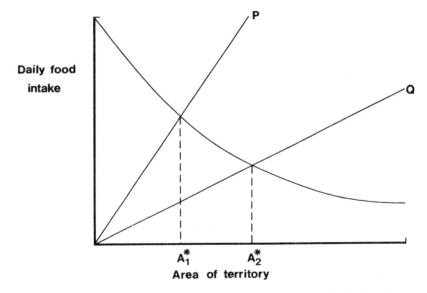

Figure 7.2: The optimal territory size depends upon territory quality. Productive territories (P) have smaller optima ($A_1^\star$) than less productive territories ($A_2^\star$).

other sunbirds (Gill and Wolf, 1975). They depend upon these flowers for their daily nectar supply. Frank Gill and Larry Wolf had observed that sunbirds defended territories containing roughly 1600 *Leonotis* flowers. Was 1600 the optimal number to defend? Was this the optimal territory size? Graham Pyke (then at the University of Utah in the United States, now at Sydney Museum) used data from their study of sunbird territoriality to predict both the time budgets and optimal territory size (number of flowers defended; see Pyke, 1979).

A typical day in the life of *Nectarinia* involves about 14 hours in certain 'fixed' activities such as sleeping (T_z). In the remaining 10 hours it must spend some time feeding (T_f) and some time defending its territory (T_d). This leaves a certain amount of time (T_s) for just sitting around. Sitting is a period of maximum vigilance during which the risk of predation is very low.

Pyke used Gill and Wolf's data to calculate the sunbird's daily energetic expenditure. This is given by the amount of time spent in each activity multiplied by the metabolic rate for that activity. That is,

$$C = T_z M_z + T_f M_f + T_s M_s + T_d M_d \qquad (6)$$

where, M_z, M_f, M_s and M_d are the metabolic rates during the fixed activities, whilst feeding, sitting around and defending the territory respectively. By definition, T_z is fixed, and the total energetic cost of these fixed activities was 5949 calories/day (that is, $T_z M_z = 5949$ calories/day). From Gill and Wolf's data, the metabolic rates were 1000, 400 and 3000 calories/h respectively whilst feeding, sitting around and defending the territory against intruders.

Pyke then used Gill and Wolf's data to estimate the production of each territory. The total energetic production of each territory per day,

$$P = np \qquad (7)$$

where n is the number of flowers on the territory, and p is the daily production of each flower in calories. In addition, the gross daily energetic gain to the territory owner,

$$G = crT_f \qquad (8)$$

where r is the rate at which the owner visits flowers during feeding time T_f, and c is the average standing crop of energy per flower (again in calories) available to a sunbird. That is, c is the *average* amount of energy obtained by a sunbird on each visit to a flower.

As in the simple model in section 7.2 we assume that the sunbird does not eat more than is available ($G > P$) and does not defend a territory bigger than absolutely necessary ($P > G$). The sunbird will be in equilibrium with its food supply when its daily energy intake (G) equals the daily production of the territory (P). That is when:

$$np = crT_f$$

Or, rearranging, when:

$$c = np/rT_f \qquad (9)$$

We use this result below. It tells us that the average standing crop per flower (c) increases with the number of flowers and their rate of production, and decreases with the time the sunbird spends feeding and rate at which it visits flowers.

We know the relationship between territory size (that is, number of flowers, n) and production (equation (7)). Now we must define the relationship between defence time and territory size (see section 7.2).

Pyke argued that the frequency of intrusions should be a function both of territory size and territory quality. That is the number of flowers, and the average energetic content of those flowers. If there is no nectar available ($c = 0$) then we would not expect intruders to persist in their intrusion. However, as territory quality improves ($c > 0$) we would expect the frequency of intrusions to increase — slowly at first, and then more rapidly. In other words the relationship between T_d and c is concave (Figure 7.3); intruders are more

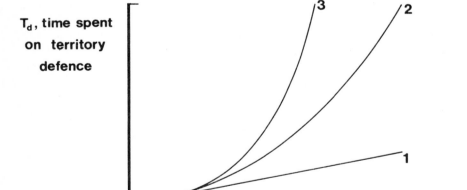

Figure 7.3: Sunbird territoriality. Pyke (1979) argues for a concave relationship between time spent in territorial defence (T_d) and territory quality (c). (Specifically $1 < \alpha < 3$, see text.)

likely to intrude upon valuable territories (high c) than they are poor territories (low c).

We also expect that time spent in territorial defence increases with territory size, n.

A suitable function relating defence times to territory size (n) and territory quality (c) is:

$$T_d = knc^\alpha \qquad (10)$$

And since we want a concave function then $\alpha > 0$, and k is a constant.

Substituting for c (equation (9)) this leaves us with,

$$T_d = kn(np/rT_f)^\alpha$$

$$= \left(\frac{kp^\alpha}{r^\alpha} \right) \left(\frac{n^{\alpha+1}}{T_f^\alpha} \right) \qquad (11)$$

And if we define a new constant,

$$k' = kp^\alpha / r^\alpha$$

then,

$$T_d = \frac{k'n^{\alpha+1}}{T_f^\alpha} \qquad (12)$$

This means that once we know one component of the time budget (say T_f) we can calculate another (T_d); and once we know T_d and T_f then we know T_s (since $T_s = 10 - (T_f + T_d)$).

Since the exact form of the concave function is unknown, Pyke allowed α to equal 1, 2 and 3 (just as we did in Example 2 in Chapter 2). He argued that if $\alpha > 3$ then tiny changes in the average energy content of a flower lead to unrealistically large defence times.

Having specified the territorial system all we need do now is to substitute for the various parameters and decide upon the currency to be maximised.

7.4 Substituting Parameters and Choosing the Right Currency

We have already specified the various metabolic rates. All that remains is to substitute values for p (the average daily energy production per flower), and the unknown constant k'. The former is 7.5 calories/flower/day. However, to calculate k' we must rearrange equation (12), and then substitute observed values of n, T_f and T_d.

Rearranging equation (12),

$$T_d = \frac{k'n^{\alpha+1}}{T_f^\alpha} \qquad \text{(equation 12)}$$

$$T_d T_f^\alpha = k'n^{\alpha+1}$$

And so,

$$k' = T_d T_f^\alpha / n^{\alpha+1} \qquad (13)$$

To calculate k', Pyke then substituted *observed* values of n, T_f and T_d into equation (13) and calculated k' for values of α of 1, 2 and 3.

When $\alpha = 1$,

$$k' = T_d \times T_f/n^2$$
$$= 0.28 \times 2.42/1600^2$$
$$= 2.65 \times 10^{-7}$$

When $\alpha = 2$,

$$k' = T_d \times T_f^2/n^3$$
$$= 0.28 \times 2.42^2/1600^3$$
$$= 4.00 \times 10^{-10}$$

And when $\alpha = 3$,

$$k' = T_d \times T_f^3/n^4$$
$$= 0.28 \times 2.42^3/1600^4$$
$$= 6.06 \times 10^{-13}$$

At first glance this procedure may seem rather circular. We have used observed values of n, T_f and T_d to estimate k', and we then go on to use k' to predict the optimal values of n, T_f and T_d. However, this is perfectly legitimate. Although we estimate k' from observed data we then use this constant to model values *other than that observed.*

The next step must be to specify the currency being maximised. Pyke actually considers four different currencies, but we shall discuss only three of these.

(1) Perhaps the most obvious candidate (see Chapter 3) is that sunbirds are maximising their net energetic returns (*net-maximising*). That is,

$$E = G - C$$

where G is the gross daily energetic gain (equation (8)) and C is the daily energy expenditure (equation (6)).

(2) Another possibility is that sunbirds are minimising their energetic costs (*cost-minimising*). Pyke argues (from interspecific data) that there may be a relationship between average metabolic rate and longevity. The lower the overall metabolic rate the greater the probability of survival and so the longer the lifespan. If sunbirds are simply 'ticking over' they may choose to minimise costs (C) rather than maximise net energetic returns. I prefer a second explanation; that maximising E may lead to increases in bodyweight. In nectar-drinking birds bodyweight may have important effects on manoeuvrability and so impose high costs. A sunbird in equilibrium bodyweight may do better than one which is increasing in bodyweight; so a sunbird which simply minimises costs and remains at equilibrium bodyweight may do better than one that maximises net returns and increases in bodyweight. Of course, if we knew the cost function or bodyweight then we could actually include this in a sophisticated (but straightforward) net-maximising type of model.

(3) The third candidate is that sunbirds maximise T_s, the time spent sitting around (*sitting-maximising*). Sitting around might be important if sunbirds are more vulnerable to predators whilst defending or feeding in their territories. Sitting around might minimise the risk of predation (Chapter 5).

Pyke calculated the gross energetic value of territories for a variety of territory sizes (equation (8)). Then, for each territory size, he looked at the effect of a chosen feeding time (T_f) on the time spent in territorial defence (T_d). And since the proportion of time spent in 'fixed' activities is (by definition) fixed, then the sitting time (T_s) is simply,

$$T_s = T - (T_f + T_d) \tag{14}$$

where T is the time available for feeding, sitting around and defending the territory (where $T = 10$ hours, see above).

With this information we can now choose a territory size, n, select a feeding time (T_f) and calculate its effect on defence times (T_d). We can then calculate how much time is left for sitting around, and we use these various times to calculate daily costs, C (using equation (6)).

Example 1

Say that $n = 2000$ flowers. Then, the daily production of the territory is,

$$P = np \qquad \text{(equation (7))}$$

$$= 2000 \times 7.5$$

$$= 15\,000 \text{ calories/day}$$

And this is the owner's gross energetic gain,

$$G = 15\,000 \text{ calories/day}$$

If we let $\alpha = 2$ then,

$$T_d = \frac{k'n^3}{T_f^2} \qquad \text{(equation (12))}$$

and $k' = 4 \times 10^{-10}$ (equation (13) *et seq.*). So,

$$T_d = \frac{4 \times 10^{-10} \times (2000)^3}{T_f^2}$$

$$= \frac{8 \times 10^{-1}}{T_f^2}$$

What happens if our sunbird decides to spend one hour foraging? When $T_f = 1$ hour, then

$$T_d = \frac{8 \times 10^{-1}}{1^2}$$

$$= 0.8 \text{ hours}$$

Knowing T_f and T_d, we can now calculate T_s using equation (14). When $T_f = 1$, $T_d = 0.8$, and so,

$$T_s = 10 - (1 + 0.8)$$

$$= 8.2 \text{ hours}$$

(since we only have 10 hours available for feeding, sitting and defence). Using equation (6) we can now calculate the costs incurred by a sunbird defending 2000 flowers and spending 1 hour feeding.

$$C = 5949 + (1 \times 1000) + (8.2 \times 400) + (0.8 \times 3000)$$
$$= 5949 + 1000 + 328 + 2400 \cdot$$
$$= 9677 \text{ calories/day}$$

So, the total net energetic returns accruing to a sunbird defending 2000 flowers and spending 1 hour feeding are,

$$E = G - C$$
$$= 15\,000 - 9677$$
$$= 5323 \text{ calories/day.}$$

We could now select another feeding time (say $T_f = 1.01$ hours) and in the same way calculate the net energetic returns for a sunbird choosing *that* feeding time. We could then select yet another feeding time. And another. And so on. In this way we could calculate the feeding time which maximises net energetic returns when defending a territory of 2000 flowers (*net-maximising*). Or we could calculate the feeding time which minimises the total costs (*cost-minimising*). And, of course, we can calculate that feeding time which maximises the time spent sitting around (*sitting-maximising*).

Once we have done this for territories of 2000 flowers, we simply repeat the process for smaller territories (1, 2, 3 ... 1999 flowers) and for larger territories (2001, 2002, 2003 ... *n*). And at the end of the day we select that territory size which maximises each of our currencies. For that territory, we then select the feeding time which again maximises each of our currencies. The only constraint is that at the end of the day, whatever the currency, the net energetic return must be greater than zero (otherwise our sitting-maximiser would simply sit and starve — not terribly optimal!).

Havng done this for $\alpha = 2$, we then repeat this entire process for $\alpha = 1$ and $\alpha = 3$. We then compare our predicted territory sizes and feeding times with those observed. As it happens, the models came closest to the observed feeding times and observed territory size when $\alpha = 2$ (Table 7.1).

The 'traditional' *net-maximising* model does very badly! However, both the *cost-minimising* and *sitting-maximising* models give answers close to the observed territory size. Of these two, the *cost-minimising* model gives the closest fit to the observed data. As might be expected the *sitting-maximising* model overestimates the sitting time, and underestimates the feeding and defence times.

One of the nice things about Pyke's sunbird study is that we have three (and in the original paper, four) different optimality models pitted against each other, each with its own set of optimisation criteria. We are not testing whether sunbirds are optimal; we are testing these optimisation criteria.

Table 7.1: Predictions and observed data for territorial behaviour in *Nectarinia*. Both the *cost-minimising* and *sitting-maximising* models accurately predict the observed territory sizes, but the *cost-minimising* model is better at predicting the observed time budgets

	Net-maximising	Model Cost-minimising	Sitting-maximising	Observed
Territory size (flowers)	7070	1595	1653	1600
Feeding time (h)	7.45	2.41	1.72	2.42
Defence time (h)	2.55	0.28	0.61	0.28
Sitting time (h)	0	7.31	7.67	7.30

In the next section we shall outline a well-worked example of territoriality — this time in the pied wagtail (*Motacilla alba*). A number of models will be introduced each examining different aspects of wagtail territorial and social behaviour. These models address questions about territory sharing, territorial versus non-territorial behaviour, and also questions about optimal territory size.

7.5 Wagtail Behaviour

Large numbers of wagtails overwinter in the Thames Valley in southern England. Nick Davies and Alasdair Houston of Oxford University studied their foraging and social behaviour on Port Meadow just to the north-east of Oxford (Davies and Houston, 1981, 1983). Every year, as many as 300 wagtails congregate there. Some feed in flocks at shallow pools in the middle of the meadow. Others defend feeding territories along the River Thames which flows along one side of the meadow.

Territory owners establish themselves along stretches of the river, defending both banks against intruders. They feed by systematically patrolling their territory, running along the water's edge picking up insects washed up on the riverbank. Occasionally territory owners tolerate 'satellite' wagtails on their territories. However, the owner's behaviour toward these satellites appears highly unpredictable. On any one day an owner and satellite may be found feeding together peacefully on the territory. The following day, the owner may evict the satellite. A few days later and the owner may be feeding with another satellite. Sometimes an owner may stay on territory all day; and sometimes the owner leaves his territory to feed with flocks in the middle of the meadow. How do we explain these changes in behaviour? The key to the problem seemed to lie in the peculiar nature of the food supply on the river-bank.

7.5.1 The Food Supply

The shallow pools in the middle of Port Meadow provide a relatively constant food supply with most birds obtaining about 20 items of food per minute. Sadly, this food supply is not always available to wagtails. Sharp frosts often cause the pools to freeze, forcing the wagtails to leave the meadow. In contrast, the river rarely freezes and although food appears on the riverbank at variable rates it is nearly always available.

Territorial wagtails forage almost exclusively by picking up insects at the water's edge. The owner systematically searches its territory working its way along one bank, crossing the river, and then working its way down the opposite bank. Why should the owner forage in this way? Well, counts of the numbers of insects washing up on the riverbank revealed an exponential relationship between the numbers of insects and time (Figure 7.4). The reason

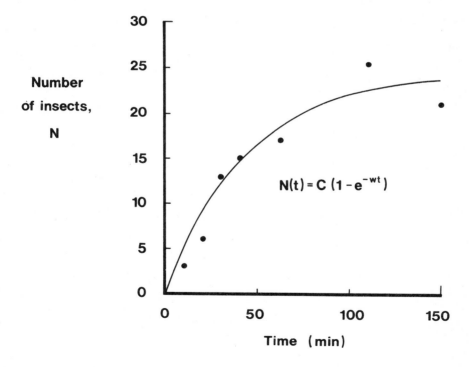

$$N(t) = C\,(1 - e^{-wt})$$

Figure 7.4: Wagtail food supply. The number of insects accumulating along a stretch of riverbank increases exponentially with time. These data were obtained by stretching a terylene net along the riverbank and recording the cumulative number of prey in the net at various intervals (from Davies and Houston, 1981).

that the numbers do not continue to increase at the same rate is because after a time these insects are washed away again by the river. (In fact, Houston had predicted such an exponential build up before the rates were measured in the field.)

This means that by searching its territory systematically the owner allows time for prey to accumulate on the riverbank. Figure 7.5 shows that the feeding rate on any stretch of the river increases with the time since that stretch was last visited (R).

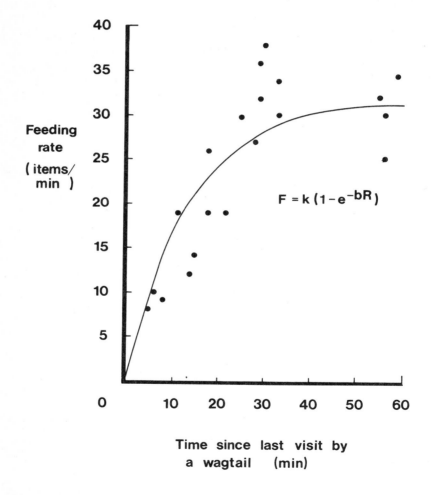

Figure 7.5: Feeding rates and return times. The feeding rate of territory owners increases with time since a particular stretch of the riverbank was last visited by a wagtail. The owner's feeding rate is given by $F = k(1 - e^{-bR})$, where k and b are constants. (After Davies and Houston, 1981.)

The problem is that an intruder landing on the territory will deplete a stretch of the riverbank. That is, the renewal time between visits to that stretch will be shortened, fewer prey will accumulate on the bank, and so the territory owner suffers a fall in feeding rate (Figure 7.6). Hardly surprising then that the owner vigorously defends its territory against intruders; as soon as an intruder is spotted the owner gives chase. However the intruder is not always spotted immediately. The further the intruder lands from the owner the less likely it is to be spotted (Figure 7.7).

The most profitable place for an intruder to land is right in front of the owner since this is the place with the highest renewal time. However, any intruder silly enough to land in front of the owner is immediately evicted. If

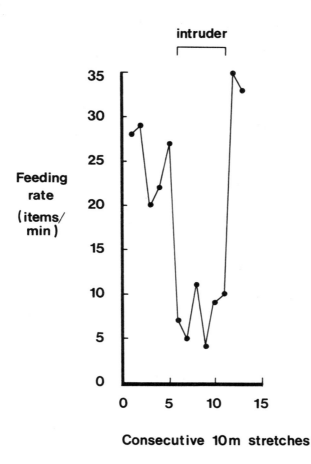

Figure 7.6: Intruders depress the owner's feeding rate. The sudden drop in feeding rate occurs when the owner encounters a stretch of the bank recently visited by an intruder.

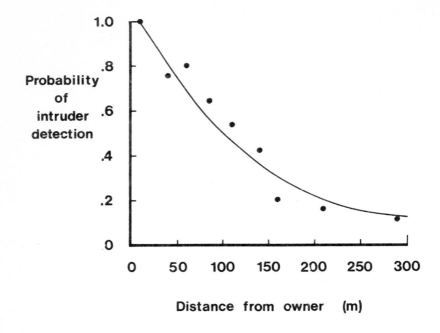

Figure 7.7: Distance from the owner and the probability of detection. The further the intruder from the owner the less likely it is to be detected. The curve is that used in the computer simulations in section 7.6. (Houston, McCleery and Davies, 1985.)

the intruder lands at some distance from the owner it is less likely to be detected but it will be feeding on a less profitable stretch. Davies and Houston (1981) found that intruders will persist in their trespass only if they obtain a feeding rate of 15 items/min or better. With feeding rates less than this the intruder will leave the territory.

The owner's feeding rate, F, on any given stretch is an exponential function of the time since that stretch was last depleted (see Figure 7.5). The interval between two successive visits to the same area is known as the *return time*, R. If there are no intruders then R will be the time since the owner last visited that stretch. Without a satellite to share its territory, the owner's feeding rate will be

$$F_{(-\text{satellite})} = k(1 - e^{-bR}) \tag{15}$$

where k and b are constants characterising the food abundance on territory and the rate of renewal respectively. These two constants will vary from day to day but can be fitted to observed feeding rate curves for any chosen day.

7.5.2 The Pros and Cons of Satellites

What happens if a territory owner decides to share its territory with a satellite? Davies and Houston (1981) found that when an owner was alone on the territory the mean return was about 40 min. When the territory was shared with a satellite this was halved to 20 min. The return time for owner and satellite was roughly the same. Usually the satellite circuited round the whole territory half a circuit behind the owner. Sometimes the owner and satellite spent most of their time in different halves of the territory. Clearly, adopting a satellite is going to halve the owner's return time, R. So the owner's feeding rate with a satellite will be,

$$F_{(+ \text{satellite})} = k(1 - e^{-bR/2}) \tag{16}$$

Example 2

We can use equations (15) and (16) to calculate the feeding rate of the owner with and without a satellite. Say that the constants k and b are found to be 15 and 0.1 respectively on one particular day (these values will also be used in several later examples). Then, if the owner is feeding alone with return time $R = 40$, its feeding rate will be,

$$F_{(- \text{satellite})} = k(1 - e^{-bR})$$
$$= 15(1 - e^{-0.1 \times 40})$$
$$= 14.73 \text{ items/min.}$$

However, with a satellite, the owner's return time is halved ($R = (40/2) = 20$ min) and its feeding rate will be,

$$F_{(+ \text{satellite})} = k(1 - e^{-bR/2})$$
$$= 15(1 - e^{-0.1 \times 20})$$
$$= 12.97 \text{ items/min.}$$

Taking on a satellite leads to a fall in the owner's feeding rate.

Although satellites reduce the owner's feeding returns they take on as much as a half share of the territorial defence. This leads to improved intruder detection. Davies and Houston (1981) found that the probability of an intruder being spotted straight away increased from 0.595 for an owner on his own to 0.848 for owners sharing their territories with a satellite.

7.5.3 The Owner's Dilemma

The territory owner faces a dilemma. On the one hand allowing a satellite on territory means that the owner suffers a reduction in its feeding rate. On the other hand it means that it has an assistant to help with territorial defence.

The decision to accept a satellite must set the costs against the benefits. But how do we calculate these costs and benefits? And what currency should we use? Time or energy? Let us start with time.

The cost is easy to calculate; we simply calculate the owner's feeding rate when the renewal time, R, is halved (equation (16)). However, the benefits are rather tricky to calculate. To work out the *benefits* of sharing a territory with a satellite we have to first calculate the *cost* of intruders alighting on the territory and depressing the renewal time (since a satellite will reduce such costs). These intruder costs can be considered as time spent not feeding. Each intrusion inflicts a time cost and so reduces the owner's feeding rate. How do we calculate these costs? Well, there are in fact three time costs involved:

(1) the *chase cost*. This is the time taken to chase away the intruder. The average time to chase off an intruder was 0.9 min. For the following calculations this is taken as 1 min.

(2) the *displacement cost*. Following each chase the owner resumes its cycle of the territory. Unfortunately, the owner does not always restart the cycle at the exact point where it left off to chase the intruder. On average, the owner was displaced by about 56 m. Davies and Houston assumed that on half of these occasions the owner was displaced forwards on the circuit and suffered no reduction in feeding rate. (In reality there will be a small cost since the renewal time will be $R - (56/14) + 1 = R - 3$ min. The term $(56/14)$ is the time taken to cover the 56 m assuming an average running speed of 14 m/min. We add 1 min because this is the extra time taken to evict the intruder during which the riverbank is renewing.) On the remaining 50% of occasions Davies and Houston assumed that the wagtail was displaced backwards on its circuit and so retraced its steps over a stretch just depleted before the chase. It will take $(56/14) = 4$ min to retrace the depleted stretch during which we assume that the feeding rate is 0 items/min. This time cost will be paid on 50% of all intrusions, and so the total time cost will be $1/2 \times 4$ min, that is 2 min. (An early version of the model omitted this displacement cost, but 2 min of lost feeding represents a considerable cost.)

(3) a *depletion cost*. Sometimes intruders landed unnoticed and depleted stretches of the territory. The mean time these intruders spent on territory before eviction was 6.9 min and this was the same with or without a satellite! Such intruders depressed the owner's feeding rate over those stretches (Figure 7.6). How can we estimate a time cost for such a fall in feeding rate? Let us suppose that the owner spends D min going over a depleted stretch. Assume that the renewal rate over this stretch is equal to a constant, r. Then the owner's feeding rate, F_d will be,

$$F_d = k(1 - e^{-br}) \tag{17}$$

What we want to do is to convert this feeding rate into a time, x min, spent feeding at rate F (the rate if no intruder was on the territory), and a time $z = D - x$, spent feeding at rate 0 items/min, such that the two cases provide the same amount of food. Thus z is our time cost due to depletion. Figure 7.8 shows what we are trying to do.

In order to calculate the time cost, z, we start by calculating the number of items, N_D, eaten in time D. This is equal to the feeding rate F_d multiplied by the time D. That is,

$$N_D = D \times k(1 - e^{-br}) \qquad (18)$$

Remember that we are looking for the time x for which this is equivalent to feeding at rate F. The number of items, N_x, eaten during time x must equal the number eaten during D.

$$N_x = x \times k(1 - e^{-bR}) \qquad (19)$$

Now $N_D = N_x$ so,

$$Dk(1 - e^{-br}) = xk(1 - e^{-bR}) \qquad (20)$$

Which means that,

$$x = D \times \frac{k(1 - e^{-br})}{k(1 - e^{-bR})}$$

And the constants (k) cancel to give,

$$x = D\frac{(1 - e^{-br})}{(1 - e^{-bR})} \qquad (21)$$

And so the time cost is equal to

$$z = D - x = D - \left[\frac{D(1 - e^{-br})}{(1 - e^{-bR})}\right]$$

Or,

$$z = D \times \left[\frac{1 - (1 - e^{-br})}{(1 - e^{-bR})}\right] \qquad (22)$$

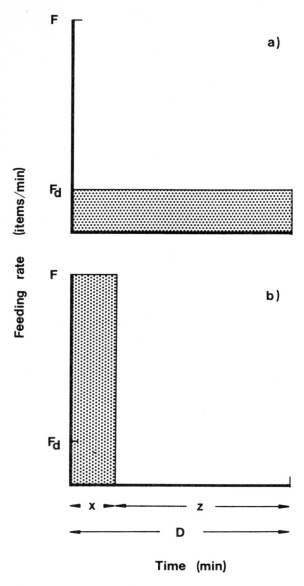

Figure 7.8: Calculating the time cost of depletion. Feeding along a depleted stretch at rate F_d for D min (a) is equivalent to feeding at rate F for x min and rate 0 items/min for z min (b). Thus z is the time cost due to depletion. A numerical example may help. If D = 4 min and F_d = 5 items/min, then feeding for 4 min at 5 items/min will yield 20 items of food. This is equivalent to feeding at the normal feeding rate (F = 20 items/min) for x = 1 min. Thus the time cost of depletion, z = D − x = 4 − 1 = 3 min. In fact the time cost is slightly more complicated than this since there is some renewal at rate r (see text).

And when a satellite shares the territory the owner's return time, R, is halved and so the time cost, z_s, for an owner with a satellite is

$$z_s = D \times \left[1 - \left[\frac{1 - e^{-br}}{1 - e^{-bR/2}} \right] \right] \tag{23}$$

Davies and Houston found that the average return time for owner and satellite to stretches depleted by intruders, r, was 10.1 min. They also assumed that it takes the owner or satellite the same time to cover a depleted patch as it does an intruder, that is, 6.9 min (in fact they used an approximate value of 7 min).

Example 3

In section 6.7 we calculated the owner's feeding rate with and without a satellite for $b = 0.1$ and $k = 15$. We can now use equations (22) and (23) to calculate the depletion costs on that day. We will use approximate values of 7, 10 and 40 min for D, r and R respectively.

Without satellites the owner incurs a depletion cost of

$$z = 7 \times \left[1 - \left[\frac{1 - e^{-0.1 \times 10}}{1 - e^{-0.1 \times 40}} \right] \right]$$

$$= 2.493 \text{ min.}$$

With a satellite the depletion cost is

$$z_s = 7 \left[1 - \left[\frac{1 - e^{-0.1 \times 10}}{1 - e^{-0.1 \times 40/2}} \right] \right]$$

$$= 1.884 \text{ min.}$$

Adopting a satellite means a smaller depletion cost because the owner has a relatively lower feeding rate anyway.

At last we have the various time costs! We are now in a position to calculate the total time cost *per* intrusion. This cost will be greater when the owner is alone because it is less likely to detect an intruder and so will have to pay the depletion cost more often.

When the owner is defending the territory alone, it detects 59.5% of intruders. These intruders are evicted immediately and so the owner pays only a chase cost (1 min) and a displacement cost (2 min), so the total time cost is $(1 + 2) = 3$ min (go back to page 140 if you have forgotten where these

values came from). On the remaining 40.5% of occasions the intruder is undetected and an owner must pay a depletion cost in addition to the chase and
displacement costs. So the total time cost following an intrusion which is not
spotted straight away is $(1 + 2 + z)$ min, where z is calculated according to
equation (22).

This means that the average time cost per intrusion when the owner is
alone is

$$T_O = (0.595 \times 3) + (0.405 \times (3 + z)) \text{ min} \tag{24}$$

However, if the owner shares a territory with a satellite then intruders are
spotted straight away on 84.8% of occasions and so the owner or the satellite
pays only the chase and displacement costs (3 min). On the remaining 15.2%
of occasions either the owner or the satellite pays a cost of $(3 + z_s)$ min, where
z_s is given by equation (23). So, on days when the owner shares its territory
with a satellite, the average cost per intrusion is given by,

$$T_S = (0.848 \times 3) + (0.152 \times (3 + z_s)) \text{ min} \tag{25}$$

which can be paid *either* by the owner or the satellite.

Example 4
We can now calculate the time costs of intrusions with and without satellites
for our hypothetical example where $b = 0.1$ and $k = 15$. We simply substitute
for z and z_s in equations (24) and (25).

Without a satellite,

$$T_O = (0.595 \times 3) + 0.405 (3 + 2.493)$$
$$= 1.785 + 2.225 = 4.010 \text{ min.}$$

With a satellite,

$$T_S = (0.848 \times 3) + 0.152 (3 + 1.884)$$
$$= 2.544 + 0.742 = 3.286 \text{ min.}$$

So, adopting a satellite not only means that wagtails pay smaller depletion
costs, but they also pay that cost less often (because of improved intruder
detection).

7.5.4 Solution to the Owner's Dilemma
We have now calculated the time costs (equations (24) and (25)) and feeding
benefits (equations (15) and (16)) with and without a satellite. What we want
to do now is to combine the two in order to calculate the owner's feeding rate

when defending the territory by itself and when sharing the territory with a satellite.

Equation (15) gives the number of items obtained by the owner in 1 min of uninterrupted foraging. However, as we have seen, wagtails are frequently interrupted while foraging. Evicting intruders leads to the chase, displacement and depletion costs outlined above. We need to know the average time cost per minute.

The defence cost per minute is equal to the number of intrusions per minute, N, multiplied by the average time cost of intrusion (T_O or T_S). In fact, N is a function of the constant k (the index of food abundance). The more food on a territory, the higher the rate of intrusion and so the greater the defence costs per minute (compare with the sunbird model in section 7.4 in which the time spent in territorial defence was a function of the number of flowers, and the territory quality c). From Figure 7.9 we see that the number of intrusions is given by,

$$N(k) = 0.00325\,k - 0.0221 \qquad (26)$$

where k is the asymptotic feeding rate on the territory.

This means that when the owner is alone on its territory, its *real* feeding rate once defence costs have been accounted for (as opposed to the simple feeding rate of equation (15)) is

$$F_O = [1 - T_O N(k)] \times k(1 - e^{-bR}) \qquad (27)$$

where T_O is the time of an intrusion (equation 24)) and $N(k)$ the number of times that cost is paid *per minute* (equation (26)). Thus $[1 - T_O N(k)]$ is the average amount of each minute for which the bird achieves a feeding rate of $F_{(-\text{ satellite})} = k(1 - e^{-bR})$.

If our territory owner decides to take on a satellite, the defence costs are reduced, and so the owner can spend more time feeding. However, it must feed at a lower rate (since the satellite shares the territory). Let us assume that the satellite does a full half of the territorial defence. This means that the owner's defence costs, T_S, are halved and so the owner's feeding rate will be

$$F_S = [1 - (1/2)T_S N(k)] \times k(1 - e^{-bR/2}) \qquad (28)$$

In other words, $[1 - ((1/2)T_S N(k))]$ is the average amount of each minute for which the territory owner attains a feeding rate of $F_{(-\text{ satellite})} = k(1 - e^{-bR/2})$ (assuming that the owner and satellite share the defence costs equally).

And so the solution to the owner's problem is simply to take on a satellite when $F_S > F_O$. What could be simpler?

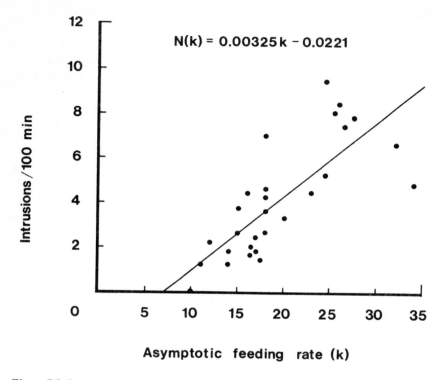

$$N(k) = 0.00325\,k - 0.0221$$

Asymptotic feeding rate (k)

Figure 7.9: Intrusions and territory quality. The daily rate of intrusions increases with the asymptotic feeding rate (k). The higher the asymptotic feeding rate the greater the number of intrusions. The regression equation is for the number of intrusions per minute. (Davies and Houston, 1981.)

Example 5

Using equations (27) and (28) we can calculate the owner's feeding rate with and without a satellite. In our hypothetical example, $b = 0.1$ and $k = 15$. The first thing to do is to calculate the rate of intrusion, N, which is a function of k.

$$N(k) = 0.00325 \times 15 - 0.0221 \qquad \text{(equation (26))}$$
$$= 0.02665 \text{ intrusions/min}$$

We have already calculated T_O and T_S (4.010 and 3.826 min respectively), and we have already calculated $F_{(- \text{ satellite})}$ and $F_{(+ \text{ satellite})}$ (14.73 and 12.97 items/min respectively — see section 7.5.3). Substituting for these values in equations (27) and (28), we get,

$$F_O = (1 - (4.010 \times 0.02665))\,14.73$$

$$= 13.16\ \text{items/min.}$$

And,

$$F_S = (1 - (1/2)(3.826 \times 0.02665))\,12.97$$

$$= 12.31\ \text{items/min.}$$

So on this particular day (when $b = 0.1$ and $k = 15$) the owner's feeding rate will be higher if it defends the territory singlehanded. The model predicts that it should *not* adopt a satellite.

7.5.5 How Well Does the Model Do?

Davies and Houston used equations (27) and (28) to predict the feeding rates which would be achieved by the owner with and without a satellite. For each day they fitted values of b and k (equation (16)) to data for feeding rates against return times. They then calculated intrusion rates $N(k)$ from equation (26), and calculated T_O and T_S from equations (24) and (25) with an approximate return time from their data of $R = 40$ min.

Table 7.2 compares the model's predictions with the owner's observed behaviour on 42 days. On 13 days the model predicted that the owner should take on a satellite; on eleven of those the owner indeed took on a satellite (and on two days it defended the territory alone). On 27 days the model predicted that the owner should not adopt a satellite and on 23 days the owner was not observed with a satellite. The figures in brackets show the expectation if the model had been 100% correct.

The model does rather well. Looking at Table 7.2 we see that the model got it right on 36/40 days or 90% of the time. Of course with this kind of all-

Table 7.2: Days on which owners were observed on territory with and without a satellite. The model assumes that the owner makes its decision to adopt a satellite on the basis of expected feeding returns. If feeding alone promises the highest return then the owner should evict intruders. Otherwise it should adopt a satellite to share the territorial defence. The figures in brackets are the predicted number of days if the model was 100% correct.

		Predicted	
		With satellite	Without satellite
Observed	With satellite	11(13)	4(0)
	Without satellite	2(0)	23(27)

or-none prediction it is difficult to put an exact figure on how well the data support the model. However, the model seems sufficiently accurate to warrant a feeling that it has at least captured the essence of the owner's dilemma.

7.6 Feeding and Flocking

One major assumption made by the above model is that wagtails attempt to maximise their feeding rates. It seems a reasonable assumption and one which is not without precedent (see Chapter 3). We assume that natural selection has produced efficient wagtails maximising their daily feeding rates. In this section we shall develop a model of wagtail social behaviour which assumes that wagtails are maximising feeding rates. As we shall see this model runs into one or two little problems.

7.6.1 Model 1
In section 7.5 we described how wagtails would sometimes abandon their territories to feed in flocks around shallow pools in the middle of the meadow. Eventually they would return to the territory and often a wagtail would spend the day alternating between flock-feeding and territoriality. This usually happens when the rate of food renewal on the territory is rather low. It seems likely that the owner leaves its territory when it can get richer pickings by feeding around the shallow flood pools. But how long should a wagtail spend in the flock and how long on territory if it is to maximise its daily feeding rate?

When food is scarce on the territory the owner may leave to feed with the flock. The longer the owner spends away from the territory the greater the number of prey accumulating during his absence. Now we already know that while the owner is off territory the number of prey accumulating on a strip of territory is:

$$N(t) = C(1 - e^{-wt}) \qquad (29)$$

(see Figure 7.4) where C and w are constants on any given day and t is the time since the owner's last visit. In this case t is made up of three components,

$$t = T + D + F\min \qquad (30)$$

where T is the time taken to circuit the territory, D is the time spent with the flock, and F is the time to fly to the flock and back again ($F = 0.75$ min on average). So we assume that the owner flies to the pool, and then it flies back to the territory in order to make one complete circuit before returning to the pool again. In this model we will assume that there is no serious depletion due to intruders while the territory owner is away. (This is reasonable because on days when the feeding returns from the territory were so bad as to force the owner to flock feed intruders rarely stayed on a territory.)

While feeding in the flock for time D the territory owner's feeding rate is R. Thus the total number of prey, N_1, captured while feeding in the flock is simply

$$N_1 = RD \qquad (31)$$

Let us divide the territory into L sections. We know (equation (29)) that the number of prey accumulating on a stretch of territory while the owner is away is given by

$$N(t) = C(1 - e^{-wt})$$

and in this case $t = (T + D + F)$ (equation (30)), and so,

$$N(t) = C(1 - e^{-w(T + D + F)}) \qquad (32)$$

Let $\theta = w(T + D + F)$. Then the number of prey accumulating on a single stretch of the territory is given by

$$N(t) = C(1 - e^{-\theta}) \qquad (33)$$

If the territory is composed of L sections then the number of prey accumulating on the entire territory, N_2, is simply,

$$N_2 = LC(1 - e^{-\theta}) \qquad (34)$$

Thus the overall feeding rate, G, is given by the number of prey captured in the flock (N_1) and on the territory (N_2) divided by the time in the flock (D), on the territory (T) and travelling between the two (F). That is,

$$G = \frac{(N_1 + N_2)}{(T + D + F)} \qquad (35)$$

Substituting for N_1 and N_2,

$$G = \frac{RD + LC(1 - e^{-\theta})}{(T + D + F)} \qquad (36)$$

Now the value of D, the flock time, which maximises the daily feeding rate, G, can be found by differentiating with respect to D. When G is at a maximum then $dG/dD = 0$ (see section 2.4 in Chapter 2). Eventually (see Appendix 7.1) we end up with,

$$\frac{R(T+F)}{LC} + e^{-\theta}(1 + \theta) = 1 \tag{37}$$

when the value of D maximises the owner's feeding rate.

This means that given the values of C and w for any one day we can calculate the flock time, D, which maximises G.

To test this model Davies and Houston (1983) grouped their predictions into three predicted flock times. According to the model an owner might:

(1) stay on territory all day $(D = 0)$
(2) spend up to 30 min on average in a flock $(30 > D > 0)$
(3) spend more than 30 min in a flock $(D > 30)$.

Table 7.3 shows the number of observed and predicted observations falling into each category. The model does rather badly! The right diagonal gives the total number of times that the model and the data agreed. The model got it right on 16/35 days (46%). Not terribly good! Where had the model gone wrong? One of the problems is that territory owners appear to be sacrificing short-term gains in feeding rate and spending extra time on their territories. This can be shown by plotting the percentage time spent on territory as a function of the difference between the feeding rate on territory and the feeding rate in the flock. We predict that when the feeding rate in the flock is greater than the feeding rate on territory then the owner should leave. However, it does not (Figure 7.10).

7.6.2 Model 2
Looking at Figure 7.10 it is clear that territory owners spend more time on their territories than we would expect if they were simply maximising their

Table 7.3: Frequency of observed and predicted times spent in a flock rather than on territory. The model assumes that territory owners are maximising their feeding returns. The model performs rather poorly.

		Observed flock times (min)		
		0	0–30	> 30
Predicted	0	9	7	1
flock	0–30	2	4	0
times (min)	> 30	1	4	3

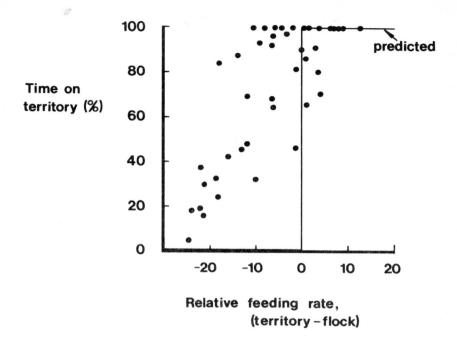

Figure 7.10: Time on territory and daily feeding rates. The step function shows the predicted time spent on territory if territory owners are maximising their daily feeding rates. The model predicts that owners should switch to flock feeding when their returns from flock feeding are greater than their returns from maintaining a territory. However, owners choose to stay on territory even when they would improve their feeding rates by joining a flock. (Davies and Houston, 1983.)

daily feeding rates. Why should they do this?

Davies and Houston observed that territorial intruders were only likely to persist in a trespass if they obtained a feeding rate greater than 15 items/min. One possibility is that the owner is periodically returning to the territory to harvest the food supply thus ensuring that any intruding wagtail does not achieve a feeding rate greater than this 15 items/min threshold. By sacrificing a short-term gain in feeding rate the owner ensures that the territory remains unprofitable to intruders. The critical question is how long dare a territory owner leave its territory before it becomes profitable to intruders? The owner must return to harvest the territory before this critical time.

Let N^* be the critical number of food items in a 10 m stretch of the river which will give an intruder the critical feeding rate of 15 items/min. Let us suppose that our territory owner leaves the territory for t min. How long will it be before the entire territory is profitable to an intruder?

We already know (from equation (29)) that

$$N(t) = C(1 - e^{-wt})$$

So,

$$N^\star = C(1 - e^{-wt_c}) \qquad (38)$$

where $N^\star$ is the critical number of items accumulating in time t_c. Rearranging,

$$t_c = \frac{1}{w} \ln[C/(C - N^\star)] \qquad (39)$$

So at time t_c an intruder landing anywhere on the territory will obtain 15 items/min. How long will it be before an intruder lands on territory and persists in its trespass? This will depend upon the rate of intrusion and the pattern of intrusions. However, we can get a rough estimate from the average time to an intrusion.

The average (expected) time to the next intrusion will depend upon the intrusion rate $N(k)$ (and this depends upon the asymptotic food level C). So, $1/N(k)$ gives us the expected time to the next intrusion, t_i. This means that the maximum amount of time a wagtail can afford to spend away from the territory, t_{max} is simply,

$$t_{max} = t_c + t_i$$

That is, the time taken for the territory to become profitable to an intruder (t_c) *plus* the expected time to the next intrusion (t_i). Any longer, and there is a good chance that our wagtail will return only to find an intruder depleting his territory.

The results are shown in Figure 7.11. It is rather better than the first model, but still not perfect. Although the observed times away from the territory all fall below the predicted maximum the precise relationship between time away from the territory and the predicted time away does not look too good. Although the data support the model qualitatively it looks as though wagtails play safe by underestimating the time they can afford to spend away from the territory.

7.7 Territory Size

Large territories mean long foraging circuits, long renewal times, and so more

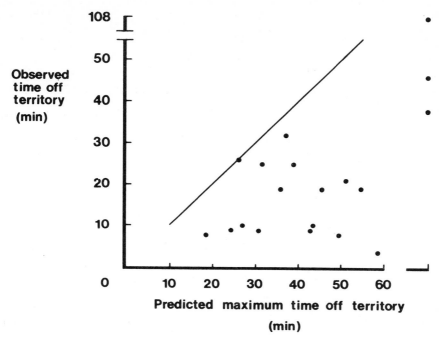

Figure 7.11: The second model of wagtail time budgeting predicts that owners should return to the territory before the territory becomes profitable to intruders. Although the wagtails never stayed away from the territory for longer than this predicted maximum, the exact relationship between observed and predicted times is rather poor. (Davies and Houston, 1983.)

food. So a wagtail can improve its feeding returns by increasing the size of its territory. However, large territories are more costly to defend. An intruder is more likely to pass undetected and so deplete stretches of the territory. In this section we are going to tackle the problem of optimal territory size. To solve this problem Houston and Davies were joined by their colleague Robin McCleery. Together they developed a *simulation* model of wagtail behaviour (Houston, McCleery and Davies, 1985).

The simulated wagtail shares many of the characteristics of real wagtails. It walks a regular circuit around the territory. It stops to evict intruders. The territory covers both banks of a model river 40 m in width. Territory sizes covered the range observed on Port Meadow: length varied from 150 m to 600 m of river that is 300–1200 m of riverbank. The model wagtail covers 1 m sections of riverbank in 4 s which corresponds with field values of 0.25 m/s for wagtail velocity. (In fact, Houston, McCleery and Davies, 1985 simulated a range of wagtail velocities, but we shall not consider the results of these simulations here.)

Every 4 s the model wagtail moves to the next 1 m section to feed, and the number of prey in this fresh section, N, is given by equation (29). Thus,

$$N = C(1 - e^{-wt}),$$

where C is the asymptotic value of N, w is the renewal rate, and t is the time since that section was last visited by a wagtail (either the owner or an intruder).

At each 4 s time step an intruder arrives with a probability dependent upon C (which is an index of territory value) and the territory size, such that,

$$p(\text{intruder}) = A_1 C + A_2 \qquad (40)$$

A_1 and A_2 being constants (values 0.109 and 1.45 respectively) derived from field data for intruders arriving in 100 min on a 600 m territory. Thus the probability of an intruder arriving in a 4 s time step is,

$$p(\text{intruder}) = (0.109 \ C + 1.45) \ [4 \ /(60 \times 100)] \qquad (41)$$

and then scaling for territory size, the probability of an intruder landing in a territory size S is simply,

$$p(\text{intruder}) = (0.109 \ C + 1.45) \times [4/(60 \times 100)] \times S/600 \qquad (42)$$

If an intruder arrives it lands with equal probability on any section of the territory and moves with equal probability in the same or the opposite direction to the territory owner.

The probability of the model territory owner detecting a model intruder d metres away was assumed to be,

$$p(\text{detection}) = e^{-\alpha(d-c)} \qquad (43)$$

where α and c are both constants. This approximates the observed probabilities (Figure 7.7). (In fact, Houston, McCleery and Davies varied α and c to simulate changes in the effectiveness of intruder detection. The interested reader is referred to Houston, McCleery and Davies, 1985.)

If the owner detects an intruder it gives chase. In the simulation each chase lasted 60 s (observed mean value in the field is 54 s) during which time the owner was unable to feed and paid a metabolic cost of 9 × BMR (the *chase cost*; BMR: basal metabolic rate). In addition the model owner paid a *displacement cost*, landing with equal probability 56 m either side of its position when the chase began.

If an intruder was not detected it moved to the next section and depleted it. If this section gave a feeding rate less than the threshold of 15 items/min then the intruder left (see section 7.6 above).

Each computer run lasted for the equivalent of a winter's day (8 h) and at the end of each run Houston *et al.* recorded the number of intrusions, chases, and the number of items taken. They then calculated the mean feeding rate. The total energetic intake was determined using a calorific value of 14.64 j/item and a digestive efficiency of 0.75 (these were determined in an earlier paper by Davies, 1977).

The energetic cost of intruder chases was given by,

$$\text{chase cost} = \text{number of chases} \times \text{duration} \times 9(\text{BMR}) \qquad (44)$$

And the foraging costs were taken to be,

$$\text{foraging cost} = \text{time walking} \times (4(\text{BMR}) + \text{correction for speed}) \qquad (45)$$

The exact costs of walking and flying are not known for wagtails, but from what is known of similar species $4 \times \text{BMR}$ and $9 \times \text{BMR}$ are fairly realistic estimates.

(Note that by including metabolic estimates we have shifted currencies — from time to energy. This reflects a general change in currency in behavioural ecology. Our choice of currency (time or energy) can have important consequences for optimality models).

These simulations allowed the wagtail's energetic gain to be calculated for a number of territory sizes. During each simulated 8 hour run the exact timing of intrusions (though not the overall rate), the location of the intrusions on territory, the direction of movement of the intruder, and the direction of displacement following a chase were determined by a random number generator. Houston *et al.* ran several series of simulations examining the effects of C (the asymptotic value for the number of prey items), w (the rate of accumulation of food items), and S the territory size, on the net gains.

We know that as territory size increases the owner increases the renewal time between successive visits. However, it pays increased defence costs because the intrusion rate increases with territory size. Not only will the intrusion rate increase, but intruders are more likely to land at greater distances from the intruder and so escape detection for longer. So, returning to the original question, given C and w what is the optimal territory size?

The simulation clearly shows that the optimum territory size depends upon the rate of renewal, w. The net gains are plotted in Figure 7.12. This shows that for a range of realistic values of w a wagtail maximises its energetic gains by opting for a territory of 600 m. As it happens (!) this corresponds to the territory size most commonly found on Port Meadow (Figure 7.13).

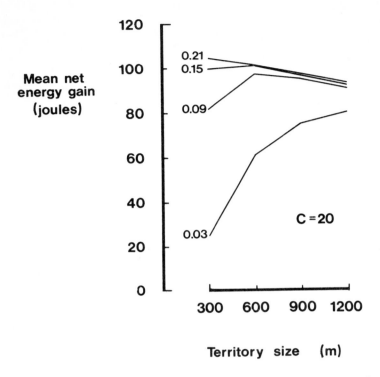

Figure 7.12: Mean energetic returns on territories of different sizes. For a range of renewal rates (w) the energetic returns are maximised on territories of about 600 m. However, if w is very small (0.03) then it pays to defend a rather larger territory (1200 m), and if w is very large (0.15) it pays to defend a small territory (300 m). (Houston, McCleery and Davies, 1985.)

7.7 Summary

The starting point for the above models of territoriality was to specify the relationship between time spent feeding and territory size, and the relationship between time spent in territorial defence and territory size. The objective was then to express these two very different behaviours in terms of a common currency. In Graham Pyke's sunbird model this was done by looking at the effect of time spent in territorial defence on the time available for feeding and other activities. It was then a relatively simple matter to measure the effect of feeding time and territorial defence on energetic intake. However, both the sunbird model (see section 7.3) and the simple model (see section 7.2) assume that the territory owner is in equilibrium with its food supply. This simplifying assumption means that the owner's intake is maximised when it equals the

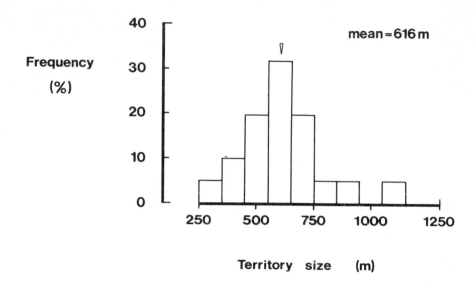

Figure 7.13: Observed territory sizes on Port Meadow, Oxford. The mean territory size (616 m) is that which maximises energetic returns for a range of realistic renewal rates (see Figure 7.12). (Davies and Houston, 1981.)

. production of the territory. Although this may be the case for sunbirds it may not be true in general. If an animal depletes its territory over time then the optimal territory size is going to be larger than if he is in equilibrium with his food supply. A starting point for further models perhaps?

In section 7.5 we switched from Pyke's relatively simple model to a rather more complex situation — territoriality in the wagtail. We looked at three aspects of wagtail territoriality: models of territory-sharing; time-budgeting between the flock and the territory; and models of optimal territory size.

In the first model (territory-sharing) the objective was to quantify the various costs and benefits in terms of their effects on the owner's feeding rate. The first important step was to identify the effect of 'return times' on feeding rates. Sharing a territory halved these return times with quantifiable effects on an owner's feeding rate. This fall in feeding rate is clearly a *cost* of adopting a satellite. However, adopting a satellite allows the owner to share the costs of territorial defence. The next step was to identify and then quantify those costs in terms of their effects on the owner's feeding rate. Once we had these costs, we were able to infer the *benefits* of territory-sharing (see section 7.5).

The second series of models looked at the effect of flock-feeding and territory-feeding on the owner's feeding rate. Again the starting point was to calculate the owner's feeding rate both on a territory and in a flock. The next step was to select a value for the flock time (D) which maximised the owner's *overall* feeding rate. I think it is fair to say that this model did very badly (see Table 7.2). This dramatic failure tells us that something very interesting is going on. Owners appear to be sacrificing *short-term* gains in feeding rate in order to spend 'extra' time on the territory. One possibility is that we are watching optimisation over a longer period of time; it may pay a territory owner to maintain its territory over the entire winter. Although this may mean that on some days it suffers a fall in feeding rate, over the entire winter it probably does better than if it switched back and forth between the flock and the territory. The second model — which assumed that territory owners are 'harvesting' their territories to deter intruders — does much better.

This story reveals one of the drawbacks of feeding rate maximising and other *short-term* optimality models. An animal's survival and reproductive fitness may depend upon optimisation over a considerable period. An animal that has sole access to a resource can afford to manage that resource in such a way as to maximise its yield over a whole season. This is to be contrasted with the 'slash and burn' mentality of the feeding-rate–maximising territorial intruder.

Similarly long-term optimisation may require some kind of environmental sampling. Survival in the long run may depend upon a knowledge of the environment. For instance, without taking time out from feeding to sample the environment an optimal forager may miss good feeding patches. This means that an animal may appear to behave suboptimally in the short-term in order to maximise returns in the long term.

This is especially important in any consideration of life-history tactics (see McNeill Alexander, 1982). A decision to postpone the first breeding season may mean a reduction in reproductive success in the short-term, but in the long-term it may mean increased lifetime fitness (see Stearns, 1976).

Environmental sampling, resource management, lifetime success, and other long-term considerations go beyond the time-frame of the short-term optimality model. This book is dominated by short-term models. All things considered, they do rather well. However, there are many situations where a *long-term* optimality model may be more appropriate. McNeill Alexander (1982) gives a detailed account of a number of such models.

In section 7.7 we returned to the question of optimal territory size. This time the objective was to predict that territory size which maximised energetic returns. This model did not simply look at feeding rates but attempted to look at net energetic intake by accounting for the various metabolic costs of feeding and territorial defence. This is such a complex task that it defies the simple kind of *analytical* approach that we have used up until now. For the first time, we see in this chapter how a computer model can be used to *simulate* wagtail behaviour. For the non-mathematician, simulation models can be especially attractive! In the next chapter we will see more extensive use of simulation methods.

Appendix 7.1

We know that,

$$G = [LC(1 - e^{-\theta}) + RD][T + D + F]^{-1}$$

If we let:

$$u = LC(1 - e^{-\theta}) + RD, \text{ and}$$
$$v = (T + D + F)^{-1}$$

and remembering our rule for the differentiation of a product,

$$G = uv$$
$$dG/dD = d(uv)/dD$$
$$= u(dv/dD) + v(du/dD)$$

(see section 2.2 in Chapter 2).

So we want dv/dD and du/dD. Let us take it one step at a time.

Step 1: du/dD

Now,

$$u = LC(1 - e^{-\theta}) + RD$$

Substitute for θ and we get,

$$u = LC(1 - e^{-w(T + D + F)}) + RD$$
$$= LC(1 - e^{-w(T + F)}e^{-wD}) + RD$$

So,

$$\frac{du}{dD} = \frac{d[LC(1 - e^{-w(T + F)}e^{-wD}) + RD]}{dD}$$

$$= (LCwe^{-w(T + D + F)} + R)$$
$$= (R + LCwe^{-\theta})$$

Step 2: dv/dD

Now,

$$v = (T + D + F)^{-1}$$

So,

$$\frac{dv}{dD} = \frac{d[(T + D + F)^{-1}]}{dD}$$

$$= -1(T + D + F)^{-2}$$
$$= -1/(T + D + F)^2$$

Step 3: *dG/dD*
Now,

$$dG/dD = u \cdot dv/dD + v \cdot du/dD$$

Substituting for *du/dD* and *dv/dD* we get,

$$dG/dD = [\mathrm{LC}(1 - e^{-\theta}) + RD]\,[-1/(T + D + F)^2] +$$
$$[(T + D + F)^{-1}]\,[R + LCwe^{-\theta}]$$

That is,

$$dG/dD = \frac{[R + LCwe^{-\theta}]}{[T + D + F]} - \frac{[LC(1 - e^{-\theta}) + RD]}{[T + D + F]^2}$$

Multiplying through by $[T + D + F]$,

$$[R + LCwe^{-\theta}] - \frac{[LC(1 - e^{-\theta}) + RD]}{[T + D + F]}$$

Now, when *G* is maximised *dG/dD* = 0. So the feeding rate is maximised when,

$$[R + LCwe^{-\theta}] - \frac{[LC(1 - e^{-\theta}) + RD]}{[T + D + F]} = 0$$

Rearranging,

$$LC(1 - e^{-\theta}) + RD = (R + LCwe^{-\theta})(T + D + F)$$

Multiplying out the brackets gives us,

$$LC - LCe^{-\theta} + RD = R(T + D + F) + LCwe^{-\theta}(T + D + F)$$
$$= RT + RD + RF + LCwe^{-\theta}(T + D + F)$$

But recall that $\theta = w(T + D + F)$. So,

$$LC - LCe^{-\theta} + RD = RT + RD + RF + LC\theta e^{-\theta}$$

And RD cancels leaving,

$$LC - LCe^{-\theta} = RT + RF + LC\theta e^{-\theta}$$
$$= R(T + F) + LC\theta e^{-\theta}$$

Rearranging,

$$LC = R(T + F) + LC\theta e^{-\theta} + LCe^{-\theta}$$
$$= R(T + F) + LCe^{-\theta}(1 + \theta)$$

And dividing through by LC leaves us with,

$$1 = \frac{R(T + F)}{LC} + e^{-\theta}(1 + \theta)$$

Chapter 8
Games Theory Models: Social Behaviour

8.1 Introduction

In this chapter we are going to tackle a group of models developed from games theory. Games theory is a branch of mathematics devoted to the analysis of decisions made by two or more players where the outcomes depend upon what an opponent chooses to do. Economists and mathematicians have used the theory of games to analyse complex decisions in a variety of situations — everywhere from the board room to the nuclear arms theatre! However, many of the decisions which animals make are also open to a games theory analysis. Animals do not make optimality decisions in a void, but in a complex social environment. In certain circumstances an animal's payoff may depend upon the responses of other animals. This chapter covers a number of areas where this is true.

The name most closely associated with the use of games theory to understand the evolution of animal behaviour is that of Professor John Maynard Smith. In the early 1970s he was asked to referee a paper on animal aggression submitted to the journal *Nature* by Dr George Price. Price was puzzled by the evolution of ritualised non-injurious behaviour in animal contests. Even in contests for a valuable resource, animals rarely use their weaponry in the most effective way. The red deer (*Cervus elaphus*), for instance, does not often use its antlers to stab or puncture, but to push and grapple with an opponent. They appear to practise restraint during aggressive encounters. It occurred to Price that if animals adopted a strategy of 'retaliation' in which an animal normally adopts conventional tactics but responds to an escalation with retaliation this might be favoured by natural selection. The end result would be the ritualised behaviours that we now see in aggressive contests. Though highly praised by Maynard Smith this paper was too long for *Nature* (30 pages!) and was rejected.

Not long after this, Maynard Smith spent 3 months in the Department of Theoretical Biology in Chicago. He decided to use his time there learning about games theory since he had seen that it might be applicable to the problem of restraint in aggressive contests. While in Chicago he developed a general model of Price's ideas. Naturally when he came to write up this model Maynard Smith contacted Price. To his surprise, he discovered that Price's paper was still unpublished. However, the two got together and jointly published a paper 'On the logic of animal conflict' (Maynard Smith and Price, 1973).

This is a rather bald account of the origin of games theory applications to behaviour. In fact, an inkling of games theory ideas is apparent in several papers written at about the same time. Maynard Smith himself gives an excellent account of the 'polyphyletic' origin of the games theory approach (Maynard Smith, 1976, 1982).

The concept central to the games theory approach to animal behaviour is that of the *evolutionarily stable strategy (ESS)*; that is, a strategy which (when common) is uninvadable by alternative strategies. An ESS need not be a 'best' strategy (that giving the highest payoff); as long as it is uninvadable by alternative strategies (Dawkins, 1980, 1982).

In Appendix 8.1 the general conditions for an ESS are described mathematically. However, in the following section we are going to look at how this concept can be used to analyse social behaviour. In fact, most of the examples consider aggression between animals, but the general approach can be applied to other aspects of social behaviour. We start with a very simple model of aggressive interactions.

8.2 The Basic Hawk–Dove Model

This model considers a population of animals choosing between two behavioural strategies. When an individual member of this population meets another individual it can do one of two things. It may threaten an opponent with an aggressive display, but flee without injury if attacked (Dove strategy). Or it may attack an opponent immediately (Hawk strategy), and risk a serious injury. It is assumed that an individual's choice of strategy is heritable. Let us assign costs and benefits to such aggressive contests. These values are in units of fitness, that is an increase or decrease in the number of offspring that individuals leave.

If an animal wins a contest the benefit is V (for *Value*) units. If an animal incurs a serious injury the cost is W (for *Wound*) units. And if it is involved in a long display the cost is T (for *Time*) units.

In order to evaluate the Hawk and Dove strategies we need to calculate their respective payoffs (shown in Table 8.1) in contests with Hawks (a) and (c) and in contests with Doves (b) and (d). The payoff is the cost or benefit that results from a dispute. We shall now calculate these payoffs (a), (b), (c) and (d).

What happens if a Hawk attacks a Hawk (a)? Let us assume that if all else is equal each Hawk has a 50:50 chance of winning. If the Hawk wins it gains V units, but if it loses it suffers a cost of W units. Since both outcomes are equally likely the average payoff for each encounter is the mean of these two values. That is,

$$\text{payoff} = (V - W)/2 \text{ units of fitness.}$$

What happens when a Hawk attacks a Dove (b)? The Hawk always wins without incurring a cost so the average payoff to the Hawk is V units.

And what happens when a Dove meets a Hawk (c)? The Hawk attacks the Dove and the Dove withdraws without incurring a cost. So, its payoff is $= 0$ units.

And when a Dove meets a Dove (d)? Assuming again that all else is equal, each Dove has a 50:50 chance of winning such a contest. Both Doves display at a cost of T units, but only one wins the resource (value V). Thus, the winner gets $(V - T)$, and the loser gets $(-T)$, so that the average payoff,

$$\text{payoff} = (V/2 - T) \text{ units}$$

We now know the payoffs (a), (b), (c) and (d) (Table 8.2). Let us see what happens if we let V, W, and T take some (fairly) arbitrary values.

Example 1
If an animal wins a contest the benefit, V, is 100 units. If an animal incurs a serious injury the cost, W, is 200 units. And if it is involved in a long display then the time cost, T, is 30 units. Realistically $T < W$ (in absolute terms the cost of injury will be greater than the cost of display).

(In some text books V, W and T are written as algebraic values (+ 100, − 200, − 30) in order to show the direction of their effects on fitness. For

Table 8.1: Payoff matrix for the Hawk-Dove game.

		Against	
		Hawk	Dove
Payoff to	Hawk	a	b
	Dove	c	d

Table 8.2: Payoffs in the Hawk-Dove game. V is the value of winning, W the cost of injury, and T the cost of a lengthy display.

		Against	
		Hawk	**Dove**
Payoff to	Hawk	$(V - W)/2$	V
	Dove	0	$V/2 - T$

example, a long display is said to increase the animal's fitness by − 30 units. However, this can be confusing; if we substitute these algebraic values into the equations for the payoffs very odd things happen. I will stick to absolute values of V, W and T.)

This gives us the payoff matrix in Table 8.3.

Let us assume that we have a population of Doves. What happens if a mutant Hawk arises in this population? When Hawks are rare, most of their encounters are with Doves against whom the payoff is + 100 units. This is considerably more than that to a Dove when it encounters a Hawk (0 units) or to a Dove which encounters another Dove (+ 20 units). Hawks are highly successful and rapidly sweep through the population. However, they do not completely dominate the population, for when Hawks are common Hawk–Hawk contests are frequent and their average payoff is only − 50 units. If a rare Dove meets a Hawk it will get 0 units. This is not a lot, but it is considerably more than − 50 units. In other words a population of Doves can be invaded by a rare mutant Hawk, and a rare Dove can invade a population of Hawks.

This means that neither Hawk nor Dove is an evolutionarily stable strategy. Both strategies are invadable by the alternative strategy. If there are a lot of Doves around it pays to be a Hawk; if there are a lot of Hawks around it pays to be a Dove. Although Hawks always beat Doves, they cannot sweep

Table 8.3: The Hawk-Dove game. Payoffs in Example 1; $a < c$ so Hawk is not an ESS; and $d < b$ so Dove is not an ESS.

		Against	
		Hawk	**Dove**
Payoff to	Hawk	−50 (a)	+100 (b)
	Dove	0 (c)	+20 (d)

completely through the population because they sustain costly injuries when fighting each other. The benefit accruing to each strategy is therefore said to be *frequency dependent.*

Although neither of the 'pure' strategies (Hawk and Dove) is an ESS, there is a mixed bag of Hawks and Doves which is stable. We can calculate the ratio of Hawks to Doves in the 'mixed' ESS.

When the average payoff to each strategy is equal the population will be at an ESS (Parker, 1984; see Appendix 8.1). Only then will the fitnesses of the two strategies be equal so that natural selection acts equally on both. And the average payoff depends upon the proportion of Hawks and Doves in the population.

Let p be the proportion of Hawks in a population, and let $(1 - p)$ be the proportion of Doves. We assume that individuals encounter Hawks and Doves at random — that is, in proportion to their relative numbers in the population. Then the average payoff to a dove, P_D, will be

$$P_D = pc + (1 - p)d \tag{1}$$

and the average payoff to a Hawk, P_H, in this population will be

$$P_H = pa + (1 - p)b \tag{2}$$

When $P_H = P_D$ then both Hawk and Dove receive the same average payoff and the population is at an ESS. Equating (1) and (2) we find that,

$$pc + (1 - p)d = pa + (1 - p)b$$

Multiplying out the brackets,

$$pc + d - pd = pa + b - pb$$

and bringing all the terms involving p to one side,

$$pc - pd - pa + pb = b - d$$

Or,

$$p(b - d + c - a) = b - d$$

So the proportion, p, of Hawks in an ESS will be given by,

$$p = (b - d)/(b - d + c - a)$$

Or,

$$p = (b-d)/[(b-d)+(c-a)] \qquad (3)$$

as it is usually written.

Substituting for a, b, c and d,

$$p = \frac{V+2T}{W+2T} \qquad (4)$$

and if $T = 0$ this reduces to,

$$p = \frac{V}{W}$$

(which corresponds to the equation for p given by Parker, 1984). In other words, the greater the value of the resource, the higher the proportion of Hawks. Conversely, the greater the cost of injury, the greater the proportion of Doves.

So if we substitute for a, b, c and d in equation (3), then in our Example 1,

$$p = (100-20)/[(100-20)+(0-(-50))]$$
$$= 80/130 = 0.615$$

And we get exactly the same answer using equation (4):

$$p = \frac{V+2T}{W+2T}$$

$$= \frac{100+60}{200+60}$$

$$= \frac{80}{130}$$

$$= 0.615$$

In other words the average payoffs to Hawk and Dove are equal when Hawks make up 61.5% of the population. If either strategy increased in frequency then the other would be at an immediate advantage and would itself increase to bring the population back to the ESS.

This mixed ESS can be realised in one of two ways. Either the population can consist of a proportion of animals, p, playing Hawk, and a proportion, $(1 - p)$, playing Dove. Alternatively the population could consist of individuals playing Hawk on a proportion p of encounters and Dove the rest of the time.

Example 2

One important point to note is that with a different set of costs and benefits we can arrive at a completely different set of answers. The following example shows how a change in the relative costs and benefits (V, W and T) can affect the ESS.

Consider what happens if the benefit of winning a dispute (V) is 200 units, injury costs (W) are rather low (100 units) and the cost of a lengthy threat display (T) the same as in the first example (30 units). The resulting payoff matrix is shown in Table 8.4. Now consider a population of Doves. A rare Hawk will encounter mostly Doves and obtain a payoff of + 200 units. A Dove will obtain only 0 or + 70 units (from encounters with the Hawk or other Doves respectively). The mutant Hawk sweeps through the population. So Dove is not an ESS. Moreover Dove cannot invade a population of Hawks. In a population of Hawks a Dove receives a payoff of only 0 units. This is considerably less than the payoff to a Hawk in a population of Hawks (+ 50 units). This time the strategy Hawk is called a 'pure' ESS.

Clearly the ESS depends upon the various costs and benefits. We could calculate the ESS for a range of values of V and W. The results are shown in Figure 8.1. We see that Hawk is only an ESS when $V > W$. When $V < W$ then the ESS is a mixed ESS with a proportion, p, of Hawks.

In general, if $V > W$ then the payoff to a Dove against a Hawk (c) will be less than the payoff to a Hawk against a fellow Hawk (a). In other words $c < a$, and so Hawk is an ESS. However, if $V < W$ then the payoff to a Dove in a population of Hawks will be greater than the payoff to a Hawk. That is, $a < c$ and so Dove will invade a population of Hawks. Note that Dove cannot be

Table 8.4: Hawk-Dove game. Payoffs in Example 2; $a > c$ so Hawk is an ESS; $d < b$ so Dove is not an ESS. In this example Hawk is the only ESS.

		Against	
		Hawk	**Dove**
	Hawk	+50 (a)	+200 (b)
Payoff to			
	Dove	0 (c)	+70 (d)

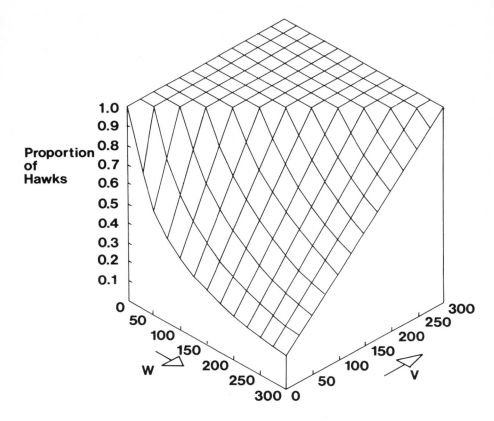

Figure 8.1: Proportion of Hawks in the Hawk–Dove ESS for Values of V and W. If
V > W then the strategy hawk is an ESS. If V < W then the ESS is a mixed strategy
with a proportion, p, of hawks. The smaller the value of the resource (V) relative to the
cost of serious injury (W), the lower the proportion of hawks in the mixed ESS. In this
example, T = 30.

an ESS; even if $T = 0$ then $b (= V)$ will always be greater than $d (= V/2)$ and
so a Hawk will always spread in a population of Doves.

In the next section we shall consider an interesting extension of the basic
Hawk–Dove model. It introduces a third strategy *Retaliator* into the game. In
fact Retaliator was the strategy introduced by Maynard Smith and Price to
account for the ritualised nature of animal contests (see section 8.1).

8.3 Hawk–Dove–Retaliator

The following game shows that Retaliator can be an ESS. Retaliator plays a
conditional strategy. Unlike Hawk and Dove, Retaliator's behaviour depends

upon its opponent's behaviour. Retaliator simply plays Dove unless its opponent chooses to escalate the contest. If the opponent escalates then Retaliator retaliates and plays Hawk. So, Retaliator plays Dove against Dove, and Hawk against Hawk. We can draw up a payoff matrix as before (Table 8.5).

The payoffs for the various Hawk–Dove interactions are exactly the same as those in the basic Hawk–Dove model (*a*, *b*, *c* and *d*, see Table 8.1). However, we are interested in the payoffs to Hawks and Doves when they meet Retaliators. When Hawk meets Retaliator, Retaliator plays Hawk and so the payoff to Hawk is the same as if it had met another Hawk (*a*). Similarly when Dove meets Retaliator, Retaliator plays Dove and so the payoff to Dove is the same as if it had met another Dove (*d*).

Exactly the same reasoning applies to the payoffs to Retaliator when encountering Hawks and Doves. Against Hawks, Retaliator plays Hawk and obtains *a*. Against Doves, Retaliator plays Dove and obtains *d*. And against other Retaliators, Retaliator plays Dove and also obtains *d*, since neither escalate the contest.

To see how this game works in practice let us look at a worked example.

Example 3
The costs and benefits are the same as those in example 1. So,

$$V = 100$$
$$W = 200$$
$$T = 30$$

This allows us to construct the payoff matrix in Table 8.6.

As Maynard Smith and Price expected (1973) Retaliator turns out to be an ESS. In a population of Retaliators the average payoff is $+ 20$. This is stable against invasion by Hawks (who get $- 50$) and by Doves (who get $+ 20$ also).

Table 8.5: Payoffs in the Hawk-Dove-Retaliator game. The payoffs *a*, *b*, *c* and *d* are those given in Table 8.2. Against Hawk the payoff to Retaliator is the same as for a Hawk against a Hawk. Against Dove or Retaliator the payoff to Retaliator is the same as for a Dove against a Dove.

		Hawk	Against Dove	Retaliator
	Hawk	*a*	*b*	*a*
Payoff to	Dove	*c*	*d*	*d*
	Retaliator	*a*	*d*	*d*

Table 8.6: The Hawk-Dove-Retaliator game. Payoffs in example 3. In this example Retaliator is the only ESS.

Payoff to		Hawk	Against Dove	Retaliator
	Hawk	−50	+100	−50
	Dove	0	+20	+20
	Retaliator	−50	+20	+20

In contrast, in a population playing Hawk the average payoff is − 50. This can be invaded by Doves (who get 0) though not by Retaliators (who get − 50 too). Similarly in a population playing Dove the average payoff is + 20. This is invadable by Hawks (who get + 100) though not by Retaliators (who get the same as Doves, + 20).

(In fact, it is not strictly true that a population of Retaliators cannot be invaded by Doves. Nor is it true that Retaliators cannot invade a population of Doves. In both cases the candidate for invasion will obtain the same payoff as a member of the main population. This means there will be no selective pressure against the mutant Dove or Retaliator. Doves could for instance drift randomly within a population of Retaliators and even displace the initial population. Maynard Smith (1982, pp. 188–91) discusses the problem of 'selective neutrality' and various modifications to the original Hawk–Dove–Retaliator model. In this chapter we will assume that a rare mutant cannot invade a population unless its payoff against members of that population is *greater* than their payoffs in encounters with other members of the same population.)

In general, Retaliator can only be invaded by Hawk when the payoff to a Hawk against a Retaliator (a) is greater than the payoff to a Retaliator against a fellow Retaliator (d). That is, when,

$$(V- W)/2 > (V/2) - T$$

Multiplying through by 2 and cancelling V tells us that this occurs when,

$$W < 2T$$

in absolute terms.

In other words Hawk will only invade a population of Retaliators when the cost of serious injury is less than twice the cost of display. The stability of Retaliator depends upon the relative size of these two costs.

So it looks as though a strategy of retaliation can be evolutionarily stable provided that the cost of serious injury is large enough. This may account for the ritualised nature of aggressive contests between animals — the original problem which puzzled George Price. In a population of Retaliators escalation into full-blooded combat would be relatively rare. Only when an opponent escalates a conflict will a Retaliator retaliate. Most of the contests will be relatively peaceable affairs.

In the following section we are going to look at another interesting extension of the Hawk–Dove game. This section introduces another strategy *Bourgeois*.

8.4 Hawk–Dove–Bourgeois

The basic Hawk–Dove model outlined above assumes that Hawks and Doves differ only in their choice of behavioural strategy. The model assumes that contestants are equally matched. Of course, in the real world this is rarely the case. Often one animal has some intrinsic advantage over another. It might be bigger, better, stronger and generally more able to contest a disputed resource than its opponent. In other words, the two contestants may not be equally matched. There may be a difference in their *resource-holding potential* or *RHP*, and this situation is described as a *RHP asymmetry* (Parker, 1974).

As well as RHP asymmetries there can exist a *payoff asymmetry*. This occurs when the value of the disputed resource is higher for one of the contestants than for the other. The contestant which values the resource more highly is likely to fight more persistently than the other. For example, a hungry individual may fight more persistently for food than a satiated individual. The value (or 'utility') of the resource is greater for the hungry individual.

In addition to RHP and payoff asymmetries, there is a third class of asymmetry called an *uncorrelated asymmetry*. For example, if two people toss a coin to decide who shall have the last 'After Eight' then they are using an uncorrelated asymmetry to settle the dispute. That is, the criterion for settling the dispute has nothing to do with the relative competitive abilities of the two contestants or the value of the payoff. If two contestants are equally matched and the value of the disputed resource (the chocolate) is small, then both contestants can avoid wasting precious time by adopting such arbitrary conventions.

Animals do not toss coins! However, they can settle a fight using some arbitrary convention such as who found the disputed resource first ('finders-keepers'). But are such conventions evolutionarily stable? We can explore the stability of uncorrelated asymmetries using games theory. The Hawk–Dove-Bourgeois game provides a model for such asymmetries.

To the simple Hawk–Dove model we are going to add a 'conditional' strategy — Bourgeois. Bourgeois follows the simple rule: play Hawk if you are the owner of the disputed resource, and Dove if you are not. We can draw up a payoff matrix as before (Table 8.7).

The payoffs for the various Hawk–Dove interactions are exactly the same as before. That is a, b, c and d in Table 8.1. We can use them to calculate the payoffs to Hawks and Doves when they meet Bourgeois. For simplicity, we assume that Bourgeois is a *resident* (and plays Hawk) half the time, and the rest of the time it is an *intruder* (and plays Dove).

When a Hawk meets a resident Bourgeois (playing Hawk) its payoff will be a; and when it meets an intruder Bourgeois (playing Dove) its payoff will be b. So the payoff to a Hawk against Bourgeois is the average of these two payoffs, $(a + b)/2$.

When a Dove meets a resident Bourgeois (playing Hawk) its payoff is c; and when it meets an intruder Bourgeois (playing Dove) its payoff will be d. So the payoff to a Dove against Bourgeois is the average of these two payoffs, $(c + d)/2$.

We now need the payoffs to Bourgeois.

When Bourgeois meets Hawk then half the time it plays Hawk and gets a and half the time it plays Dove and gets c. So the payoff to Bourgeois against Hawk is the average of these $(a + c)/2$.

When Bourgeois meets Dove then half the time it plays Hawk and gets b, and half the time it plays Dove and gets d. So the payoff to Bourgeois against Dove is the average of these $(b + d)/2$.

Finally, when Bourgeois meets Bourgeois half the time it is the owner, the intruder retreats and the resident gets payoff b; and half the time it is an intruder, it retreats and gets c. So the payoff to a Bourgeois against a fellow Bourgeois is the average of these $(b + c)/2$. Win or lose Bourgeois suffers no injury or display costs.

To see how the game works in practice we can try another worked example.

Example 4

In this example we are going to keep the same costs and benefits we used in Example 1. So,

Table 8.7: Payoffs in the Hawk-Dove-Bourgeois game. The payoffs a, b, c and d are given in Table 8.2.

		Hawk	Against Dove	Bourgeois
	Hawk	a	b	$(a + b)/2$
Payoff to	Dove	c	d	$(c + d)/2$
	Bourgeois	$(a + c)/2$	$(b + d)/2$	$(b + c)/2$

$$V = 100$$
$$W = 200$$
$$T = 30$$

This allows us to construct the payoff matrix for the Hawk–Dove–Bourgeois game (Table 8.8).

It turns out that Bourgeois is an ESS. In a population playing Bourgeois the average payoff is $+50$. This is stable against invasion by Hawks (who get $+25$) and Doves (who get $+10$). In contrast, in a population playing Hawk the average payoff is -50. This can be invaded by Doves (who get 0) and Bourgeois individuals (who get -25). Similarly, in a population playing Dove the average payoff is $+20$. This is invadable both by Hawks (who get $+100$) and individuals playing Bourgeois (who get $+60$).

Thus Bourgeois is the only strategy which is uninvadable. Uncorrelated asymmetries such as Bourgeois *can* be evolutionarily stable. But do they really occur in nature? Perhaps the best known example of such an uncorrelated asymmetry is that seen in territorial disputes between speckled wood butterflies, *Pararge aegeria* (Davies, 1978).

Pararge males defend patches of sunlight on the woodland floor. Nick Davies of Oxford University observed speckled wood butterflies during the summer of 1976 in Wytham Wood. He found that 60% of males hold territories and the remainder patrol the canopy. If a male intruder stumbles into a territory, the resident male approaches the intruder, and a brief (3–4 s) spiral flight follows after which the *resident* returns to his sunspot. The *resident* always wins (Davies, 1978). Davies was able to show that these butterflies use *ownership* as a convention to settle these territorial disputes. If a male was removed from a territory and replaced with another male, then on the 'owner's' return it was the new owner which won the dispute. In addition, when Davies introduced two males to the same territory (so that each 'thought' he was the owner) there followed a protracted spiral flight. Davies argued that sunspots are

Table 8.8: The Hawk-Dove-Bourgeois game. Payoffs in example 4. Only Bourgeois is an ESS. In a population playing Bourgeois the average payoff is +50. This cannot be invaded by Hawks (who get +25) or Doves (who get +10). In general, if $V < W$ then Bourgeois is an ESS.

| | | | Against | |
		Hawk	Dove	Bourgeois
	Hawk	−50	+100	+25
Payoff to	Dove	0	+20	+10
	Bourgeois	−25	+60	+50

so abundant in Wytham Wood that they are relatively low in value (an intruder can always move on and find another). As the Hawk-Dove-Bourgeois game shows, arbitrary conventions can work when the value of the disputed resource is low. However, if the value of the disputed resource changes Bourgeois may not be the ESS.

Per-Olof Wickman and Christer Wicklund of the University of Stockholm obtained some rather different data for *Pararge* territorial disputes (Wickman and Wicklund, 1983). They studied *Pararge aegeria* in a dense spruce forest at Agesta (about 20 km from Stockholm). Unlike Davies (1978) they found that the resident did not always win. On 17 occasions they observed a territory owner regain his territory from an intruder after the owner had temporarily left his territory unattended. Why this discrepancy between the two studies? They suggest that in the spruce forest sunspots are a rather valuable resource. In Sweden ambient temperatures are often very low. By sunbathing, butterflies can increase their body temperature and so fly more efficiently. And this means that when ambient temperatures are low sunspots attract female speckled wood butterflies. Owning a territory means more females for a male to court. Effectively, the value of the disputed resource (V) is much higher in the Swedish study. The effect of increasing V relative to W is to make Hawk the ESS. This is shown in the following example.

Example 5
In this example we are going to use the same costs and benefits that we used in example 2. So,

$$V = 200$$
$$W = 100$$
$$T = 30$$

where $V > W$. From these values we can construct the payoff matrix as described above. This matrix is shown in Table 8.9.

Now, only Hawk is an ESS. In a population of Hawks the average payoff is + 50. This is stable against invasion by Doves (who get 0) and Bourgeois (who get + 25). In a population playing Bourgeois the average payoff is + 100. This can be invaded by Hawks (who get + 125). In a population playing Dove the payoff is + 70. This is invadable both by Hawks (who get + 200) and Bourgeois (who get + 135).

As we saw earlier the ESS is very sensitive to the various costs and benefits. In fact, Bourgeois can be invaded by Hawk whenever the payoff to a Hawk against a Bourgeois is greater than the payoff to a Bourgeois against a fellow Bourgeois. That is, whenever,

$$(b + c)/2 < (a + b)/2$$

Table 8.9: The Hawk-Dove-Bourgeois game. Payoffs in Example 5. Only Hawk is an ESS. In a population playing Hawk the average payoff is +50. This cannot be invaded by Bourgeois (who get +25) or Doves (who get 0). In general if $V > W$ then Hawk will be an ESS.

| | | Against | | |
		Hawk	Dove	Bourgeois
	Hawk	+50	+200	+125
Payoff to	Dove	0	+70	+35
	Bourgeois	+25	+135	+100

Multiplying through by 2 and cancelling b this simplifies to

$$c < a$$

Now, if $V > W$ then $a = (V - W)/2$ is positive, and so it is greater than c ($c = 0$, see Table 8.2). However, if $V < W$ then $c < a$, and Bourgeois is an ESS. The stability of Bourgeois depends critically upon the relative value of the resource, V. The implication is that in Davies' study $V < W$ (as in Example 4) and so Bourgeois is an ESS. In the Wickman and Wicklund study $V > W$ (as in example 5) and so Hawk is an ESS.

We have now discussed several of the games that we need in order to introduce our detailed case studies. New and exciting games are emerging all the time. Maynard Smith (1982) introduces some of these in his very readable book *Evolution and the Theory of Games*. However, in the next section we press on and consider a very specific application of games theory.

8.5 Games Spiders Play

Although the models presented above are jolly interesting it is difficult to see how we might use games theory to model a *particular* case. However, in this section we are going to remedy this by examining aggressive contests between individual spiders of the species *Agelenopsis aperta* (Maynard Smith and Riechert, 1984).

For some years Dr Susan Riechert of the University of Tennessee has studied these spiders in Arizona and New Mexico. Female *Agelenopsis* build webs to catch prey and good web sites are in short supply. As a result fights over web sites are fairly common (Riechert, 1979).

Size is an important determinant of the outcome of these fights and much of the contest involves weighing up an opponent. As soon as an intruder arrives, the web owner springs into action. At first the two spiders 'locate' each other, adjusting their positions and preparing for action. Then one of the contestants makes an approach and the two spiders 'signal' to each other (by vibrating the web). One of the spiders might then 'threaten' the opponent, feigning an attack but without making contact. Finally, the two spiders make 'contact', shoving and biting at each other (Figure 8.2).

Spider contests are often made up of several bouts with one or other opponent making a 'retreat' at the end of each bout. Eventually one of the contestants 'withdraws' from the fight (Figure 8.3).

Locate

Signal

Threaten

Contact

Figure 8.2: The behaviour of Agelenopsis *in web disputes. The four behaviours represent increasing escalation from locate and signal to threat and contact.*

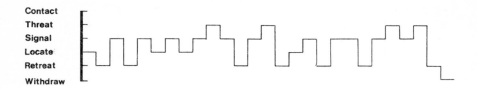

Figure 8.3: Typical sequence of behaviours in an Agelenopsis *dispute. This short sequence shows the choices made by a small owner defending an excellent web site against a large intruder. At first, the owner alternates between signal and locate. There follows a rapid escalation to contact followed by the alternation of retreat and signal. Towards the end of the contest the owner alternates between signal and threaten before retreating and then withdrawing from the contest. (After Riechert, 1979.)*

The history behind the various *Agelenopsis* models is rather interesting. They owe their origin to the Hawk–Dove–Bourgeois game outlined above. At first Maynard Smith considered the Hawk–Dove–Bourgeois game to be an interesting mathematical curiosity without biological relevance. However, in 1974 he gave a talk at Austin, Texas on games theory and the Hawk–Dove models. At the end of the talk Larry Gilbert approached Maynard Smith and described his as yet unpublished work on swallowtails (*Papilio zelicaon*). These butterflies hold hilltop territories. Like *Pararge* they appear to use an ownership convention to settle disputes; the resident *Papilio* always wins. However, if two *Papilio* perceived themselves as owners (they had held the same hilltop, but on alternate days) there followed a protracted territorial dispute.

Gilbert's work suggested that the Bourgeois strategy might indeed have some biological validity, and this prompted Maynard Smith to make a search of the literature for further relevant data. One of the studies which turned up was Susan Riechert's *Agelenopsis* work.

There were three features of *Agelenopsis* contests which attracted Maynard Smith's attention (Maynard Smith, 1982).

(1) Body weight is an important factor determining the outcome of disputes. Experimentally doubling the weight of an intruder (by glueing lead weights to its abdomen) meant that the intruder usually won. The shortest fights took place when the owner was substantially larger than an intruder.

(2) If the difference in size between the two opponents was small then contests lasted longer, but the owner usually won.

(3) The longest and most vicious contests took place when the owner was defending a good web site against a slightly larger intruder.

Thus *Agelenopsis* disputes possess many of the features of animal contests discussed in sections 8.3 and 8.4. They show aspects of all three kinds of asymmetry (RHP, payoff and Bourgeois). Riechert and Maynard Smith corresponded and there followed an exchange of visits with Riechert spending a year in Sussex. From this exchange two models of *Agelenopsis* disputes emerged. (As it happens the 'Bourgeois' component of *Agelenopsis* disputes is rather unimportant!)

8.5.1 The First Model
This model assumes that intruders can choose between two alternatives; escalation (Hawk) and retreat (Dove). The model assumes that,

(1) the two contestants differ in size so that in an escalated contest there is a probability, x, that the owner will win. The larger the owner relative to the intruder, the greater the value of x;
(2) in an escalated contest the winner receives V or v (where $V > v$) depending upon web site quality, and the loser incurs a cost of C;
(3) the probability that the owner will win (x) is known both to the owner and the intruder;
(4) a proportion, p, of all webs are of value V. The rest $(1 - p)$ are of value v;
(5) the value of the web (V or v) is known only to the owner.

Condition (5) was included because in experimental tests in which the web owner was removed and two 'intruders' were introduced to a web site the duration of a contest bore no relation to the value of that site (but see below).

Maynard Smith and Riechert assumed that an intruder can choose only Hawk (H) or Dove (D). The owner, on the other hand, has a third option Conditional Hawk (CH). Conditional Hawk chooses H if the web is valuable (V) but Dove if the web is of value v.

Before setting up our payoff matrix we want to know the *expected* value (E) of a web site to our intruder. If an intruder wins she can expect either V or v units. Her expected payoff will depend upon the relative frequency, p, of each web type. On p occasions the site will be worth V units; and the rest of the time $(1 - p)$ it will be worth v units. So the expected value will be,

$$E = pV + (1 - p)v$$

We can now set up our payoff matrix. The complete matrix is shown in Table 8.10. To show how the various payoffs are derived we shall give some examples.

(1) What is the payoff to an intruder adopting the strategy H when the owner replies with H? Remember that x is the probability that the owner will win. So, on $(1 - x)$ occasions the intruder will win and on average she can

Table 8.10: The payoff matrix for *Agelenopsis* disputes (After Maynard Smith, 1982). Owners can opt for Hawk, Dove or Conditional Hawk. Intruders can opt only to play Hawk or Dove.

		Payoff to intruder	
		Hawk	**Dove**
	Hawk	$E(1 - x) - Cx$	0
		$Ex - C(1 - x)$ E	
Payoff to owner	Conditional hawk	$p[V(1 - x) - Cx]$ $+ (1 - p)v$	$(1 - p)v/2$
		$p[Vx - C(1 - x)]$ $(E + pV)/2$	
	Dove	E	$E/2$
		0 $E/2$	

expect to gain E units. However, on x occasions the intruder loses and pays a cost of C units. So the average payoff to the intruder of playing H will be the average benefit $(E(1 - x))$ minus the average cost (Cx), or,

$$\text{payoff} = E(1 - x) - Cx \tag{5}$$

(2) What happens if the owner replies to H with a CH strategy? Remember that p is the proportion of webs of value V. Then on $(1 - p)$ occasions the web will be worth only v units, the owner will play D and the intruder will take over the web. So, on these occasions, the intruder will obtain v units. However, on p occasions the web will be worth V units and the owner will play H. If the owner loses (which happens on $(1 - x)$ occasions) the intruder gains V units. If the owner wins (on x occasions) the intruder pays a cost of C units. So on p occasions the intruder obtains $[V(1 - x) - Cx]$ units, and on $(1 - p)$ occasions she obtains v units. So the average payoff to an intruder playing H to the owner's CH is

$$\text{payoff} = p[V(1 - x) - Cx] + (1 - p)v \tag{6}$$

(3) And what is the intruder's payoff when the owner plays CH to the intruder's D? On p occasions the web will be worth V units, the owner plays H and the intruder backs down. The payoff to the intruder will be 0 units. However on $(1 - p)$ occasions the web will be worth v units, the owner plays D to the intruder's D. Let us assume as in sections 8.3 and 8.4 that an intruder will win half of these contests. Her payoff will be $[(1 - p) \, v/2]$, and the average payoff will be

$$\text{payoff} = p(0) + [(1 - p) \, v/2] \tag{7}$$

We can work out the owner's payoffs in exactly the same way to complete Table 8.10.

We can now use this table to predict the owner's best reply to various plays by the intruder. We assume that the owner chooses that strategy which gives the highest payoff. For example, if the intruder chooses H then the owner's best reply is H, CH or D depending upon which gives the highest payoff. If $H > CH$, and $H > D$ then the owner should opt for H. That is, if,

$$Ex - C(1 - x) > p[Vx - C(1 - x)], \text{ and}$$
$$Ex - C(1 - x) > 0$$

then the owner should opt for H.

Now what we want to do is to calculate the ESS for this game between spiders. In other words we want the best replies to an opponent's play for a range of values of x (the probability that the owner will win).

If the intruder chooses D then it always pays the owner to opt for H since there is no risk of injury and the owner always wins. If the intruder chooses H then there is a range of values of x for which the owner's best reply is D. If the owner is very small, for instance, it pays the owner to opt for D rather than waste time in an escalated contest which she is likely to lose.

Now if a pair of choices, I for the owner and J for the intruder, is each the best reply to the other then the strategy pair (I, J) is an ESS. For instance, if the owner's best reply to H is H, and H is itself the intruder's best reply to H then (H, H) is an ESS. However, if the owner's best reply to H is CH and the intruder's best reply to CH is D then (CH, H) is not an ESS.

Using this kind of logic Maynard Smith (1982) shows that for certain values of V, v and p, the strategy shown in Figure 8.4 is an ESS. (In fact there were two ESSs, but only the ESS shown here approximated real contests when different values of V, v and p were used.) This ESS reproduces the three features of interest.

(1)   if the size difference is not great ($x \sim 0.5$) then the owner's choice depends upon the value of the web;
(2)   if the size difference is large then the larger spider wins without escalation; and
(3)   there is a region with $x \sim 0.5$ in which escalated contests occur when the site is valuable (V) and which the intruder wins without escalation when the site is not valuable (v).

Although this model reproduces the qualitative features of *Agelenopsis* disputes, it is too crude to produce a blow by blow account of such contests. In particular the model spiders can choose between only two strategies (H and

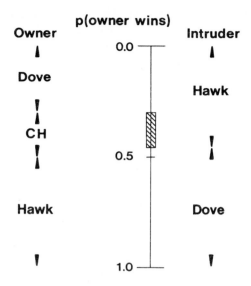

Figure 8.4: ESS for Agelenopsis *disputes. The probability that the owner wins = x (see text). Between x = 0.00 and x = 0.30, the strategy pair (D,H) is an ESS. Between x = 0.45 and x = 1.00, the strategy pair (H,D) is an ESS. Between these two (shaded area) is the zone of escalation. The strategy pair (CH,H) is an ESS. The chances of the owner winning may be less than 50:50 but the owner will escalate the contest if the web site is valuable. (After Maynard Smith, 1982.)*

D). In real life spiders can choose to escalate from 'locate' to 'signal' to 'threat' to 'contact' with the option to 'retreat' or 'withdraw' anywhere along the line (Figure 8.2). The second model attempts a more detailed analysis of *Agelenopsis* disputes.

8.5.2 The Second Model

To capture the behavioural complexity observed in spider contests requires a rather complex model. In fact, the problem is too complex for a simple analytical model. In Chapter 7 we found that complex problems are often susceptible to computer simulation.

The model begins with two spiders playing a game in which each spider makes one move at a time. On each move a spider can decide to locate, signal, threaten or make contact with an opponent depending upon its level of aggression (X). However, the decision to retreat or withdraw is determined by two conflicting tendencies; aggression (X) and fear (Y). The model assumes that both tendencies increase during a bout until they reach a point where the level of fear (Y) outweighs the level of aggression (X). At this point the simulated spider retreats. If the difference between fear and aggression exceeds a critical, threshold value then a spider withdraws altogether. As each spider moves it imparts information about its relative size to its opponent. This information affects the opponent's level of fear.

There were two main objectives. The first was to predict the outcome of spider contests, and the second to predict the costs of fights as a function of relative size and web site value.

There were three requirements of the model:

(1) it should reproduce the general features of spider fights outlined above;
(2) each act performed by the simulated spiders should be determined by the values of the two internal variables X and Y;
(3) the values of X and Y should be determined by:
   (a) genetic differences in the rate of increase of X and Y; (relatively unimportant in the contests described in this chapter, but see Maynard Smith and Riechert (1984) for further details);
   (b) a variable which models the effect of ownership;
   (c) a variable D which models the effect of relative size;
   (d) a variable V which models the effect of web site value;
   (e) the previous course of the fight.

This completes the logical plan of the model. Although some effort went into fitting values of D, V etc. to give a rough qualitative fit, the logic behind the model changed very little during further development (though see below). It is unnecessary to run through all of the model's parameters, and the following account is intended only to give a taste of the full model.

All acts are determined by the values of aggression (X) and fear (Y). If $(X - Y)$ is large and negative a spider withdraws (W). If $(X - Y)$ is small and negative a spider retreats (R). Otherwise a spider locates, signals, threatens or makes contact according to the value of X.

If $X <$ 4 then the spider locates, L,
If $4 < X <$ 10 then the spider signals, S,
if $10 < X <$ 14 then the spider threatens, T,
if $14 < X$ then the spider makes contact, C.

The model assumes that aggression and fear $(X$ and $Y)$ are made up of temporary components $(X_T$ and $Y_T)$ which rise during a bout but fall to zero as soon as a spider retreats; and permanent components $(X_P$ and $Y_P)$ that change as information is received about the opposition's fighting ability. This information is obtained during a fight from the acts L, S, T, and C. In the model the *opponent*'s permanent aggression X_P is increased by

$$(GD) + E$$

at the end of each move, where D is the actual size difference (which can be negative if the opponent is larger than the spider making the move), G is a constant depending upon the act performed ($G = 1, 2, 3,$ or 4 for L, S, T or C respectively) and E is a random variable between -1 and $+1$. G means that acts like T and C reveal more information than L and S. E was included to allow for errors in information transfer. In this simple model Maynard Smith and Riechert assumed that only one spider (the non-mover) obtains information about D. In real life of course both spiders are grappling with each other and each will obtain information about relative size. However, to keep the model simple this was ignored.

Following each move the level of temporary aggression X_T was increased by a constant A. This constant represented the rate of increase of X_T for each population of spiders. The level of temporary fear Y_T was increased by (GF). Once again F is a constant representing the rate of increase of Y_T for each population, and G is a constant ($1, 2, 3$ or 4) depending upon the move (L, C, S or T) as before. If a spider retreated its temporary aggression and temporary fear (X_T and Y_T) dropped to zero; and permanent aggression (X_P) increased by one and permanent fear (Y_P) increased by two. (Since the rate of increase of fear was greater than that of aggression, this ensured that contests did eventually end!) Which spider made the next move depended upon the value of Z ($Z = X - Y$, see above).

In order to simulate the effects of web site value, V, on ownership an intruder withdrew, W, if $Z < -5$, but an owner withdrew only if $Z < -(5 + V)$. In the simulations, V took the values $+8, +3$ or -3 depending upon whether the owner was defending an excellent, average or poor site respectively. In addition ownership played a part in the decision to retreat, R. Intruders retreat if $Z < -2$; owners retreat only if $Z < -(2 + V)$. So an owner is less likely to withdraw and less likely to retreat in a way that depends on the site value, V. The dependence of these two decisions (retreat, withdraw) on site value represents the only major modification to the original logic of the model (see section 8.8).

The results of such computer-simulated fights are compared with real fights in Figure 8.5. Not only did the computer model predict the outcome of *Agelenopsis* disputes, but it made a fair attempt at modelling contest costs (Figure 8.6). The general features hold good; the most costly fights occur when the owner of an excellent site is slightly smaller than an intruder, and contest costs increase with site value. There was only one notable failure; the model predicted little difference between large owners defending excellent sites and large owners defending average sites. In both cases the owners should have won with consummate ease. In fact, the cost of defending an excellent site was almost twice that of defending an average site. This suggests that the intruder sometimes knows that she is in with a chance of an excellent web site. Quite how she does this is a mystery.

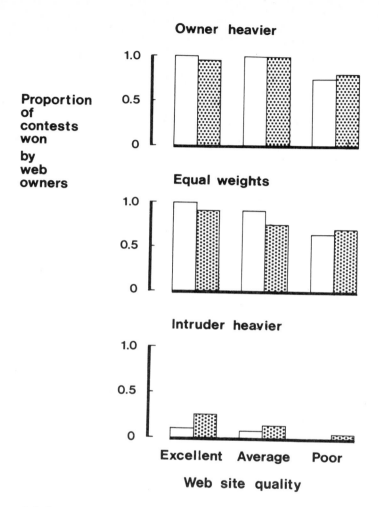

Figure 8.5: Outcome of Agelenopsis *disputes. These show the proportion of contests won by web owners at excellent, average and poor sites when the owner is heavier, the same weight as, or lighter than the intruder. Simulated outcomes (open bars) show a close approximation to observed outcomes (shaded bars). (After Maynard Smith and Riechert, 1984.)*

Clearly this model takes account of a far greater number of relevant variables than the formal models developed in sections 8.2 to 8.4. It shows how a games theory approach can be integrated with other modelling techniques to simulate the fine details of aggressive contests as well as revealing general principles about the evolution of aggressive behaviour. In the next section we are going to look at a rather different series of models.

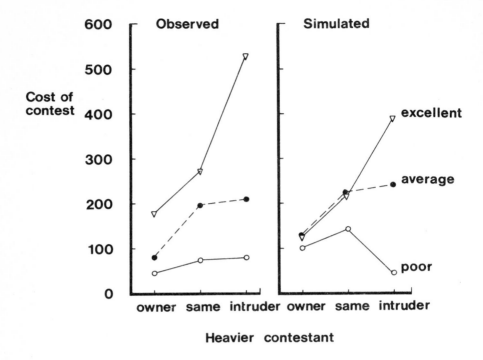

Figure 8.6: The cost of Agelenopsis *disputes. The units are rather arbitrary, but contest costs were estimated using weighted sums of each type of move (see Maynard Smith and Riechert, 1984). The simulated costs show a close approximation to the observed costs, though the simulations do tend to underestimate the cost of disputes over excellent webs.*

8.6 The Prisoner's Dilemma

We have seen how games theory has been applied to the analysis of aggressive contests. In this section we shall look at what games theory can tell us about the evolution of cooperation. In particular we shall focus on a simple model developed by Robert Axelrod of the Institute of Social and Policy Studies at Michigan University and the evolutionary biologist William Hamilton (then at Michigan now at Oxford) (Axelrod and Hamilton, 1981).

The *Prisoner's Dilemma* is a classic game which has been used extensively in the analysis of conflict in human behaviour. In this game we have an imaginary situation in which two people are arrested on suspicion of joint involvement in a serious crime. They have indeed committed the crime, but the police have insufficient evidence to obtain a conviction unless one or both prisoners makes a confession. Each prisoner can make one of two choices. He can stay silent (cooperate), or he can squeal on his partner (defect). If they both cooperate then the police are forced to release them. However if one of the prisoners defects he earns a substantial reward and his partner gets a life sentence (the sucker's payoff). If both prisoners defect they each implicate the other and both are imprisoned for 10 years.

The only 'rational' strategy is to defect; whatever your opponent does, you do better by defecting. On the one hand, if your opponent cooperates then you gain the maximum payoff; and on the other hand, if your opponent defects you avoid the 'sucker's payoff'. The paradox is that it pays both prisoners to defect, but if they both defect (result, 10 years in prison) they do less well than if they both cooperate (result, freedom).

Psychologists have used this relatively simple game to investigate cooperative and competitive behaviour in people. Usually the game is played for points with each contestant obtaining, say, three points if they both cooperate. If both opponents defect then they each get two points. And if one cooperates while the other defects, then the defector gets the maximum payoff (four points) and his partner gets the 'sucker's' payoff of a single point (Table 8.11).

An interesting extension of the prisoner's dilemma game is the N-Person Prisoner's Dilemma Game, or NPDG. In the NPDG each player can choose to cooperate or defect. If a player defects he will obtain a larger payoff than if he cooperates. But if everyone cooperates they do better than if everyone defects. This may sound rather familiar! An individual householder may benefit by ignoring a hosepipe ban, but everyone will be better off if they all heed an appeal to conserve water. Only if they all conserve water will supplies be maintained. Or an individual member nation may sell its oil cheaply in contravention of an OPEC agreement, but if the oil-producing nations stick together they will do better than if they all go it alone. Interestingly, in experimental versions of the NPDG the chances of an individual member defecting increase with group size (Colman, 1982). This is not simply because a large barrel is more likely to have one rotten apple: in games in which stooges have

Table 8.11: Payoffs in the Prisoner's Dilemma Game. The rational strategy is for each prisoner to defect even though they do rather better if they both cooperate. For each set of consequences, the payoff to prisoner 1 is given first, and the payoff to prisoner 2 second.

| | | Prisoner 2 | |
		Cooperate	Defect
Prisoner 1	Cooperate	3,3	1,4
	Defect	4,1	2,2

been used to increase group size the 'real' group members respond to the increase in group size by making more competitive (defect) choices (Hamburger, 1979).

Unlike people, animals are not bound by agreements or treaties so competitive animals will exploit cooperative animals. Competitive animals which do well leave more young behind and very quickly the population is swamped by defecting animals. Defect is likely to be an ESS (see Craig (1984) for an interesting biological example). How then can cooperation evolve in the tooth and claw atmosphere of natural selection?

8.7 TIT FOR TAT

In many biological settings the same two individuals may meet more than once, If an individual can recognise an opponent and remember the outcomes of previous encounters then this allows cooperation to get a foot in the evolutionary door. The problem becomes that of the *reiterated* prisoner's dilemma.

Robert Axelrod investigated what happens when individuals play repeatedly against the same opponent. He invited a number of people to write computer programs to play the reiterated PDG. The programs were submitted by game theorists in economics, sociology, political science and mathematics. The 14 entries and a totally random strategy were paired in a round robin tournament, each contest lasting for 200 moves. The programs were scored according to their total payoff. The winning program, submitted by Anatol Rapoport of the Institute for Advanced Study in Vienna, was also the shortest. Called TIT FOR TAT, it always cooperates on the first move, and thereafter makes the move adopted by its opponent on the previous move.

A second tournament was held. This time each contest was of random duration (to stop strategies with special rules for the last move) with a median of 200 moves. There were 62 entries from six countries. This time entrants included biologists, physicists and computer scientists. TIT FOR TAT won again. Moreover, if a succession of tournaments were played with programs increasing in representation if they did well, then ultimately TIT FOR TAT swept the board displacing all the others. In fact TIT FOR TAT is stable against invasion by any other strategy providing that the sequence of games is long enough.

What makes TIT FOR TAT so successful?

Well, it has three interesting properties. TIT FOR TAT is never the first to defect (it is nice). It is quick to retaliate (provokable). And should an intransigent opponent have a change of heart then TIT FOR TAT will cooperate straight away (it is forgiving).

Let us take a look at TIT FOR TAT in more detail. A match consists of a sequence of games between the same two players. The payoffs from each game are given in Table 8.12. At the end of each game there is a probability, p, of a further game. What is the expected number of games? Well, at the end of their first game the probability of one further game is p. The probability of two further games is p^2. Three games? p^3. And so on. So, the expected number of games is,

$$E_n = 1 + p + p^2 + p^3 \ldots \ldots p^\infty$$
$$= 1/(1 - p) \tag{9}$$

(see section 2.6 in Chapter 2).

Thus if $p = 0.99$ then the expected number of games will be 100. However, if $p = 0.90$ then the expected number is 10.

Remember that TIT FOR TAT has a memory for only one game (it is forgiving). Also TIT FOR TAT always plays cooperate (C) on its opening move. If at any point an alternative strategy Q makes a play of C then TIT FOR TAT will reply with a C. And if the first play by Q is D then a play of D by Q at any later point resets the match to its initial state. Note also that if a strategy Q is the best reply to TIT FOR TAT, then it must make the same play as it did on the first move if the initial state ever recurs. It must be consistent. If there was a better play then it should have played it the first time round.

If we accept these two points then we need to consider only three alternative strategies, Q_1, Q_2 and Q_3 (Table 8.13).

Let us consider the first strategy Q_1. TIT FOR TAT begins the contest with a C choice. Q_1 replies with a C choice. TIT FOR TAT makes the same

Table 8.12: Payoffs in the reiterated Prisoner's Dilemma Game. R, S, T and P are the payoffs to player A. In the Prisoner's Dilemma $T > R > P > S$ and $R > (S + T)/2$ (see Axelrod and Hamilton, 1981). If a contestant chooses to cooperate and his opponent cooperates, then his payoff will be R. However, if his opponent defects then his payoff is S.

		Player B	
		Cooperates	Defects
Player A	Cooperates	R Reward for mutual cooperation	S Sucker's payoff
	Defects	T Temptation to defect	P Punishment for mutual defection

Table 8.13: The three alternative strategies against TIT FOR TAT.
Q_1 **makes a run of cooperative choices (***CCCC***...).** Q_3 **makes a run of defections (***DDDD***...).** Q_2 **alternates between defection and cooperation (***DCDC***...).**

TFT Q_1		TFT Q_2		TFT Q_3	
C		C		C	
	C		D		D
C		D		D	
	C		C		D
C		C		D	
	C		D		D
.		.		.	
	.		.		.
.		.		.	
	.		.		.
.		.		.	
	.		.		.

Sequence (*CCC*...)   (*DCDC*...)   (*DDDD*...) for *Q*.

choice as its opponent — another *C*. Q_1 cannot change its mind and select *D*. By the rules above, if *D* was a best reply to *C* then it should have chosen *D* first time round. Since it chose *C* then it must choose *C* again. And again. And again. And so the contest continues.

Now look at Q_2. TIT FOR TAT opens with a *C*. Q_2 replies with a *D*. TIT FOR TAT retaliates with a *D*. Q_2 replies to *D* with a *C*. TIT FOR TAT cooperates, *C*, and the game is back to its initial state. Since Q_2 replied to *C* with a *D* on its first turn it must reply with *D* again (if it is to be consistent). And so Q_2 alternates between *D* and *C* for the reasons outlined above. So Q_2 is a run of *DCDCDC* . . . . .

And the third strategy, Q_3? As for Q_2, Q_3 replies to TIT FOR TAT's opening *C* with a *D*. And once again TIT FOR TAT retaliates with a *D*. However, unlike Q_2, Q_3 replies to TIT FOR TAT's *D* with another *D*. TIT FOR TAT retaliates again. And so begins a long run of defections *DDDDD* . . . .

How well does each of these strategies do? And can any of them invade TIT FOR TAT?

The payoff to TIT FOR TAT against itself is

$$R + pR + p^2R + p^3R \ldots = R/(1-p) \tag{10}$$

The payoff to Q_1 (*CCCC*...) against TIT FOR TAT is the same, so Q_1 cannot invade (though it could drift randomly through the population since it is selectively neutral — see section 8.3 above).

The payoff to Q_2 $(DCDCD\ldots)$ is

$$T + pS + p^2T + p^3S\ldots = (T + pS)/(1 - p^2) \tag{11}$$

And the payoff to Q_3 $(DDDD\ldots)$ is

$$T + pP + p^2P + p^3P\ldots = T + pP/(1 - p) \tag{12}$$

This means that TIT FOR TAT is uninvadable providing that the payoffs to Q_2 and Q_3 are less than or equal to the payoffs to TIT FOR TAT. That is,

$$[T + pP/(1 - p)] < R/(1 - p) > [(T + pS)/(1 - p^2)]$$

That is, when

$$p > (T - R)/(R - S),$$

and

$$p > (T - R)/(T - P) \tag{13}$$

(see Appendix 8.2). In other words TIT FOR TAT is an ESS providing that the probability of a further game is high.

Though TIT FOR TAT is an ESS it is not the only ESS. Although Q_3 cannot invade a population of TIT FOR TAT players, it is itself an ESS, and cannot be invaded by TIT FOR TAT except in special circumstances. A discussion of these special circumstances goes beyond the scope of this book and the reader is referred to Maynard Smith (1982), p. 169 *et seq.*

8.8 Summary

In this chapter we have explored the application of games theory thinking to just two problems: the evolution of aggressive behaviour and the evolution of cooperative behaviour. However, games theory has much wider applications; it can be used to model any situation in which an animal's decisions depend upon the choices of other animals. In the previous chapters the optimal behaviour was easily identifiable because it was in some sense the best of two or more alternatives. However, in this chapter we have focused on contests and conflicts between animals; and in a contest the best way to behave depends upon what your opponent is doing. Maynard Smith (1982) provides a survey of games theory applications, and Parker (1984) summarises some of the important models and their applications.

In sections 8.2 to 8.4 some very simple games theory models were intro-

duced and developed to a point where we were ready to tackle the more difficult models in section 8.5. Eventually the models of spider contests became so
complex that we abandoned analytical methods and outlined a simulation
model of aggressive behaviour in *Agelenopsis*.

It is obvious that some time was spent fiddling with the model parameters in
order to get a loose qualitative fit to *Agelenopsis* disputes. However, no
attempt was made to produce an optimal fit. A much closer match could have
been obtained. For instance, the model parameters were all integers and a
much better fit could have been obtained by trying real numbers. In fact, the
only conceptual change during the development of the model was to make the
decisions retreat and withdraw dependent upon the value of a web site (see
page 184). The dependence of these two decisions on site value represents the
only major modification to the logic of the original model. Without it, site
value had very little effect on the course of a contest (contradicting all the
evidence).

In the second half of the chapter we returned to classical games theory
models with the problem of the reiterated Prisoner's Dilemma. Not for the first
time in this book, we saw how ideas borrowed from economics and psychology
can be readily transferred to animal behaviour. One of the most interesting
aspects of this chapter is the backgrounds of the contestants entering the
reiterated Prisoner's Dilemma competition. Here we saw economists, soci-
ologists, political scientists, mathematicians, physicists, computer scientists
and biologists joining in to tackle an interesting problem. The winning program (TIT FOR TAT) was submitted by Professor Anatol Rapoport who was
one of the first researchers to establish the Prisoner's Dilemma Game as a
model of cooperative and competitive behaviour in people. In particular he
was interested in repeated plays of the Prisoner's Dilemma. In repeated plays
of the Prisoner's Dilemma, Rapoport and his colleague Albert Chammah
reported interesting sex differences in behaviour (Rapoport and Chammah,
1965). They found that men show a greater tendency to make cooperative
plays than women. This does not appear to be due to any inherent male
tendency to cooperation. Both sexes are equally likely to make cooperative
choices in the initial stages of a game. However, men are more likely to
reciprocate cooperative choices than women; they are more 'forgiving'. In
contrast, women are more likely to retaliate against 'defect' choices; they are
more provokable! These empirical findings of differences in the 'reciprocity'
or 'tit for tat' behaviour suggested the TIT FOR TAT strategy. There can be
no better testimony to the interdisciplinary nature of mathematical modelling
than the TIT FOR TAT story!

In the final chapter we shall move on to discuss some general points about
modelling in behavioural ecology.

Appendix 8.1: Conditions for an ESS

Consider two strategies, I and J, and let the payoffs from encounters be a, b, c and d (below):

		Against	
		I	J
		-------	-----
	I	a	b
Payoff to	J	c	d

The strategy I is an ESS if either,

$$a > c, \text{ or}$$
$$a = c \text{ and } b > d.$$

Conversely, J is an ESS if either,

$$d > b, \text{ or}$$
$$d = b \text{ and } c > a.$$

It is possible for both I and J to be ESSs; if I becomes established first then it is uninvadable by J, but if J becomes established first then it too is uninvadable. Which strategy becomes established is then a matter of historical precedence.

Parker (1984) discusses these conditions in more detail and outlines some more general conditions proposed by Hammerstein.

Appendix 8.2

We want to show that TIT FOR TAT is an ESS providing that the probability, p, of another encounter is sufficiently large (equation (13)). From equation (12),

$$T + \frac{pP}{(1 - p)} < \frac{R}{(1 - p)}$$

Multiply through by $(1-p)$,

$$(1-p)T+pP< R$$

Or,

$$T-pT+pP< R$$

And so,

$$T+p(P-T) < R$$

Subtracting R from both sides of the inequality gives us,

$$T-R+p(P-T) < 0$$

Or,

$$(T-R) < p(T-P)$$

And so,

$$p>(T-R)/(T-P)$$

In other words TIT FOR TAT will not be displaced by strategy Q_3 provided that p is sufficiently large. And what about Q_2?

From equation (12) we know that TIT FOR TAT is stable against invasion by Q_2 provided that,

$$\frac{R}{(1-p)} > \frac{(T+pS)}{(1-p^2)}$$

Or,

$$\frac{R}{(1-p)} > \frac{(T+pS)}{(1+p)(1-p)}$$

Multiplying through first by $(1-p)$ gives,

$$R>(T+pS)/(1+p)$$

And then by $(1+p)$,

$$R(1+p) > T+pS$$

Or,

$$R+pR > T+pS$$

Collecting terms,

$$p(R-S) > (T-R)$$

And dividing by $(R-S)$,

$$p > (T-R)/(R-S)$$

So provided that the probability of a further encounter (p) is sufficiently high TIT FOR TAT is stable against invasion by all three strategies, and so it is stable against all possible strategies.

Chapter 9
Conclusions

9.1 Modelling and Assumptions

Mathematics provides a broad framework for modelling events in the real world. The reason we use mathematics is because it is a well-worked system with known properties. We can take advantage of these known properties to predict the behaviour of the system that we are modelling. However, in adopting a mathematical framework we must be clear about the assumptions made by the model. We must ask ourselves if the mathematical framework is appropriate for the system we are trying to model.

In Chapter 5, we looked at a model of vigilance in birds which assumed a Poisson process generating scanning events. We then used the known properties of Poisson processes to predict the probability of an event (scan) occurring in time T. With one or two further assumptions about the behaviour of the predator, we identified this as the probability of predator detection. We then took advantage of some further known properties of Poisson processes to calculate the probability of flocks of birds detecting a predator. But how good are Poisson processes as models of the process generating scanning events?

Unfortunately, they turn out to be rather poor models of avian scanning processes (see sections 5.3 and 5.4 in Chapter 5). This means we have a problem. The assumptions that we adopt in order for a Poisson process to be a good model of scanning in birds are unrealistic. And this restricts the application of the model. It does not make the model wrong; there may be many applications where a Poisson model is fine.

Pulliam, Pyke and Caraco (1982) apply the simple Poisson model to calculate ESSs for individuals feeding in flocks. They look at several different strategies of scanning behaviour including purely 'selfish' strategies (in which

196

individuals exploit the behaviour of their flock companions — these individuals do not 'pull their weight' in maintaining corporate vigilance), and 'cooperative' strategies (in which individuals scan cooperatively in order to maximise corporate vigilance). Neither of these strategies is evolutionarily stable. However, the strategy 'judge' (in which individuals cooperate if their flock companions are behaving cooperatively, but behave selfishly if they are not) is an ESS. What is more, the predicted scanning rates of individuals employing the 'judge' strategy are much closer to those observed in real life.

It would be entirely inappropriate to throw out this very important paper just because juncos do not meet some trivial assumption about random scanning. If, on the other hand, we wanted to model scanning patterns then clearly a Poisson model would not be appropriate. It all depends upon what you are trying to do with the model. Of course if you use a model with assumptions that are known not to hold you have to be very careful that a failure of those assumptions is not going to wreck your predictions.

Clearly, the significance of individual assumptions depends upon what you are trying to do with the model. Having said this, some assumptions are more important than others; and some assumptions may identify a subgroup of related models. In Chapter 3 we outlined a number of the classical optimal foraging models. The major assumption (which defines the *general* model) is that animals are maximising their net rate of energetic intake, E/T. Throughout the chapter we saw how the various models simply redefined net energetic intake (E) and the time over which maximisation takes place (T).

At the start of Chapter 3 we saw how a variety of models simply redefined the time over which maximisation occurs (T). If there are no searching or travelling time costs then T is simply the handling time (T_h). In the optimal diet model $T = T_s + T_h$ (the searching and handling time). And in the marginal value theorem $T = T_t + T_p$ (the travel and patch times). Turning to the definitions of energetic returns in the Kacelnik models (see section 3.5), we see increasing refinement of E. In *Yield* it is metabolisable energetic return. In *Delivery* it is metabolisable energetic return *minus* the parent's metabolic costs. And in *Family Gain* it is metabolisable energy *minus* the parent's metabolic costs *minus* the chicks' metabolic costs. Each model makes different assumptions about E and T, but they are (more or less) the same model. These models are simply *strong* or *special* versions of the general model.

In Chapter 4 we saw the advent of a whole new series of models which question the major assumption of rate-maximisation. These risk-sensitive foraging models assume that animals are minimising their probability of starvation rather than maximising their feeding returns. The shift from rate-maximising to risk-sensitive models represents a major switch in thinking, and the adoption of a whole new mathematical framework. The assumption of risk-minimisation identifies a family of related models (Krebs, Stephens and Sutherland, 1983).

9.2 Testing Models

In order to test a model we can test the individual assumptions upon which the model is based, or we can test the model's predictions. The adoption of a new mathematical framework (model) is followed by a period of verification, in which researchers test the model's predictions, and the model's assumptions. And if the model's assumptions are found to be inadequate then another framework may be adopted (a shift of *paradigm*). In this section we want to consider the testing of predictions and assumptions.

9.2.1 Assumption Testing

The first requirement of any model is that its conclusions should follow from its assumptions. However, in many cases we find that the conclusions do not follow *directly* from the assumptions. Many depend upon assumptions that are not formalised mathematically, and may therefore escape our attention.

The models of vigilance in Chapter 5 for instance depend upon some very strong assumptions about the behaviour of predators and prey. They assume, for example, that detection is always followed by escape; and they assume perfect detection while scanning and no detection while feeding. In real life, neither of these assumptions will hold, and their failure suggests new directions for models of animal vigilance.

Although the aim of most behavioural ecologists is to test a set of *optimality criteria* (Krebs, Stephens and Sutherland, 1983), when we test a model we are actually testing a set of assumptions about *constraints* (such as the strategy set), *optimisation criteria* (such as maximising payoffs or minimising losses), and *mechanisms of heredity* (sexual or asexual reproduction) (McNeill Alexander, 1982, Maynard Smith, 1982). Although the optimisation criteria are usually explicit, the other types of assumption may not be. For instance, in their original games theory paper (Maynard Smith and Price, 1973), many of the assumptions underlying the Hawk-Dove models were not made explicit. They assumed, of course, that they had defined the full 'strategy set' (that no alternative strategy was lurking in the wings), and they made assumptions about the mechanism of heredity (asexual reproduction) (see Maynard Smith's self-critique, 1982).

In recent years a greater awareness of the importance of assumptions has compelled many authors to make lengthy lists of model assumptions (see Krebs and McCleery's, (1984, pp. 97 and 101) treatment of the optimal diet and marginal value models). However, we have already seen that even when assumptions are clearly violated this need not have devastating consequences for a model. For example, on hearing that animals appear to be sensitive to both reward mean *and* variance, the naive reader might be tempted to throw out optimal foraging models in favour of their risk-sensitive cousins. Of course, in Chapter 4 we did find important differences between the two. However this does not mean that optimal foraging models will always fail. So far, risk-sensitivity is very much a laboratory phenomenon. It is a matter of debate whether the conditions for risk-proneness are likely to arise in the field (see Krebs, Stephens and Sutherland, 1983). There may be situations where optimal foraging models do not hold and where we might want to adopt a risk-sensitive model. However, it is unnecessary to evaluate the two approaches in some kind of arbitrary contest. It is sufficient to know that there may be some situations where one of the models will break down. Which model we use depends upon what we want to do with the model. Perhaps the emphasis should be on model *evaluation* rather than model testing.

9.2.2 Testing Predictions

In Chapter 1 we saw that one of the principal objectives of modelling in behavioural ecology is to make precise, quantitative predictions about how an animal will behave when behaving according to a particular combination of optimality criteria. When a model breaks down then we are forced to reconsider our particular combination of optimality criteria. This leads us to make fresh predictions.

It is the failure of a model to account for data that leads to new ideas and new research. The partial failure of the optimal diet model, for instance (Chapter 3; Krebs *et al.*, 1977), led to the introduction of the 'optimal sampling' and 'misidentification' hypotheses (Krebs *et al.*, 1977; Rechten, Avery and Stevens, 1983). The former suggests that animals sample prey in order to gain information about prey quality; the latter that they are taking small prey accidentally (mistaking them for larger prey). In an extremely elegant test of these hypotheses Rechten and co-workers (1983) found support for an interaction of both these factors. (Krebs and McCleery (1984) identify at least six other explanations of such 'partial preferences'; but see Stephens (1985) for a discussion of whether we are making too much of partial preferences.)

The work of Davies and Houston on wagtail time budgeting is another good example (Chapter 7). They began with a simple model that assumes territory owners should divide their time between feeding on territory and in flocks in such a way as to maximise their daily feeding rate. The failure of this model forced Davies and Houston to develop a second model accounting for longer-term 'cropping' of wagtail territories. According to this model the owner should alternate between the territory and the flock in such a way as to minimise the chances of the vacant territory becoming profitable to an intruder.

Of course, the fact that a model is retained may only be an indication of the low power of the test or of the poor quality of the data. And if no attempt is made to test the goodness-of-fit of behavioural models to data then departures from the model will not be detected. One obvious statistical option when testing a model is to adopt a more aggressive attitude to the criterion levels for statistical significance. Often the modeller will compare the performance of the model with some real data, and seem to confirm the null hypothesis of no difference between the model and the data. When seeking to confirm a null hypothesis it should be standard practice to adopt a less conservative significance probability value of, say 0.20 (instead of the usual 0.05), but this rarely happens. In part, this is due to an understandable reluctance on the part of modellers to reject their own models, and partly to the fear which many behavioural ecologists have of 'tinkering' with criterion levels for statistical testing. Wickens (1982) gives an excellent introduction to statistical procedures for testing both the overall goodness-of-fit of a model, and various model parameters.

Often the most interesting models are those which do not work. It is these models which stimulate further research. 'Rigging' the model to fit the data stifles further research. There are several ways of rigging the model, and several checks to model-rigging.

9.3 Ad hocery

Special assumptions which are introduced to ensure that the model fits the data deserve a special mention. *Ad hocery* (the practice of introducing special assumptions in order to make the proposed model 'behave properly') is fraught with danger (McNeill Alexander, 1982).

Several authors (including myself!) have, for instance, attempted to save the random scanning assumption (the cornerstone of Poisson models of avian vigilance) by the introduction of a constraint on the minimum interscan interval (Elcavage and Caraco, 1983; Lendrem, 1983). Although this 'works' in some circumstances it does not always (Sullivan, 1984; Lendrem *et al.*, in press). Introducing this arbitrary assumption has disguised the fact that scanning is better described by a *time-dependent* rather than a *time-independent* process (Lendrem *et al.*, in press). In other words, the longer the interscan interval the more likely an animal is to make a scan.

Similarly, in Chapter 5 we saw how Thompson and Lendrem (1985) introduced a 'recognition time' constraint to their model of vigilance in plovers (see also Barnard and Thompson, 1985). However, they make no attempt to test this assumption. As it happens this is probably not too damning. On the one hand it is not especially crucial to their model; they get a reasonable fit without it (but an even better one with it!). What is more they make a strong case for such a constraint. However, some kind of independent corroboration would be nice!

Of course, the distinction between *ad hocery* and a more 'constructive' change in a model can be rather blurred. It depends upon the strength of the case for the change. Without empirical support or strong theoretical grounds, a change in the model is suspect. However, there is an element of subjectivity; one man's milk may be another's poison. 'Empirical support' may not be as supportive as we imagine, and 'strong theoretical grounds' may be open to question.

9.4 Sensitivity Analysis

Many models contain a number of parameters that are difficult to estimate. In order to evaluate such models it is often useful to estimate how sensitive these models are to such parameters. To do this we can, as in Chapter 3, perform *sensitivity analyses* for such parameters. If the performance of a model is very sensitive to variation in a parameter that cannot be estimated accurately then we must proceed with great caution. Usually some kind of rough and ready sensitivity assessment is made during the initial model construction (see, for example, the *Agelenopsis* model in Chapter 8). In developing a model some attempt is made to work with a range of parameter values which give a reasonable fit to the behaviour we are trying to model ('model-fitting'). After spending some time playing around to get a loose qualitative fit, we can carry out a sensitivity analysis to pinpoint those parameters with large effects on model predictions. These can then be made the object of closer scrutiny.

In Chapter 7 for instance we described Pyke's (1979) model of sunbird territoriality. This model predicts the optimal territory size for values of the model parameter $\alpha = 1, 2$ and 3. Now α is an important parameter describing the relationship between the time spent in territorial defence and territory quality (c). The predictions of the model are quite sensitive to the value of α. However, if we look at these predictions (Table 9.1) we see that although sensitive to α this does not prevent us from distinguishing between the various currencies. Whatever the value of α the *cost-minimising* model gives the best approximation to the observed data. Having said that, α is still open to closer scrutiny. One could measure the relationship between time spent in territorial defence and territory quality and so derive α empirically.

Table 9.1: Predicted territory size (number of flowers defended) and territorial defence times. All three models are sensitive to the arbitrary parameter α. However, the *cost-minimising* model performs best whatever the value of α.

	Model	1	2	3
Predicted territory size (n)	Net-maximising	9628	7070	6381
	Sitting-maximising	1643	1653	1638
	Cost-minimising	1576	1595	1541
	Observed: 1600 flowers			
Predicted defence time (h)	Net-maximising	4.32	2.55	1.87
	Sitting-maximising	0.73	0.61	0.48
	Cost-minimising	0.39	0.28	0.20
	Observed: 0.28 hours			

Similarly, in Chapter 6 Houston, McCleery and Davies (1985) show that for a variety of renewal rates (w) the optimal territory size for wagtails is 600 m. The parameter w is open to further scrutiny; we could measure the renewal rates on Port Meadow (where the wagtails live) and see how they compare with the range of values used in the simulations. Better still we could look at the effect of variation in renewal rates (between stretches of the river, or between years) on territory sizes. The model predicts that the higher the renewal rate, w, the smaller the territory size.

9.5 Top-down or Bottom-up?

Mathematical models are not plucked from thin air. They are developed against a backdrop of previous research, and the modelling process can be quite prolonged. We start by defining the problem. We then attempt to identify all the relevant variables. We define their functions, specify parameters, and from this a model emerges requiring validation of parameters and verification of the predictions.

So, given that we want to do some modelling, where do we start?

Broadly speaking we can identify two slightly different types of direction. The *top-down* approach takes a branch of mathematics and looks for situations which are amenable to that particular mathematical framework. The classic example is the Hawk-Dove-Bourgeois model (see section 8.4, Chapter 8). This began as a mathematical anomaly of dubious biological significance; the search for biological examples began only after the model had been developed.

In contrast, the *bottom-up* approach takes observed empirical findings, fits functions to those data, and looks at how those functions interact. The resulting models can be quite complex, and the modellers may have to resort to the quasianalytical approach adopted by Davies and Houston to model wagtail behaviour. Their models of territory-sharing combine analytical derivation with empirically derived parameters for renewal rates, intrusion rates etc.

At the extreme of the bottom-up approach, we see instances of *data-driven modelling*. In 1981, for instance, while working on vigilance in birds I tested the effects of flock size and apparent predation risk on scanning rates in Barbary doves, *Streptopelia risoria* (Lendrem, 1984). I found no relationship between flock size and scanning rates (though this is not reported in Lendrem, 1984!) but there was a close relationship between time spent scanning and flock size. A detailed inspection of the data revealed marked differences in the scanning *patterns* of these birds. Scanning rate itself gives an inadequate description of these patterns. This focused my attention upon interscan intervals as the critical periods during which predators could make an attack. Parallel developments in risk-sensitive foraging models eventually produced the models outlined in sections 5.5 and 5.6 (Chapter 5). However, it was the empirical findings that stimulated the models.

Of course, in real life, both processes go hand in hand. Models of risk-sensitive foraging provide a good example of the roles of top-down and bottom-up modelling. Economic models of risk-sensitivity in man were the starting point for the junco experiments by Caraco, Martindale and Whitham (1980). Their findings stimulated Stephens' models of risk-sensitive foraging (Stephens, 1981; Stephens and Charnov, 1982). And Stephens' models stimulated tests by Barnard and Brown (1984).

9.6. Constraints on Perfection

Most of the models in this book are optimality models: models which minimise costs, maximise benefits, or obtain the best compromise between the two. Optimality models make assumptions about the costs and benefits of various behaviours and seem to predict which particular combination of costs and benefits will give the maximum net benefit.

So far, when discussing optimality models, we have assumed that the animal always gets it right. If our models break down we assume that our cost-benefit functions are unrealistic, our parameters suspect, or our assumptions awry. If our data fail to support a model then we assume that the model is wrong. We use our models to test our understanding of the animal's behaviour. But what happens if the animal has got it wrong? What if the animal is not perfect? Dawkins (1982) identifies several important 'constraints on perfection'. However, I am going to concentrate on just one kind of constraint — evolutionary lag.

If the pace of environmental change has outstripped the behaviour of our animals, then they may *not* be perfectly adapted to their new environment. A classic example is that of the gannets (*Sula bassana*) of Bass Rock in Scotland. A pair of gannets incubates a single egg until the chick hatches. On hatching, the parents feed the chick for several weeks. However, Nelson (1964) found that if a second egg is added, to a nest then gannets can successfully raise two young. So why do the gannets of Bass Rock lay only one egg? One possibility is that raising two may exert enormous costs on the parents, prohibiting reproduction in the following breeding season. But there are other species of gannet which do lay two eggs and successfully raise both chicks. Lack (1966) suggests that only recently has the food supply off Bass Rock improved sufficiently to allow gannets to raise two young. The implication is that *Sula bassana* has not kept pace with ecological change.

Evolutionary lag is one of the most serious obstacles to the testing of optimisation models. There is no easy way out; the best we can do is to invoke evolutionary lag (and other constraints) sparingly, and only when there is independent evidence for such a constraint (Dawkins, 1982; Maynard Smith, 1978).

However, such constraints may mean that animals are behaving sub-optimally. Optimality models in biology have been heavily criticised when presented as tests of whether such and such an animal is/is not optimal (see, for example, Lewontin, 1979). Although some authors might think of optimality models in this way, the vast majority would maintain that testing optimality *per se* is not their intent (Maynard Smith, 1978; Dawkins, 1982; McNeill Alexander, 1982; Krebs, Stephens and Sutherland, 1983). Rather, the aim is to test whether a particular set of optimisation criteria correctly predicts an animal's behaviour.

There are those (for example, Myers, 1983) who think that whilst this is a neat point, it leaves the underlying issue (of optimality) unanswered. It does; and so it should! Behavioural ecology is a very pragmatic discipline. The counsel for despair states that there are so many constraints acting upon an animal that the chances of it behaving according to a set of identifiable optimality criteria are minute. In reality, modelling in behavioural ecology has proven remarkably successful at identifying those criteria.

9.7 Concluding Remarks

I hope that this book has shown how models arise and how they develop. For those readers new to these methods, I hope that I have taken some of the mystique out of modelling. By showing the nuts and bolts of the models and spelling out how the various equations are derived, one can get a real feel for how the models behave. It does not require a great deal of mathematical sophistication to follow what is going on or indeed to come up with interesting models. The trick is to find an interesting problem and then look for a suitable framework.

Appendix 1: Greek Symbols

Name	Lowercase	Uppercase
alpha	α	A
beta	β	B
gamma	γ	Γ
delta	δ	Δ
epsilon	ε	E
zeta	ζ	Z
eta	η	H
theta	θ	Θ
iota	ι	I
kappa	κ	K
lambda	λ	Λ
mu	μ	M
nu	ν	N
xi	ξ	Ξ
omicron	o	O
pi	π	Π
rho	ρ	P
sigma	σ	Σ
tau	τ	T
upsilon	υ	Y
phi	φ	Φ
chi	χ	X
psi	ψ	Ψ
omega	ω	Ω

Appendix 2: Indices

Much of the algebra in this book involves little more than manipulating indices. In this appendix we outline the most important results used in this book.

A number x multiplied by itself n times is written x^n where x is the *base* and n is called the *exponent*. The base x is said to be *raised* to the *power n*, and if

$$y = x^n$$

then y is said to be an exponential *function* of x.

There are certain simple rules for the manipulation of indices and I outline those used in this book:

Rule 1: $x^m \times x^n = x^{(m+n)}$

Rule 2: $x^m / x^n = x^{(m-n)}$

Rule 3: $x^0 = 1$

Rule 4: $x^{-m} = 1/x^m$

Rule 5: $x^{1/n} = \sqrt[n]{x}$

> A particularly useful instance of this is $x^{1/2} = \sqrt[2]{x}$, or simply $\sqrt{x}$. A second useful instance is $x^{-1/2} = 1/\sqrt{x}$ which crops up time and time again in this book.
>
> And a further useful instance combining Rule 1 with Rule 5 is $x^{1/2} = x(x^{-1/2})$ which crops up in Chapter 6.

Rule 6: $(x^m)^n = x^{mn}$

Rule 7: $(x^{1/n})^m = x^{m/n}$

Several models in this book employ *the* exponential function, e^x. If,

$$y = a^x$$

then we can choose a constant k such that,

$$y = a^x = (e^k)^x$$

where e is *the* exponential constant, and $e = 2.71828\ldots$

And, by Rule 6,

$$(e^k)^x = e^{kx}$$

By Rule 4,

$$e^{-x} = 1/e^x$$

Newby (1980) gives further details and several more useful rules and instances which do not make an appearance in this book.

References

Axelrod, R. and Hamilton, W.D. (1981) 'The Evolution of Cooperation', *Science*, *211*, 1390–6.

Barnard, C.J. and Brown, C.A.J. (1984) 'Risk-sensitive Foraging in Common Shrews (*Sorex araneus L.*)', *Behav. Ecol. Sociobiol.*, 13, 1–4.

—— and —— (In press) 'Risk-sensitive Foraging in Common Shrews: Effects of Mean and Variance in Reward Rates', *Behav. Ecol. Sociobiol.*

—— and Thompson, D.B.A. (1985) *Gulls and Plovers: The Ecology and Behaviour of Mixed-species Feeding Groups*, Croom Helm, London/Columbia University Press, New York.

Bertram, B.C.R. (1980) 'Vigilance and Group Size in Ostriches', *Anim. Behav.*, *28*, 278–86.

Caraco, T. (1981a) 'Risk-sensitivity and Foraging Groups', *Ecology, 62*, 527–31.

—— (1981b) 'Energy Budgets, Risk and Foraging Preferences in Dark-eyed Juncos (*Junco hyemalis*). *Behav. Ecol. Sociobiol.*, *8*, 213–17.

—— and Chasin, M. (1984) 'Foraging Preferences: Response to Reward Skew', *Anim. Behav.*, *32*, 76–85.

—— and Lima, S. (1985) 'Foraging Juncos: Interaction of Reward Mean and Variability', *Anim. Behav.*, *33*, 216–24.

——, Martindale, S. and Whitham, T.S. (1980) 'An Empirical Demonstration of Risk-sensitive Foraging Preferences', *Anim. Behav.*, *28*, 820–30.

Charnov, E.L. (1976) 'Optimal Foraging: The Marginal Value Theorem', *Theor. Popul. Biol.*, *9*, 129–36.

Colman, A.M. (1982) 'Experimental Games', in *Cooperation and Competition in Humans and Animals* (ed. A.M. Colman) pp. 113–40, Van Nostrand Reinhold, London and New York.

Cook, R.M. and Cockerell, B.J. (1978) 'Predator Ingestion Rate and its Bearing on Feeding Time and the Theory of Optimal Diets', *J. Anim. Ecol.*, *47*, 529–47.

Craig, J.L. (1984) 'Are Communal Pukeko Caught in the Prisoner's Dilemma?' *Behav. Ecol. Sociobiol.*, *14*, 147–50.

Dawkins, R. (1980) 'Good Strategy or Evolutionarily Stable Strategy?' in *Sociobiology: Beyond Nature/Nurture?* (eds G.W. Barlow and S. Silverberg) pp. 331–367, Westview Press, Boulder, Colorado.

—— (1982) *The Extended Phenotype*, W.H. Freeman, Oxford and San Francisco.

Davies, N.B. (1977) 'Prey Selection and Social Behaviour in Wagtails (*Aves: Motacillidae*)', *J. Anim. Ecol,*, *46*, 37–57.

—— (1978) 'Territorial Defence in the Speckled Wood Butterfly (*Pararge aegeria*), the Resident Always Wins', *Anim. Behav.*, *26*, 138–47.

—— and Houston, A.I. (1981) 'Owners and Satellites: the Economics of Territory Defence in the Pied Wagtail, *Motacilla alba*', *J. Anim. Ecol.*, *50*, 157–80.

—— and —— (1983) 'Time Allocation Between Territories and Flocks and Owner-satellite Conflict in Foraging Pied Wagtails, *Motacilla alba*', *J. Anim. Ecol.*, *52*, 621–34.

Einhorn, H.J. (1982) 'Learning from Experience and Suboptimal Rules in Decision Making', in *Judgement Under Uncertainty: Heuristics and Biases* (eds D. Kahneman, P. Slovic and A. Tversky), pp. 268–83, Cambridge University Press, Cambridge.

Elcavage, P. and Caraco, T. (1983) 'Vigilance Behaviour in House Sparrow Flocks', *Anim. Behav.*, *31*, 303–4.

Elgar, M.A. and Catterall, C.P. (1981) 'Flocking and Predator Surveillance in House Sparrows: Test of an Hypothesis. *Anim. Behav.*, *29*, 868–72.

Elner, R.W. and Hughes, R.N. (1978) 'Energy Maximisation in the Diet of the Shore Crab, *Carcinus maenas.*' *J. Anim. Ecol.*, *47*, 103–16.

Gill, F.B. and Wolf, L.L. (1975) 'Economics of Feeding Territoriality in the Golden-winged Sunbird', *Ecology*, *56*, 333–45.

Hamburger, H. (1979) *Games as Models of Social Phenomena*, W.H. Freeman, San Francisco.

Hart, A. and Lendrem, D.W. (1984) 'Vigilance and Scanning Patterns in Birds', *Anim. Behav.*, *32*, 1216–24.

Houston, A.I. and McNamara, J. (1982) 'A Sequential Approach to Risk-taking', *Anim. Behav.*, *30*, 1260–1.

—— and —— (1985) 'The Variability of Behaviour and Constrained Optimisation', *J. Theor. Biol.*, *112*, 265–73.

——, Kacelnik, A. and McNamara, J. (1982) 'Some Learning Rules for Acquiring Information', in *Functional Ontogeny* (ed. D.J. McFarland), pp. 140–91, Pitman, London.

——, McCleery, R.H. and Davies, N.B. (1985) 'Territory Size, Prey Renewal and Feeding Rate: Interpretation of Observations on the Pied Wagtail (*Motacilla alba*) by Simulation', *J. Anim. Ecol.*, *54*, 227–39.

Krebs, J.R. (1978) 'Optimal Foraging: Decision Rules for Predators', in *Behavioural Ecology: An Evolutionary Approach* (eds J.R. Krebs and N.B. Davies), pp. 23–63, Blackwell, Oxford/Sinauer Associates, Sunderland, MA.

—— and Davies, N.B. (1981) *An Introduction to Behavioural Ecology*, Blackwell, Oxford.

—— and McCleery, R.H. (1984) 'Optimization in Behavioural Ecology', in *Behavioural Ecology: An Evolutionary Approach* (eds J.R. Krebs and N.B. Davies), pp. 91–121, 2nd edn. Blackwell, Oxford/Sinauer Associates, Sunderland, MA.

——, Erichsen, J.T., Webber, M.I. and Charnov, E.L. (1977) 'Optimal Prey Selection in the Great Tit, *Parus major*', *Anim. Behav.*, *25*, 30–8.

——, Stephens, D.W. and Sutherland, W.J. (1983) 'Perspectives in Optimal Foraging', in *Perspectives in Ornithology* (eds G.A. Clark and A.H. Brush), pp. 165–216, Cambridge University Press, New York.

Lack, D. (1966) *Population Studies of Birds*, Clarendon Press, Oxford.

Lazarus, J. (1972) 'Natural Selection and the Functions of Flocking in Birds: A Reply to Murton', *Ibis*, *114*, 556–8.

—— (1979) 'The Early Warning Function of Flocking in Birds: An Experimental Study with Captive Quelea', *Anim. Behav.*, *27*, 855–65.

Lendrem, D.W. (1982) *Vigilance in birds*, DPhil. thesis, Oxford University.

—— (1983) 'Predation Risk and Vigilance in the Blue Tit (*Parus caeruleus*)', *Behav. Ecol. Sociobiol.*, *13*, 9–13.

—— (1984a) 'Flocking, Feeding and Predation Risk: Absolute and Instantaneous Feeding Rates', *Anim. Behav.*, *32*, 298–9.

—— (1984b) 'Sleeping and Vigilance in Birds, II. An Experimental Study of the Barbary Dove (*Streptopelia risoria*)', *Anim. Behav.*, *32*, 243–8.

——, Stretch, D.D., Metcalfe, N.B. and Jones, P.L. (In press) 'Scanning for Predators in the Purple Sandpiper (*Calidris maritima*): A Time-dependent or Time-independent Process?', *Anim. Behav.*

Lewontin, R.C. (1979) 'Fitness, Survival and Optimality', in *Analysis of Ecological Systems*. (eds D.J. Horn, R.D. Mitchell and G.R. Stairs), pp. 3–21. Ohio State

University Press, Columbus.

Maynard Smith, J. (1976) 'Evolution and the Theory of Games', *Amer. Sci.*, *64*, 41–5.

—— (1978) 'Optimization Theory in Evolution', *Ann. Rev. Ecol. Syt.*, *9*, 31–56.

—— (1982) *Evolution and the Theory of Games*, Cambridge University Press, Cambridge.

—— and Price, G.R. (1973) 'The Logic of Animal Conflict', *Nature (Lond.)*, *246*, 15–18.

—— and Riechert, S.E. (1984) 'A Conflicting-tendency Model of Spider Agonistic Behaviour: Hybrid-pure Population Line Comparisons', *Anim. Behav.*, *32*, 564–78.

McCleery, R.H. (1977) 'On Satiation Curves', *Anim. Behav.*, *25*, 1005–15.

McFarland, D.J. (1977) 'Decision-making in Animals', *Nature (Lond.)*, *269*, 15–21.

—— (1985) *Ethology*, Pitman, New York and London.

—— and Houston, A.I. (1981) *Quantitative Ethology: the State Space Approach*, Pitman, London.

McNeill Alexander, R. (1982) *Optima for Animals*, Edward Arnold, London.

Mendenhall, V.M. and Milne, H. (1985) 'Factors Affecting Duckling Survival of Eiders *Somateria molissima* in Northeast Scotland', *Ibis*, *127*, 148–58.

Myers, J.P. (1983) 'Is Foraging Always Optimal?' in *Perspectives in Ornithology* (eds G.A. Clark and A.H. Brush), pp. 216–21, Cambridge University Press, New York.

Neave, H.R. (1981) *Elementary Statistics Tables*, Allen and Unwin, London.

Nelson, J.B. (1964) 'Factors Influencing Clutch-size and Chick Growth in the North Atlantic Gannet *Sula bassana*'. *Ibis*, *106*, 63–77.

Newby, J.C. (1980) *Mathematics for the Biological Sciences*, Clarendon Press, Oxford.

Orians, G.H. and Pearson, N.E. (1979) 'On the Theory of Central Place Foraging', in *Analysis of Ecological Systems* (eds D.J. Horn, R.D. Mitchell and G.R. Stairs), pp. 155–77, Ohio State University Press, Columbus.

Parker, G.A. (1974) 'Assessment Strategy and the Evolution of Fighting Behaviour', *J. theor. Biol.*, *47*, 223–43.

—— (1978) 'Searching for Mates', in *Behavioural Ecology: An Evolutionary Approach* (eds J.R. Krebs and N.B. Davies), pp. 214–44, Blackwell, Oxford/Sinauer Associates, Sunderland, MA.

—— (1984) 'Evolutionarily Stable Strategies', in *Behavioural Ecology: An Evolutionary Approach* (eds J.R. Krebs and N.B. Davies), pp. 30–61, 2nd edn, Blackwell, Oxford/Sinauer Associates, Sunderland, MA.

Pulliam, H.R. (1973) 'On the Advantages of Flocking', *J. Theor. Biol.*, *38*, 419–22.

——, Pyke, G.H. and Caraco, T. (1982) 'The Scanning Behaviour of Juncos: A Game Theoretical Approach', *J. Theor. Biol.*, *95*, 89–103.

Pyke, G.H. (1979) 'The Economics of Territory Size and Time Budget in the Golden-winged Sunbird'. *Amer. Natur.* *114*, 131–45.

Rapoport, A. and Chammah, A.M. (1965) 'Prisoner's Dilemma: A Study of Conflict and Cooperation', University of Michigan Press, Ann Arbor.

Real, L.A. (1980) 'Fitness, Uncertainty and the Role of Diversification in Evolution and Behaviour', *Amer. Natur.*, *115*, 623–38.

—— (1981) 'Uncertainty and Pollinator–Plant Interactions: The Foraging Behaviour of Bees and Wasps on Artificial Flowers', *Ecology*, *62*, 20–6.

Rechten, C., Avery, M.I. and Stevens, T.A. (1983) 'Optimal Prey Selection: Why do Great Tits Show Partial Preferences?' *Anim. Behav.*, *31*, 576–84.

Regelmann, K. (1984) 'A Remark on the Theory of Risk-sensitive Foraging', *J. Theor. Biol.*, *110*, 217–22.

Riechert, S.E. (1979) 'Games Spiders Play, II. Resource Assessment Strategies'.

Behav. Ecol. Sociobiol., *6*, 121–8.

Schaller, G.B. (1972) *The Serengeti Lion*. University of Chicago Press, Chicago.

Sibly, R.M. and McFarland, D.J. (1976) 'On the Fitness of Behaviour Sequences', *Amer. Natur.*, *110*, 601–17.

——, Calow, P. and Nichols, N. (1985) 'Are Patterns of Growth Adaptive?', *J. Theor. Biol.*, *112*, 553–74.

Slovic, P., Fischoff, B. and Lichtenstein, S. (1980) 'Facts vs Fears: Understanding Perceived Risk', in *Societal Risk Assessment: How Safe is Safe Enough?* (eds R. Schwing and W.A. Albers, Jr), pp. 463–89, Plenum Press, New York.

Stearns, S.C. (1976) 'Life-history Tactics: A Review of the Ideas', *Q. Rev. Biol.*, *51*, 3–47.

Stephens, D.W. (1981) 'The Logic of Risk-sensitive Foraging Preferences', *Anim. Behav.*, *29*, 628–9.

—— (1982) *Stochasticity in foraging theory: risk and information*, DPhil thesis, Oxford University.

—— (1985) 'How Important are Partial Preferences?', *Anim. Behav.*, *33*, 667–8.

—— and Charnov, E.L. (1982) 'Optimal Foraging: Some Simple Stochastic Models', *Behav. Ecol. Sociobiol.*, *10*, 251–63.

Sullivan, K.A. (1985) 'Vigilance Patterns in Downy Woodpeckers', *Anim. Behav.*, *33*, 328–9.

Thompson, D.B.A. (1984) *Foraging economics in flocks of lapwings, golden plovers and gulls*, PhD thesis, University of Nottingham.

—— (1986) 'The Economics of Kleptoparasitism: Optimal Foraging, Host and Prey Selection by Gulls', *Anim. Behav.*

—— and Barnard, C.J. (1984) 'Prey Selection by Plovers: Optimal Foraging in Mixed Species Groups', *Anim. Behav.*, *32*, 554–63.

—— and Lendrem, D.W. (1985) 'Gulls and Plovers: Host Vigilance, Kleptoparasite Success and a Model of Kleptoparasitic Detection', *Anim. Behav.*, *33*, 1318–24.

Tversky, A. and Kahneman, D. (1982) 'Judgement Under Uncertainty: Heuristics and Biases', in *Judgement Under Uncertainty: Heuristics and Biases* (eds D. Kahneman, P. Slovic and A. Tversky), pp. 3–20. Cambridge University Press, Cambridge.

Weaver, W. (1977) *Lady Luck*, Penguin Books, Harmondsworth.

Wickens, T.D. (1982) *Models for Behaviour*, W.H. Freeman, San Francisco.

Wickman, P–O. and Wicklund, C. (1983) 'Territory Defence and its Seasonal Decline in the Speckled Wood Butterfly (*Pararge aegeria*), *Anim. Behav.*, *31*, 1206–16.

Ydenberg, R.C. (1982) *Territorial vigilance and foraging, a study of trade-offs*, DPhil thesis, Oxford University.

—— (1984a) 'Great Tits and Giving Up Times: Decision Rules for Leaving Patches', *Behaviour*, *90*, 1–24.

—— (1984b) 'The Conflict Between Feeding and Territorial Defence in the Great Tit', *Behav. Ecol. Sociobiol.*, *15*, 103–8.

—— and Houston, A.I. (In press) 'Optimal Trade-Offs Between Competing Ecological Demands in the Great Tit, *Amer. Natur.*

—— and Krebs, J.R. (In press) 'The Trade-off Between Territorial Defence and Foraging in the Great Tit (*Parus major*)', *Amer. Zool.*

Subject Index

Species Index